FORBIDDEN
FAITH

FORBIDDEN
FAITH

THE SECRET HISTORY
OF GNOSTICISM

RICHARD SMOLEY

HarperSanFrancisco
A Division of HarperCollinsPublishers

FIRST HARPERCOLLINS PAPERBACK EDITION PUBLISHED IN 2007

Text design by Martha Blegen

Library of Congress Cataloging-in-Publication Data is available.
ISBN: 978–0–06–085830–8
ISBN–10: 0–06–085830–3

07 08 09 10 11 RRD(H) 10 9 8 7 6 5 4 3 2 1

Contents

Acknowledgments

Inevitably an enterprise like this one benefits from the contributions of innumerable people. It would be difficult to list all of those whose written works and personal insights have made it possible to write this book.

Nonetheless, a few names stand out as worthy of special mention, particularly my agent, Giles Anderson, whose support and guidance were essential in helping me navigate the waters of the submissions process, and Eric Brandt, my editor at Harper San Francisco, whose comments and suggestions have proved invaluable in revising the manuscript. I am also obliged to Elizabeth Berg for a fine job of copyediting. In addition, I would like to thank Jay Kinney, John Carey, and John Connolly, whose comments on specific sections of the manuscript helped me avoid a number of errors. Any that remain are, of course, my responsibility and not theirs. And my friend Christopher Bamford has, as usual, been extraordinarily generous in lending me books from his magnificent personal library.

JUNE 2005

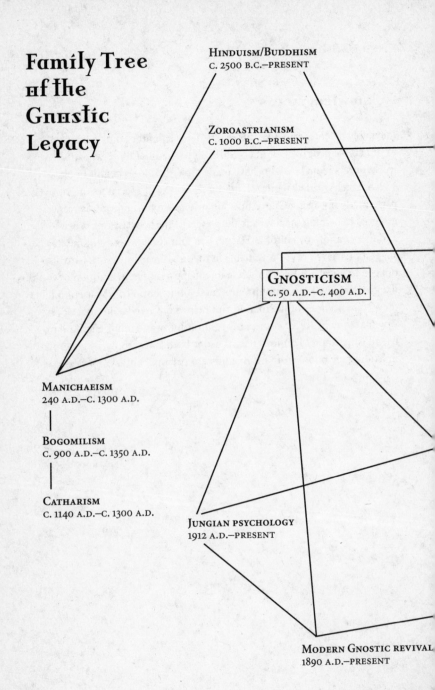

Family Tree of the Gnostic Legacy

HINDUISM/BUDDHISM
C. 2500 B.C.–PRESENT

ZOROASTRIANISM
C. 1000 B.C.–PRESENT

GNOSTICISM
C. 50 A.D.–C. 400 A.D.

MANICHAEISM
240 A.D.–C. 1300 A.D.

BOGOMILISM
C. 900 A.D.–C. 1350 A.D.

CATHARISM
C. 1140 A.D.–C. 1300 A.D.

JUNGIAN PSYCHOLOGY
1912 A.D.–PRESENT

MODERN GNOSTIC REVIVAL
1890 A.D.–PRESENT

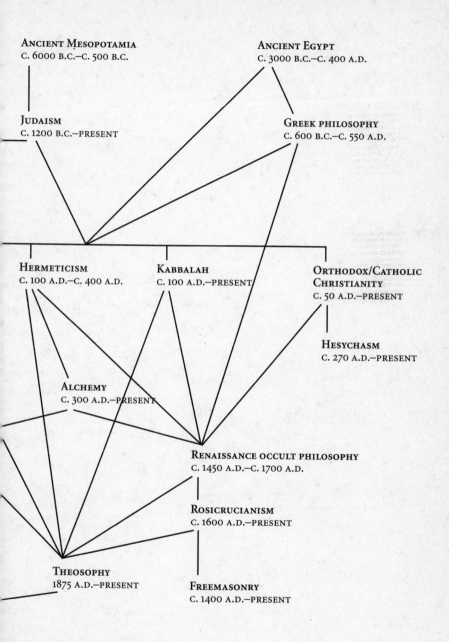

Introduction

Even the name is strange. *Gnosis*: glancing at it on the page, you may wonder how it is pronounced. (In fact the *g* is silent, and the *o* is long.) The meaning of the word is more perplexing still. Some may know that it has to do with the Gnostics or Gnosticism, and that this was a movement dating from the early days of Christianity. A person with some background in religion might add that Gnosticism was a heresy — a teaching that allegedly distorted Christ's doctrine — and that it died out in ancient times. Few would be able to say more.

And yet the subject keeps coming up. G. R. S. Mead, a British scholar who published a study of Gnosticism in 1900, could call his work *Fragments of a Faith Forgotten*, but the faith is not quite as forgotten as it was a hundred years ago. In a world that is restlessly searching for the newest and the fastest and the easiest of everything, the ancient and cryptic teachings of Gnosticism have edged their way onto best-seller lists and into television documentaries and newsmagazines. Recently *Time* magazine noted, "Thousands of Americans follow Gnosticism avidly in New Age publications and actually recreate full-dress spiritual practices from the early texts and other lore."[1] The literary critic Harold Bloom has even gone so far as to say that Gnosticism is at its core the American religion.

Why has this once-forgotten faith regained its allure? Some of it no doubt stems from the persecution it has suffered in its history. During most of Christian history, Gnosticism was forgotten because it was forbidden; to orthodox Christian theologians, it was not only a heresy but the arch-heresy. Such denunciation by the official church might have served as a deterrent in other eras, but today, in our age of self-conscious individualism and revolt against authority, it often has the opposite effect: condemnation endows a movement with glamour.

But even this explanation doesn't take us far. You can pick up any history of Christianity and find pages and pages devoted to Ultramontanists, Pelagians, Nestorians, Waldenses, and dozens of other sects and schisms that flourished for a brief time before vanishing into the afterlife of memory. All of them were duly labeled as heresies and duly condemned. Indeed one of the most impressive accomplishments of the Christian church has been the astonishing number of epithets it has devised for groups and individuals who do not see things as the officials do. Of all these dead branches in the family tree of Christianity, why should Gnosticism exercise such a peculiar and powerful fascination?

This isn't an easy question to answer, but the effort is worth making, because it will tell us a great deal not only about Gnosticism itself, but about ourselves and our spiritual aspirations. For the Gnostics to have such appeal, they must offer solutions to problems overlooked by mainstream religion. To see what these are, it would be useful to step back and look at the religious impulse with a wider lens.

Broadly speaking, religion fulfills two main functions in human life. In the first place, it's meant to foster religious experience, to enable the individual soul to commune with the divine. In the second place, it serves to cement the structure of society, upholding values and ideals that preserve the common good. The word *religion* derives from the Latin *religare*, meaning "to bind back" or "bind together." Religion's function is to bind individuals both to God and to one another.

There is no real contradiction between these two purposes; ideally they should work together in perfect harmony. But this rarely happens. More often than not, these two functions conflict in various ways, just as individual needs frequently clash with collective ones. One problem arises when an individual has some kind of spiritual experience that doesn't fit with accepted theology. This person poses an apparent threat to the established order, which regards him with suspicion and at times with hostility. He becomes a heretic and an outcast. If he has some personal charisma — and spiritual experience can endow a person with precisely this sort of charisma — he may start a church or a movement of his own. Thus are new religions born.

Whether or not this happens, someone with access to an inner source of spiritual insight does not need the church — or does not need it as ordinary people do. Furthermore, such a person often has an inner authority lacking in many leaders of established religions. This was precisely the response Jesus evoked when he began to preach: "And they were astonished at his doctrine: for he taught them as one that had authority and not as the scribes" (Mark 1:22). Naturally, the "scribes" — those with a purely external knowledge of religion — are bound to regard this person as a threat to their own power.

Of course the scribes see things differently. They view themselves as guardians of the social order. They say that society needs to have consistent patterns of belief and practice as a way of reinforcing common values. A person with an individual and independent experience of the divine threatens (or is believed to threaten) these values. If the religious authorities have some measure of secular power — as they did in Christ's time and in the Middle Ages — the mystic will be persecuted or put to death. If the authorities have little secular power — as they do today — they will have to content themselves with condemning or at least criticizing him.

It's probably unwise to indulge in too much tongue-clicking over this situation; as usually happens, people end up acting mostly as the logic of their circumstances dictates. The spiritual visionary may say, with Luther, "Here I stand: I can do no other," but the authorities on the other side of the bench could no doubt say much the same thing. They have the task of supporting and strengthening the faith of the majority, of helping them pass through the ordeals of births and deaths and marriages. They can see that most people are not interested in the subtleties of religious experience and would rather ignore them. Besides, as the clergy have long since learned, many supposedly mystical revelations are little more than symptoms of mental disorder.

Consequently, religious authorities tend to downplay or discourage such experiences; they are too troublesome and unmanageable. Take, for example, the numerous apparitions of the Virgin Mary. Many of these — at Lourdes, Fatima, Medjugorje, for example — were greeted with hostility by the local clergy, who doubted the good faith of the visionaries and also feared the challenge to their own authority. After all, people are apt to say, if the priests are so holy, why didn't the Virgin appear to them? Only later, if at all, did the church grudgingly accept the legitimacy of these visions.

As a result, the powers that be tend to discourage spiritual experience beyond a certain safe and harmless minimum. Unfortunately for them, religion exists partly because of the human need for direct communion with the divine, so they turn out to be sacrificing one part of their job to another. Thus it happens that the history of religion follows a predictable cycle: the initial vision of a charismatic founder (himself usually persecuted by the clerics of his time) degenerates, as time goes on, into a collection of secondhand dogmas. At this point, anyone who goes to the religion thirsting for spiritual experience is likely to be told she is looking for the wrong thing, or simply to be turned away.

Such is Christianity today. A modern priest or minister might be well schooled in the theology of Bultmann, Tillich, and Karl Barth and may be intimately familiar with the question of the Q document and its strata of composition, and yet find himself at a total loss when a parishioner tells him she has seen an angel. And people *do* see angels — or what they experience as angels. After over twenty-five years of spiritual exploration from both personal and professional points of view, I'm constantly amazed by how many apparently ordinary people have had profound and often dazzling spiritual experiences. They're often unwilling to talk about them, because they don't know whom to ask. They may be afraid — with some reason — of seeming strange or mad. If they go to their clergyman, usually he will give them some meaningless reassurance (if they are comparatively lucky) or (if they are not) he will tell them their experience was a visitation by the devil.

Over and against this indifference or hostility from mainstream Christianity, spiritual seekers have encountered a flood of teachings that have come to the West from Asia during the last century. These teachings have spread in mass culture to such a degree that words like *Zen*, *karma*, and *yang* and *yin* are now part of our standard vocabulary. And one thing Eastern teachings have stressed is precisely the need for spiritual experience — the need for a genuinely religious person to verify within herself the truths she has heard or read about. Indeed this is probably the main reason Hindu and Buddhist teachings have found such a huge audience in Europe and America. The idea that inner illumination is not an aberration or an embarrassment has proved to be a godsend for many.

Here is where Gnosticism comes in. It is based on *gnosis*, a Greek word that means "knowledge" but knowledge of a very specific kind — a direct inner experience of the divine. The closest equivalent in common parlance is probably *enlightenment* as described in a Hindu or Buddhist context. Many people today are excited to hear that the quest for enlightenment is not an exotic import but deeply rooted in Christianity, and may actually have been the original impetus for it. The fact that Gnosticism has been despised or ignored by the official hierarchy is not a drawback; for many, it no doubt mirrors the dismissal of their own experience by the same hierarchy.

Another reason for Gnosticism's appeal has to do with its attitude toward the world we see. The Gnostics of antiquity generally regarded the visible world as a defective creation, the handiwork of a second-rate deity called the demiurge (from a Greek word meaning "craftsman"). While this is at odds with the glaring artificial sunshine of American mass culture, the appeal of the Gnostic vision is understandable if we look a bit beneath the surface.

The great sociologist Émile Durkheim said that religion is essentially a collection of internalized social forces: "Society in general, simply by its effect on men's minds, undoubtedly has all that is required to arouse the sensation of the divine. A society is to its members what its god is to its faithful. . . . The ordinary observer cannot see where the influence of society comes from. It moves along channels that are too obscure and circuitous, and uses psychic mechanisms that are too complex, to be easily traced to the source. So long as scientific analysis has not yet taught him, man is well aware that he is acted upon but not by whom. Thus he had to build out of nothing the idea of those powers with which he feels connected."[2] Those powers are, of course, the gods.

It is both natural and somewhat comical for a sociologist to try to reduce all religious experience to mere internalizations of social forces. Even so, Durkheim's insight has much truth to it. The religious mindset tends to view the divine order in terms of the society it knows. To take an obvious example, medieval theologians portrayed the cosmos as a kind of feudal state, with the Lord at the top, the angels as the equivalents of the clergy and nobility, and humanity as the commoners.

Another example can be found among the Gnostics themselves. The classic Gnostic systems arose in the second century A.D. At this time the Roman Empire was at its zenith. For most of its subjects, the empire was the world: the Greek word *oikoumene*, literally meaning the "inhabited world," was more or less synonymous with the Roman Empire. The only parts of the known earth that were not under its sway, such as present-day Ireland, Germany, and Iran, were remote, forbidding, and for most people all but unreachable.

The Roman citizen of the time thus lived in an all-encompassing social order that had reached an extremely high level of material culture and intellectual sophistication. On the other hand, its very size and complexity dwarfed the individual. Rome, the center of political power, was not only omnipotent but also distant and frequently capricious in behavior.

In such a milieu, it's easy to see how the intellectual systems of the Gnostics sprang up. They taught that we live in a realm of delusion, ruled by inferior gods called the "archons." The true, good God was far above these dimensions, and would not even be knowable at all had he not sent divine messengers, including Jesus, to restore this lost knowledge to humanity. The Gnostics thus cast the universe in the form of the milieu they knew, where layers and layers of usually unfriendly figures stood between the individual and the main source of political authority.

Today we don't live in a world ruled by one all-encompassing political system. But it's also true that modern civilization has spread over the globe and now seems every bit as pervasive and inescapable as the Roman Empire did in its day. While our political processes still have a democratic guise, many people feel they as individuals have little actual say in them. And they are right, since a great deal of present-day power rests in the hands of corporate and bureaucratic entities over which the public has little control.

This situation has given birth to a paranoid worldview. Its fears and anxieties focus on political and economic elites — sinister combinations of the Jews, Freemasons, Bilderbergers, and various others — but some see the conspiracies in quasi-metaphysical terms — for example, malevolent extraterrestrials who have concluded secret pacts with world leaders.

These theories are not to be taken seriously on their own terms, but they *are* worth taking seriously as reflections of the discomfort aroused by a society which often seems hostile or at best uncaring. It's not surprising that such a milieu should take a fresh interest in the teachings of the Gnostics.

A third element lies in the changing psychological and philosophical orientation of our culture. Until recently, the dominant worldview in the English-speaking world was logical positivism, which says there is a reasonably close correlation between our sensory experience and reality; we can investigate this reality through scientific research and understand it through logic.

This view is now being discredited and discarded, ironically thanks to scientific research. We are increasingly aware of how the brain and the nervous system condition and limit our experience of reality. We know that we perceive things not as they are but as they're filtered through the screens of our own perceptual systems: bees can see colors we can't. Even when we extend our capacities of perception with such tools as telescopes and microscopes, we remain highly limited in what we can perceive, and we are more aware of this fact than ever. The apostle Paul said that "we see through a glass darkly," but we have a far more vivid and intricate sense of that "glass" than he ever had.

These filters of our perception bear a powerful resemblance to the archons of the Gnostics, who keep humanity imprisoned in a world of suffering and delusion. The chief difference is that in antiquity people tended to view them as external gods, whereas today we're more likely to regard them as innate parts of the structure of our own minds. But the conclusion is no less terrifying, and in some ways is more so. Biologically we have evolved our senses to enable us to live and act and move in the world we see. If we can't trust these very senses, if they shackle us to a quasi-delusional world they have made, what *can* we trust?

These ideas have percolated into mass culture rapidly and deeply. To take one well-known example, the 1999 film *The Matrix* created a world in which practically every living human was being kept asleep by a collective hallucination created by evil machinelike entities. These figures bear an astonishingly close resemblance to the archons of the Gnostics. (I will discuss *The Matrix* in more detail in chapter 9.)

All these reasons suggest why Gnosticism has enjoyed such a tremendous revival today. And yet there is one more factor, which I believe is far more compelling than any of these. It is quite simply this: there is a widespread sense that *something is missing in Christianity*. Somewhere between the time of Christ himself and the churches we know today, a vital ingredient was lost. David Hawkins, a well-known spiritual author, suggests one possibility: "A major decline [in the level of truth in Christianity] in the year 325 A.D. was apparently due to the spread of misinterpretations of the teachings originating from the Council of Nicaea."[3] This view, or something like it, has been stated in dozens of books and articles.

Usually this missing element, whatever it is, is conceived in factual terms. And it's true that many crucial facts are missing from our picture of Christian origins. Curiously, there are no surviving eyewitness accounts of Christ. Here is a man who was revered as a divine being almost immediately after his death, and yet not one of his closest disciples left any firsthand account of his experiences with him. The Gospels of the New Testament are not eyewitness accounts and do not claim to be. Luke says that the materials in his Gospel were related to him by those "which from the beginning were eyewitnesses" (Luke 1:2).[4] John ends with the peculiar statement that the beloved disciple "testifieth of these things, and wrote these things: and we know that his testimony is true" (John 21:24). No one would say "we know that his testimony is true" if he himself had been the eyewitness. Nowhere in any of the Gospels does anyone state that he himself saw these things with his own eyes.

Since conventional Christianity stresses that the events in the Gospels are factually true, this omission is extremely odd. Could it really be the case that none of Christ's disciples ever thought to write anything down about their own experience? There is no evidence that they did, but we can wonder whether such things may have been written down only to be destroyed or suppressed later — for what reasons we do not know.

Most scholars, for example, acknowledge that the ending to Mark, reckoned to be the oldest of the Gospels, was lost. The existing Gospel ends at Mark 16:8: "And they went out quickly, and fled from the sepulchre: for they trembled and were amazed: neither said they any thing to any man; for they were afraid." This ending is even more abrupt in the Greek than in the English; the last word in the verse is a conjunction. (Several alternative endings exist; you can find them in most editions of the Bible.) Did the last page of this text simply get lost, or was it deliberately removed and replaced with something else?

As usual, attempting to answer this question says more about one's preconceptions than about the actuality, so I will go no further in this direction. I will limit myself to saying that some crucial material about the earliest era of Christianity seems to be missing. The reading public has taken up this idea with enthusiasm: Dan Brown's novel *The Da Vinci Code* owes much of its extraordinary success to this fact. As most people know by now, the novel centers around a legend that Jesus was married to Mary Magdalene and that they had a child, whose bloodline entered into the Merovingian dynasty of France.

I will say more about this legend in chapter 1, but for now let me simply say I don't think the missing element in Christianity can be reduced to a collection of facts, however fascinating, about who Jesus was or what he did. Nor is it merely a matter of loss of faith. Something far greater and yet far more subtle is lacking. Christianity today often resembles an egg into which someone has poked a hole and sucked out all its contents, and then taken the shell, encrusted it with gold and jewels, and set it up as an object of veneration. In many ways, it remains a beautiful shell, but more and more people are finding that it no longer offers any nourishment. If they complain, they're usually told that they just need to have more faith — which is of course no answer at all.

On its own, faith is not enough. In many ways the twentieth century was an age of tremendous faith — much of it placed in insane political theories that brought disaster on the nations that were unwise enough to put them into practice. And even at its best, faith is merely a halting first step. Say I need to drive to Mexico and I have never been there before. In front of me I have a map. I may have faith in the map, but unless I actually test it out by attempting to follow it to my destination, my faith is not justified. And if I follow the map and find it leads me nowhere, what good does it do me to be told I should still have faith in the map? Today we are in this exact position regarding Christianity. Although the title of the present book points to a forbidden faith, very frequently it is knowledge rather than faith that has been forbidden.

What is missing in Christianity as we know it now is not merely a collection of facts but a connection to some vital inner experience that enables us to know directly the truth of what we seek. And this is what the Gnostic vision holds out to us — the possibility of experience rather than hearsay, of verification rather than blind trust. I'm not, of course, trying to resurrect the Gnostic teachings wholesale. That would be impossible in any case, because we don't understand their systems well enough to reconstruct them in practice. Any such attempt would, I suspect, turn out to be unworkable and even somewhat ridiculous. The truth remains the same throughout the ages, but the names and forms into which it is poured vary with the needs of circumstance. What made sense in the second century A.D. may seem like gibberish today.

This book is not about the direct survival of the ancient Gnostic schools. We have no evidence that they survived the end of classical antiquity. But one thing *has* survived: the quest for gnosis, for direct knowledge of higher realities, as the centerpiece of the human experience. This goal has been sought — and has apparently been reached — by many seekers over the last two thousand years. In the words of Elaine Pagels, whose book *The Gnostic Gospels* was a prime stimulant of today's appetite for Gnosticism:

> The concerns of gnostic Christians survived . . . as a suppressed
> current, like a river driven underground. Such currents resurfaced
> throughout the Middle Ages in various forms of heresy; then with
> the Reformation, Christian tradition again took on new and diverse
> forms. Mystics like Jacob Boehme, himself accused of heresy, and
> radical visionaries like George Fox, themselves unfamiliar, in all
> probability, with gnostic tradition, nevertheless articulated analogous
> interpretations of religious experience.[5]

In this sense the Gnostics' legacy still continues, in many guises and under many names. My goal here is to give a history of that legacy. As neglected and reviled as it has frequently been, it may have some lost treasures that we can take into the future. It may even offer a key to that haunting verse from the Bible: "The stone which the builders refused is become the head stone of the corner" (Ps. 118:22).

CHAPTER 1

Who Were the Gnostics?

Until fairly recently, if you were to ask about the origins of Christianity, you would hear much the same story no matter whom you asked. Jesus Christ, the incarnate Son of God, came down from heaven. He taught the apostles the true faith and commissioned them to preach the Gospel to all nations. He also founded a church and appointed the apostles as its leaders. Sometime in the second century A.D., this organization started to call itself the Catholic Church, from the Greek *katholikos*, or "universal." All Christian churches today are, in one way or another, its offspring.

Human nature being what it is, however, things did not always proceed so smoothly. Groups of people sprang up who introduced their own distortions into Christ's doctrine. Some said that Christians still had to observe the Jewish Law. Others said that Christ wasn't really divine. Still others said he wasn't really human.

Throughout the centuries, the church, aided by the power of the Holy Spirit, managed to face down these heretics, as they came to be called (from the Greek *hairesis*, or "sect"). To this day, the Christian church has preserved Christ's teaching in its pure form, thanks to the countless Church Fathers and theologians who fended off the assaults of error.

As I say, this was the standard picture of Christian history until comparatively recently (although, of course, certain details had to be adjusted depending on which denomination was telling the story). And this is the picture in which many sincere Christians still believe. Unfortunately, as modern scholarship has discovered, it's not entirely accurate.

If you read the Gospels carefully, you will notice that Christ does not talk much about theology. He has a lot to say about ethics, about loving your neighbor, and about going to God with inner sincerity. He argues often and heatedly with scribes and Pharisees about sacrificing the spirit of the Law to the letter. But he does not argue with them about the nature of God, nor does he even say who or what he himself is. His disciples keep asking him, but he never gives them a clear answer. If you were to summarize Christ's teaching as found in the Gospels, you might turn to a verse from the prophet Micah: "What doth the Lord require of thee, but to do justly, and to love mercy, and to walk humbly with thy God?" (Mic. 6:8). Christ says much the same thing in the episode of the Two Great Commandments (Matt. 22:35–40; Mark 12:28–31). There's not much theology in that.

This was the heart of Christ's teaching, and he no doubt had good reasons for stressing the things he stressed. But once Christ himself was no longer on the scene, his disciples began to teach his message in their own ways, and these ways soon began to diverge. Some stayed close to the Jewish religion; others moved away from it. You can see this in the New Testament, where Paul quarrels with the church leaders over whether Gentile converts need to follow the Mosaic Law. (The dispute is described both in Acts and in Paul's letter to the Galatians. Acts makes the whole affair sound considerably more peaceful and dignified than Paul does: Acts 15:1–31; Gal. 2:1–16.) There were other differences as well. Some emphasized a more external faith; others saw Christ's teaching in a more mystical light.

By the second century A.D., if you were to take a look at the Christian community in the Roman Empire, you would undoubtedly find a number of different, often conflicting, groups who understood the master's teaching in various ways. Some would see Jesus as a great spiritual master and nothing more. Some would resemble early versions of the Catholic or Orthodox churches today, with bishops and sacraments; others would probably look more like philosophical study groups or mystical schools. And although it would be far from true to say that these different bodies lived in perfect harmony, none of them had any special privileges, and so they all had to coexist. This picture would change radically only in the fourth century A.D., when the emperor Constantine first legalized Christianity and then began to turn it into the state religion of the Roman Empire. At this point the proto–Catholic Church — which was previously only one strain of the Christian tradition — consolidated its power by suppressing its Christian as well as its pagan rivals.

Christian history is, as a result, a sad and often heartbreaking story, where great Church Fathers (some of them later canonized as saints) heaped anathemas upon alleged heretics over points of doctrine that Christ and his disciples would in all likelihood neither have cared about nor even understood. At the same time the essential teaching of Christ — to "love thy neighbor as thyself" — was often sacrificed to this doctrinal squabbling, turning the church itself into a merciless persecutor.

The ancient Gnostics were one of those lost strains of Christianity. Who were the Gnostics, and what were they like? This isn't always easy to figure out, because much of the material we have about them comes from Church Fathers who were writing anti-Gnostic polemics. We are thus somewhat in the position of a future historian who would have to piece together a Democratic Party platform using only Republican campaign commercials as sources (or vice versa).

Fortunately, the situation has improved of late, thanks to the discovery of Gnostic texts at various archaeological sites in the Middle East over the last century. The most celebrated of these took place at Nag Hammadi, Egypt, in 1945. Two peasants, digging for fertilizer, unearthed a cache of scriptures, many of them previously unknown, that cast an entirely new light on Gnostic teachings. This discovery is so important that it in itself is one of the main reasons for the resurgent interest in Gnosticism. The Nag Hammadi texts were written by different authors at different times and represent the views of a number of sects and teachers. But they still offer an extremely valuable window onto a tradition that had previously been known mainly through the words of its enemies.

The First Gospel?

Perhaps the most interesting of the Nag Hammadi scriptures is an enigmatic work called *The Gospel of Thomas*. It is extremely short — in one standard edition, it fills only twelve pages — but it has received more attention than any of the other Gnostic scriptures.[1] This is partly because, although it never found a place in the New Testament, it may be older than the Gospels that did.

The age of *Thomas* is not easy to determine. Many scholars have placed it in the mid-second century A.D., on the grounds that it is a supposedly Gnostic document. But this begs the question, because it assumes that Gnosticism did not arise before the second century.[2] If *Thomas* is older than that, it would force scholars to push the origins of Gnosticism back to the first century. And there is reason to believe that this Gospel does date from earlier than the second century.

The most compelling argument is the form this Gospel takes. It tells no story and has no narrative beginning or ending. It is simply a collection of sayings, some of them parables, some of them proverbs, "that the living Jesus spoke," as we read in the opening verse. Remarkably, this makes the *Gospel of Thomas* resemble early sayings collections whose existence had long been postulated by New Testament scholars based on similarities and differences among the canonical Gospels. The most famous of these hypothetical sayings collections is called Q (from the German *Quelle*, or "source"). No text of this document has been discovered yet, and one may never be. Scholars can only infer what Q was like from similarities and differences between Matthew and Luke, both of whom evidently made use of it.

The Gospel of Thomas is not Q. But it bears a striking resemblance to Q in its literary form, which, as a bare collection of sayings, is more primitive than the ordered narratives of the four New Testament Gospels. Scholars generally assume that the simpler a text is, the older it's likely to be, since later versions tend to acquire embellishments and additions that were not in the first versions. To take one example, there is an apocryphal Gospel called the *Protevangelion of James*, which is about Christ's birth and infancy. (It is, by the way, the origin of the idea of Mary's Immaculate Conception.) It has a more elaborate nativity than either Matthew or Luke, and other details indicate that it's based on them. Precisely for this reason, it cannot be older than they are; it's generally dated to around 150 A.D.[3]

Thomas is not like these apocryphal works. It is not based on the canonical Gospels, it is in a more primitive form than they are, and besides, it takes exactly the form that scholars had long supposed the earliest texts about Jesus had. For this reason, some New Testament scholars go so far as to call it the "fifth Gospel." It could have been written as early as 50 A.D. Matthew, Mark, Luke, and John are usually dated to between 70 and 100 A.D.

If so, this is rather troubling to those who believe that Jesus taught a version of Christianity like those of the mainstream denominations, whether Catholic, Orthodox, or Protestant. The *Gospel of Thomas* does not present Jesus as the incarnate Son of God who takes away the sins of the world, or as the second person of the Trinity. In fact, Jesus makes no special claim to divinity or divine authority. At one point, he asks his disciples what he is like. Peter tells him he is like a righteous angel. Matthew says he is like a wise philosopher. Thomas says, "Teacher, my mouth utterly will not let me say what you resemble."[4]

Jesus chides him, saying, "I am not your teacher. You have become intoxicated from the bubbling wellspring that I have poured out." So, far from asserting his own divinity, Jesus even balks at being honored with the comparatively humble title of "teacher." Moreover, *Thomas* never speaks of Jesus as "Christ" — the Greek equivalent of the Hebrew *Messiah*, or "anointed one." These facts also point toward an early date for this Gospel, since under most circumstances, the image of charismatic figures grows in status and prestige as their living memory fades. Eventually they may attain divine or semidivine status. (In our own time, this has happened with Mao Zedong in China and even with Elvis Presley in the United States.) The doctrine of Jesus's divinity was not formulated until the Council of Nicaea, convened by the emperor Constantine in 325.

Just as important as these considerations is the kind of teaching that the Jesus of *Thomas* presents. Many of Jesus's sayings in *Thomas* resemble those in the New Testament Gospels. Those that don't are often extremely cryptic: "Be passers-by" (*Thomas*, 42). "I have cast fire upon the world, and see, I am watching until it blazes" (10). "When you see one not born of woman, fall upon your faces and prostrate yourself before that one: it is that one who is your father" (15). Most striking, however, is the declaration made at the very beginning of the Gospel: "Whoever finds the meaning of these sayings will not taste death" (1).

It is this characteristic of *Thomas* that has led scholars to regard it as Gnostic. Here, in essence, is the central difference between Gnosticism and conventional Christianity. "Whoever finds the meaning of these sayings will not taste death." What is most important in *Thomas* is not sin, repentance, and redemption, but an enigmatic mystical illumination that is somehow encoded in these verses. Jesus's sayings in *Thomas* are like koans, those unanswerable riddles given by Zen masters to their pupils as a way of cutting through the ordinary mind. They are meant not to convey information but to awaken. The goal of Gnosticism is not salvation, but enlightenment.

This was, no doubt, the main reason conventional Christianity repudiated Gnosticism, for illumination is too hard, too uncertain of attainment, to form the basis for a popular religion. It is much easier to see things in light of sin and atonement or appeasing the wrath of an angry God, particularly in pagan antiquity, which adopted exactly this attitude toward its own deities.

What of Thomas the man? We do not know much about him. His name means "twin" in Aramaic, but that tells us little. Some argue that he was Jesus's twin brother or resembled Jesus enough to be his twin, but most likely it simply means that he was born as a twin to someone else and had *Thomas* as his nickname. His most famous appearance in the Bible comes in John's Gospel, where he doubts Christ has risen from the dead and only believes when he sees (John 20:24–29). But scholars have in turn doubted that this story is historical. They say it most likely does not reflect a real incident; instead it was a jab at the Gnostics, followers of Thomas, some of whom did not believe that Christ had suffered and died in the flesh.

Apart from these sketchy details, scholars believe that Thomas most likely preached in Syria, where he was venerated for centuries by Christians (and where his Gospel may have been written). Afterward he may have gone as far afield as India, where to this day an extremely ancient Christian community traces its origins to his preaching. Thomas left his mark in the East, in areas where mystical enlightenment would find a more congenial home than among the rationalistic Greeks or the hard-headed Romans.

The Roots of Gnosticism

But India was not to prove the central stage for the development of Christianity. The Roman Empire provided this context, and late Roman culture and thought would leave an indelible mark on Christianity in all its forms. This was a world similar to our own in many respects. It was vast, far-flung (encompassing the entire Mediterranean basin), and remarkably unified. During the first two centuries of the Christian era, wars were rare, and the empire's inhabitants "enjoyed and abused the advantages of wealth and luxury," in the words of the historian Edward Gibbon.[5] Trade and commerce flourished, and as usually happens, along with goods and money, there also flowed ideas, philosophies, and religions. New cults and sects burgeoned in a generally tolerant pagan culture. (The Christians were persecuted not because they believed in a different god but because they refused to honor the others — a slight that pagans believed ran the risk of bringing on divine wrath.)

This religious culture helped shape the infant Christian faith. Its first and greatest influence was, of course, Judaism, the mother faith. From Judaism,

Christianity took its sacred scripture as well as its view of a single, monotheistic God. At the same time, from the outset Christianity has always had a problematic relationship with Judaism. One of the key problems has to do with the nature of God himself. The God of the Hebrews is not always good; he is capable of wrath and vengeance and is unapologetic about it. "I form the light and create darkness; I make peace and create evil; I the Lord do all these things" (Isa. 49:7). "Out of the mouth of the most High proceedeth not evil and good?" (Lam. 3:38). This was not always easy to reconcile with the good, loving God preached by Jesus.

In addition to Judaism, there were also the philosophical schools, which did not occupy themselves with philosophy as we know it today, but explained the nature of the gods and the universe and taught their pupils how to live in harmony with them. Of these the most important for Christianity and Gnosticism was the school of Plato. Although Plato himself lived in the fourth century B.C., he left an institution of higher education called the Academy in Athens, where his doctrines were taught and continued to evolve in the following centuries. It would be hard to overestimate his influence. In fact, it's sometimes said that all Western philosophy is a footnote to Plato.

Plato explains reality in a way that could be described as *esoteric*. This word does not refer to the difficulty or obscurity of his thought. Originally it meant that many of his teachings were given only to relatively advanced pupils, people who were "further in" the circle (the word comes from the Greek *esotero*, which means "further in"). But it points to another meaning as well: it indicates that these teachings are essentially about inner experience. Unlike modern thought, which views the invisible and internal dimensions of life and thought as purely subjective (and hence unreal), esotericism says these inner dimensions have a genuine reality and can be known and intelligently described. Plato even went so far as to flip conventional wisdom on its head and say that the world we see is itself unreal. The solid objects of ordinary reality are merely copies or imitations of ideal entities that he called "forms" — abstract images that exist in the realm of thought. The forms alone are real, Plato said, because they are eternal and unchanging, unlike the ceaselessly shifting world here below.[6]

Plato's influence on Gnosticism was profound, but it's often overlooked. The most important of Plato's works from this point of view is a late dialogue called the *Timaeus*. It is the book that introduced the myth of the lost continent of Atlantis. (According to Plato, who said these records had been preserved in Egypt, Atlantis was destroyed around 9600 B.C.) After talking about Atlantis, the *Timaeus* goes on to paint an esoteric portrait of the creation of the universe. God is good, Plato says, and "the good can never envy anyone anything." Consequently, "God wanted everything to be good, and nothing bad, insofar as this was possible."[7] So he created a world that was as perfect — as like himself — as it could be.

As part of this project, God creates the seven planets, which (in accordance with Greek myth) are also gods. He then charges these gods with making the human race. God does not make them himself, because, he says, "If I created them and gave them life, they would be equal to the gods."[8] Nonetheless, God says, he himself will sow the seed of divine consciousness in them. They will be a mixture of mortal and immortal.

In the *Timaeus*, Plato sometimes refers to God — and he *does* speak of one true God, who is above all the others and who in fact created them — metaphorically as the "craftsman." The Greek word for this is *demiourgos*, which has been anglicized into "demiurge." The later Gnostics would adopt this name for the creator. But they changed Plato's system by saying that this demiurge was a second-rate deity who created the visible world. They added the idea of another God — a true, good God who remained above, unmoved and aloof from this degenerate piece of cosmic handiwork. Plato's philosophical descendants objected to these views; Plotinus, the great Neoplatonic philosopher of the third century A.D., even wrote a treatise refuting them.[9] Despite these crucial alterations, it's easy to see how Plato's ideas fed into Gnostic currents.

Finally, there were the mystery cults, which introduced their followers to higher states of consciousness through secret rituals devoted to such gods as Demeter, Dionysus, and Isis, the beloved Great Mother of the Egyptians (from whom the Virgin Mary would later take many of her attributes). Initiates swore to remain silent about what they had learned and done in their rites, and they kept their oaths so well that we have only a vague idea of what went on. We do know, however, that a common theme had to do with death and resurrection. Some said the chief benefit of initiation into the mysteries was that you would no longer have a fear of death.

Even this brief picture shows some of the roots out of which Gnosticism grew. We see themes of hidden knowledge, mystical experience, and the greatest mystery of all — death and rebirth. Then there is the nature of God himself. Is he good? If so, why is the world in such terrible shape? Maybe, as Plato said, the world is not real — and maybe it's not all that good either. If this is true, what does it say about the God who created it?

The Gnostic teachers turned these questions into a system of thought that remains powerful and compelling. It's not always a cheerful picture, nor is it always easy to understand. But it has a strange allure for the modern — or rather postmodern — mind, obsessed with texts that mean the opposite of what they say on the surface, with realities that drop away from us under our feet, with forces that shape our lives and fates beyond our ken. Most importantly, it speaks to the nagging need inside many of us for awakening, for recollecting a lost truth that is central to our existence but which we have somehow mislaid.

The Gnostic Teachers

The most prominent Gnostics were charismatic teachers and philosophers who lived in the second century A.D. They taught their doctrines in lectures and private sessions and published them in books (which have come down to us only in fragments, if at all). Our information about them is extremely sketchy, because their own surviving writings have no autobiographical material, and the Church Fathers were more interested in denouncing them than saying who they were. But the little we know points to a fascinating cast of characters.

The earliest known Gnostic teacher makes a brief appearance in the book of Acts. He was named Simon, and he "used sorcery, and bewitched the people of Samaria, making out that he was some great one" (Acts 8:9).[10] Simon converts to Christianity but somehow seems to miss the point. Seeing Peter and John heal by the Holy Spirit, he offers to buy this power from them. Peter rebukes him, saying, "Thy money perish with thee, because thou hast thought that the gift of God may be purchased with money" (Acts 8:20). Although Simon repents, the Catholic Church gave him the unusual honor of naming a sin after him — simony, that is, buying or selling spiritual things for money.

The New Testament tells us no more about Simon, but it's probably not true that he repented, since later Church Fathers traced all the Gnostic schools back to him and indeed considered him the father of all heresy. In fact, there is good reason to doubt that he was ever a Christian to begin with.

Simon Magus (as he came to be called) must have been a rather wild individual. Living in the first century, at roughly the same time as Christ and his disciples, he was one of a swarm of pseudo-messiahs that abounded in the Palestine of that era, claiming to be a divine incarnation, "making out that he was some great one," as Acts puts it. Accompanying him was a woman he said was the embodiment of the fallen "Thought" of God as well as a reincarnation of Helen of Troy, whom he had found working in a whorehouse in Tyre, in what is now Lebanon.

Simon's version of Gnosticism focused on this fallen Thought of God, of which Simon's prostituted consort was only the last and lowliest incarnation. In essence, he seems to have been saying that what is primordially creative is the mind. The power to think, the capacity to think, he called the "Father." This capacity produced the Thought of God. Unfortunately, once this Thought had an existence independent from God, it felt lonely and alienated. It began to produce thoughts of its own, each of which was still more es-tranged from the primordial God, resulting in our own world of separation and isolation. Simon's own reincarnated Helen symbolized the condition of this fallen and degraded thought, exiled from the mind of God, condemned to life in this world in the most degraded of occupations.

It's not hard to cast Simon Magus as a pseudo-guru of the sort we can rec-ognize from our own time. The presence of his reincarnated Helen, the res-cued harlot, must have added a theatrical touch to his preaching. On the other hand, we also have to bear in mind that everything we know about him comes from the writings of his enemies. They managed to weave an intricate (but al-most certainly fictitious) story around him. Educated in Alexandria, Simon was allegedly a pupil of John the Baptist, who so admired his ability that he would have appointed him his successor, except that Simon happened to be in Egypt at the time of John's death. Simon, Helen, and thirty of his disciples eventually went to Rome, where he vied with Peter for the allegiance of the Christian community, and there he met his end. Apparently he wanted to prove that he would rise from the dead, so he had himself buried alive, but unfortunately failed to resurrect himself.

As I have suggested, this story is almost certainly legendary, and from it we can only gather some strands of truth, chiefly that Simon had followers in Samaria and that he or his disciples had some presence in Rome.

One apocryphal text has Simon debating with Peter, and in it Simon Magus makes this highly revealing assertion: "But you will . . . constantly stop your ears that they should not be defiled by blasphemies, and you will turn to flight, for you will find nothing to reply; but the foolish people will agree with you, indeed will come to love you, for you teach what is customary with them, but they will curse me, for I proclaim something new and unheard of."[11]

This passage reveals the issue that perhaps most sharply divided the Gnostics from the proto-Catholics. The Gnostics did not want to make their teaching easy; they saw it as difficult and not for the many. Peter and his successors, on the other hand, preached a doctrine that was accessible to nearly everyone, particularly since it fit in well with the deeply embedded notions of sin and sacrifice that were so prevalent in the ancient world. It would prove to be a key element in the triumph of Catholic Christianity.

I will not go into any more detail about Simon's system here, except to say that in its broad outlines it sets out the central Gnostic myth of alienation and redemption through illumination. Although no one today is going to resurrect Simon's teaching as a whole, there is some wisdom in his fundamental insight about the alienated "Thought" of God.

Another of the great Gnostic teachers was named Marcion.[12] The son of a wealthy shipowner from the shores of the Black Sea, he was probably born at the end of the first century. Around 140 he went to Rome, where he began to articulate his own theological views. In 144 he tried to gain acceptance for them in the Roman church but didn't succeed, and went off to start his own church, teaching until his death around 160. His influence was considerable, especially in the Middle East: there were whole communities in Syria that followed his version of Christianity as late as the fifth century.

Marcion inadvertently made a major contribution to the development of orthodox Christianity. He taught a theory of two gods: the good, true God far above, who sent Jesus Christ as a redeemer, and a lower, evil deity, the ruler and creator of this world, whom he identified with the God of the Old Testament. Naturally this led him to take a hostile view of the Hebrew Bible, so he created the first canon of Christian scripture, which was extremely stripped-down. Eliminating the entire Old Testament, Marcion's bible consisted of the Gospel of Luke, with its more Jewish elements removed, along with nine of Paul's Epistles. It was in reaction to Marcion's canon that the nascent Catholic Church would begin to draw up its own canon of the New Testament — a process that would not be complete until the fourth century.

One curious detail about Marcion's skeletal bible is the weight it gives to the writings of Paul; actually, it includes little else. This may seem odd, because Paul is generally credited as the founding genius of orthodox Christianity. Many have said he was more crucial to the development of Christian

thought than Christ himself. But there is much in the Pauline writings that
has a Gnostic flavor. In Galatians 3:19, Paul says that the Law "was ordained by
angels in the hand of a mediator." The Gnostics understood this to mean that
the Law of the Old Testament had been given not directly by God but by a
kind of intermediary on God's behalf. This would give rise to views like
Marcion's, in which the God of the Old Testament is a lesser and indeed
somewhat malevolent figure.[13] And while most scholars today don't believe
that Paul himself wrote Ephesians (they date it to the late first century, some
thirty or forty years after Paul's death), Marcion did; he made it part of his
canon. And in Ephesians we read, "For we wrestle not against flesh and blood,
but against principalities, against powers, against the rulers of the darkness of
this world, against spiritual wickedness in high places" (Eph. 6:12).

Here we find an echo of a key theme in Gnosticism: the existence of the
archons, invisible rulers of the heavenly realm that stand between us and
God. According to the esoteric worldview that was widely held in antiquity,
there were celestial "principalities" and "powers" that mediated between the
One God far above and the world of matter and appearances here below.
The Gnostics and the orthodox Christians disagreed not so much about
whether these powers existed, but about whether they were fundamentally
good or evil.

In any event, Paul was cited as a major source among the Gnostics. Valentinus,
the greatest and most influential of all Gnostic teachers, traced his spiritual
lineage to Paul. Valentinus was born in Lower Egypt around the end of the
first century A.D.[14] He was educated at Alexandria, where he converted to
Christianity. He was taught the inner doctrines of Gnosticism by an individual named Theudas, who is otherwise unknown but was apparently a disciple
of Paul's. Thus Valentinus traced his spiritual lineage directly back to Paul.

Eventually, like Marcion, Valentinus moved to Rome and began to teach
there, gaining considerable status in the Christian church. Some sources say
he was put up for election as bishop of Rome (there was no pope as such in
those days) and only lost by a narrow margin. Nonetheless, he continued to
teach, either in Rome or Cyprus. In addition, refuting the preconception that
the Gnostics were removed from ordinary reality, he was intensely active in
community work. He died sometime around 160. Even his enemies acknowl-
edged his brilliance and his literary genius. Here is one of his hymns, entitled
"Summer Harvest":

> I see in spirit that all are hung
> I know in spirit that all are borne
> Flesh hanging from soul
> Soul clinging to air
> Air hanging from upper atmosphere
> Crops rushing forth from the deep
> A babe rushing forth from the womb.[15]

With its ethereal beauty, this hymn shows one of the key features of Valentinus's thought, and indeed that of Gnosticism as a whole. The references to "soul" and "flesh" and "air" may seem baffling, but to someone who understands their symbolic language, their meaning is clear. Valentinus is speaking of three levels of being: the "air," the realm of the spirit; the "soul" or psyche, an intermediate level that depends upon the spirit; and finally the "flesh," the physical form that emanates from the soul. Above the spirit is the "upper atmosphere," the abode of God himself.

This picture of reality appears in countless instances in Western esoteric thought, not only in Gnosticism, but in other forms of esoteric Christianity and in the Jewish Kabbalah. Despite the variations that we often see among these systems, the symbolic language is remarkably consistent over an extremely long period of time. It is, in fact, this symbolic consistency that largely makes it possible to understand what the Gnostics were saying and what experiential realities they were pointing to.

The distinction between the soul and the spirit may seem academic or obscure to us, but it was not so to the Gnostics. Unlike today, when no one seems to have anything more than the vaguest idea of what these words even mean, the distinction between the soul and spirit was crucial in early Christianity. For the Gnostics and for the early Christians in general, the soul was the whole of the mental and emotional complex that makes up our inner life. The closest equivalent we have for this concept in modern English is "psyche" — and it's no coincidence that when the word *soul* appears in most English translations of the New Testament, the Greek word it is translating is *psyche*. The spirit, by contrast, was pure consciousness, the Self, the true "I" — what other religions have called by such names as the "Atman" or "Buddha nature."

This distinction was extremely important to Valentinus and indeed to most of the Gnostics, who separated humanity into three fundamental types.[16] The first, and the lowest, are the *carnal* or *fleshly* ones (sometimes called the *hylic*, from the Greek *hyle*, or "matter"): those who are oriented toward the external world of things and toward physical desires such as food and sex. Next come *psychic* individuals. This has nothing to do with "psychic powers" as we speak of them today, but rather points to a middle orientation between the body and the spirit. Such people have begun to awaken from the dream of ordinary life but have not awakened entirely. The Gnostics tended to see ordinary Christian believers, those who lived by faith rather than knowledge, as "psychic" individuals. Finally, there are the *spiritual* ones, who are also sometimes called the *pneumatic* (from the Greek *pneuma*, "spirit"). These have transcended their bonds to the world and are totally free. They are beyond earthly attachments and are no longer tempted or distracted by them (at least in theory).

It may seem arrogant and exclusive to sort people into three different classes, and no doubt some of the Gnostics must have made it look very much that way. A tendency toward elitism was one of the chief flaws of Gnostic teaching and no doubt contributed to its downfall. Even so, it's not entirely wrong, especially if we realize that this is essentially a process of self-selection. You yourself choose the category you will fall into simply by virtue of what interests you. "Where your treasure is, there your heart will be also" (Matt. 6:21). If you are oriented toward the external world and preoccupied with the satisfactions of the body, you are a "fleshly" person, no matter how well-born or well-educated you are. If you are drawn toward the unseen, toward the realms of the divine that seem to haunt us even as they elude us, you are more likely to be a spiritual, or *pneumatic*, individual — or at least have the potential to become one.

There is one work by Valentinus whose title alone survives. It was called *On the Three Natures*, and according to the ancient author who mentions it, it contained the first discussion of the Father, Son, and Holy Spirit as the three Persons of the Trinity.[17] This fact shows how complex and contradictory the whole question of Christian origins can be. Apparently the doctrine of the Trinity — the linchpin of orthodox Christianity — was first formulated by an alleged heretic.

The fourth great Gnostic teacher was Basilides.[18] Like Marcion and Valentinus, he lived in the early second century; unlike them, he did not go to Rome but stayed and taught in Alexandria. He taught a fabulously intricate esoteric system, in which the earth was surrounded by 365 heavens (which was, he said, why there were that many days in the year). The ruler of these heavens was called Abraxas or Abrasax, whose name in Greek numerology adds up to 365. It was only the angels of the lowest of these heavens — extremely insignificant figures in the celestial hierarchy — who fashioned the earth and all that is in it. Their ruler was worshipped as the God of the Old Testament.

Christ came down to save us from bondage to this unpleasant and humiliating state of affairs, but Christ, said Basilides, didn't really suffer on the cross. Instead he switched places with Simon of Cyrene (who, according to Luke, bore Jesus's cross for him) and stood aside, laughing at the folly of those who believed the world was real, while the unfortunate Simon died in his stead. In fact, said Basilides, anyone who pledged allegiance to Christ crucified was still in bondage to the low-grade rulers of this world.

Basilides, like many other Gnostics, did not attach much value to the body. We see this tendency as far back as the *Gospel of Thomas*, where Jesus says, "Wretched is the body that depends on a body. And wretched is the soul that depends upon these two" (*Thomas*, 87). Believing the world of matter was an inferior creation, the Gnostics generally regarded the body with contempt. For most of them, this led to asceticism, to cutting themselves off from carnal desires by abstaining from meat and sex, but some, including Basilides, came to the opposite conclusion: since the body was not worth much, it hardly mattered what you did with it. Of Basilides, the second-century Church Father Irenaeus of Lyons (a heresy-hunter to whom we owe much of our knowledge of Gnosticism) wrote, "He enjoined [his followers] not to worry about meat sacrificed to idols, to consider that it is nothing, and to use it without concern. Furthermore, one should consider use of the remaining modes of behavior and all kinds of pleasure as matters of indifference."[19]

Basilides himself probably had some affinities with the Stoics, the ancient philosophic school that exhorted its members to live with philosophical detachment, but some Gnostics went further and advocated antinomianism, which basically says the rules don't matter. If we are living in an illusory world created by a second-rate God, we can do anything we like down here.

Other Gnostic teachers have left even fainter impressions on history. Some are little more than names, with a fact or two attached: Cerdo, the teacher of Marcion; Cerinthus, an "enemy of truth" whom John the Evangelist on one occasion allegedly fled the baths in Ephesus to avoid; Carpocrates, whose disciples were accused of indulging in lurid rituals in which they ate semen and menstrual blood as sacraments. It's hard to know how many of these details are true. Sometimes they're contradictory. One tradition, for example, says that John wrote his Gospel in opposition to Cerinthus; another tradition says Cerinthus himself wrote it. So much knowledge has been lost, and so much of what has survived has been changed to suit various agendas, that we have to content ourselves with broad outlines.

Mary Magdalene, Christ's Consort

One figure whose name often appears in a Gnostic context is Mary Magdalene. She is a familiar figure in Catholic piety: "the woman taken in adultery," a repentant whore who anointed Jesus's feet with fragrant oil and wiped them with her own hair. Unlike most of the apostles, who left town as soon as Jesus was arrested, she stayed with him and, along with his mother and some other female disciples, stood at the foot of the cross. When she went to the tomb on Easter morning, she was the first to discover that Jesus was risen.

This version of Mary Magdalene has formed the subject for innumerable works of art, and her name has even entered the language: *magdalen* is an archaic word for "reformed prostitute," and *maudlin* owes its meaning to the tearful sentimentality she seemed to show when wiping Christ's feet with her hair. For centuries this picture, based on various incidents in the Gospels, has been taken as accurate. But recent findings suggest that in some key details it is wrong.

In the first place, there is no reason to connect Mary Magdalene with "the woman taken in adultery" in John 8:1–12. The woman is not named; she is not connected with Mary Magdalene in that passage or elsewhere. The link between the two is completely arbitrary, having been first suggested by Pope Gregory the Great in the sixth century. Nor, for that matter, is she likely to be the Mary "which anointed the Lord with ointment, and wiped his feet with his hair, whose brother Lazarus was sick" (John 11:2). As this verse suggests, the Gospel is quite clear about which Mary was which. There was one Mary who was the sister of Martha and Lazarus and who anointed Christ's feet; another Mary who was his mother; and a third one who was Mary Magdalene. Of this last figure we only know some small details from the canonical Gospels. She was with a group of other women "looking from afar off" when Jesus was crucified (Mark 15:40), and she was the first to see the risen Jesus (John 20:14–15). Perplexingly, the only other thing we know from these sources is that Jesus had cast "seven devils" out of her (Mark 16:9; Luke 8:2). But the Gospels do not tell the story of this exorcism.

When we turn to apocryphal works — particularly those connected with the Gnostics — the story is quite different. Here Mary Magdalene is presented as a disciple at least equal to the male disciples. The Gnostic *Dialogue of the Savior* characterizes her as "a woman who knew the All."[20] In another Gnostic text, the *Pistis Sophia,* or "Faith Wisdom," Jesus tells her, "thou art she whose heart is more directed to the Kingdom of Heaven than all thy brothers."[21] Most strikingly, there is this strange passage in *The Gospel of Philip*:

> The companion of the [Savior is] Mary Magdalene. [But Christ
> loved] more than [all] the disciples [and used to] kiss her [often] on
> her [mouth.] The rest of [the disciples were offended] by it [and ex-
> pressed disapproval.] They said to him, "Why do you love her more
> than all of us?" The Savior answered and said to them, "Why do I not
> love you like her?"

The answer is presumably obvious.

Elsewhere the same text tells us that "there were three who always walked with the Lord: Mary his mother and her sister [sic] and Magdalene, the one who was called his companion. His sister and his mother and his companion were each a Mary."[22] This Gospel, which is admittedly a late one, generally dated to the second half of the third century, attempts to clarify the identities of the several Marys. Mary Magdalene is Jesus's "companion" — a term that implies some sexual connection, as we see from the passage above.

The Mary Magdalene of the Gnostic texts is thus the opposite of the penitent whore of Catholic hagiography. There is no stain on her character. She has a status at least equal to that of the male apostles; her spiritual illumination surpasses theirs; she is Jesus's "companion" and possibly his wife. How did she lose this eminence? Elaine Pagels, in her well-known book *The Gnostic Gospels*, suggests that Mary Magdalene's demotion reflects the reduced status of women in the early Christian church. At first regarded as equals to men, they were gradually reduced to being second-class citizens, forbidden to have authority over men or to serve as clergy. The demotion of Mary Magdalene mirrors this shift.[23]

How are we to make sense of all these various and contradictory accounts of a woman who was one of Christ's earliest and most devoted followers? We can easily discard the familiar picture of the ex-prostitute, but what are we to do with the rest? The canonical Gospels, being older than all the other accounts, are probably closest to factual truth but do not say much. The apocryphal works, such as the *Gospel of Philip* and the *Pistis Sophia,* show that Mary Magdalene was held in the highest regard by Gnostic groups, but they are so late that their connection to historical fact is extremely tenuous. They may contain some genuine oral traditions about Mary Magdalene, but there is no way of verifying if any of these traditions are correct.

The past generation has seen a great resurgence of interest in Mary Magdalene. Much of this is due to two highly popular works: *Holy Blood, Holy Grail,* by Henry Lincoln, Michael Baigent, and Richard Leigh, and Dan Brown's enormously successful novel, *The Da Vinci Code.* I will discuss these accounts of Mary Magdalene in chapter 9, but for now let me merely say that the rediscovery and rehabilitation of this powerful but elusive figure reflects shifts in the spiritual mores of our time.

As women move into positions of social equality the old feminine ideals of Christianity are falling into the background. While there is still tremendous devotion to the Virgin Mary worldwide — as the waves of Marian apparitions suggest — she is less and less taken as the ideal for Christian womanhood. The docile, submissive virgin of Catholic and Orthodox teaching has limited appeal to the sexually liberated woman of today who wishes to stand shoulder-to-shoulder with men. A rehabilitated Mary Magdalene, consort of Jesus — possibly his wife — and the equal if not the superior of the apostles, fits modern aspirations much better. It's unlikely that this revised picture of Mary Magdalene is totally due to such social needs, but it does fit them extremely well.

Ultimately, perhaps, the story of Mary Magdalene is woven of thin strands of legends and allusions, many of which say more about the cultural aspirations of the milieu that created them than about the historical Mary. What, then, can we really say about her? We know only two things about her from the canonical Gospels, summarized in Mark 16:9: "Now when Jesus was risen early the first day of the week, he appeared first to Mary Magdalene, out of whom he had cast seven devils."

These facts — that Christ first appeared to Mary Magdalene and that he had cast seven devils out of her — are not as unrelated as they may appear. But they only make sense in terms of the symbolic language in which the Bible was written, which has always been known and understood in esoteric Christianity.

The number seven is key here. Ancient cosmology saw the earth as surrounded by the spheres of the seven planets then known: the moon, Mercury,

Venus, the sun, Mars, Jupiter, and Saturn. The spiritual forces of these planets were portrayed by ancient esoteric traditions, including Gnosticism, as malign gatekeepers of the heavenly realms who sought to keep man bound to earth. They are in fact the "rulers of the darkness of this world" mentioned in Eph. 6:12. As we'll see in the next chapter, the liberation of the soul was seen as an ascent through the seven spheres and an undoing of the bonds of these malign planetary powers. Thus one who is liberated from these powers could be described as having had "seven devils" cast out of her. In its figurative language, the Gospel could be saying that the "second birth" of the spirit, symbolized by the Resurrection, is attained first and foremost by one who has transcended the influences of the planets, that is, by one out of whom "seven devils" have been cast.

If this is true, it would help explain the extremely high esteem for Mary Magdalene in early Christianity of both the orthodox and heterodox strains. In all likelihood, she was neither a rehabilitated whore nor the "woman with the alabaster jar" who anointed the feet of Christ. But the Gnostic texts may be hitting upon some truth when they imply that she, of Christ's students, best understood the deepest truths he was trying to impart. Perhaps this was why he was able to tell her, "Thou art she whose heart is more directed to the Kingdom of Heaven than all thy brothers."

CHAPTER 2

The Heirs of Egypt

When and where he lived — or whether he ever existed on this planet at all — we do not know. He is sometimes identified with the Greek Hermes, the Egyptian Thoth, the biblical Enoch, and the Muslim Idris. But he is best known as Hermes Trismegistus, "Thrice-Greatest Hermes." A legendary divine being, part god, part man, whose life has been dated to remote antiquity, Hermes Trismegistus is revered as the father of alchemy, the occult sciences, and the Western esoteric tradition itself. He's most famous for appearing in a collection of texts that bear his name: the *Corpus Hermeticum,* or "Hermetic body" of writings.

The *Corpus Hermeticum* caused an enormous stir when it came to Western Europe in the fifteenth century, along with other treasures of Greek literature. A monk named Leonardo da Pistoia found a copy of this text in Macedonia and presented it to Cosimo de' Medici, the great Florentine patron of the arts. At the time (around 1460), the humanist Marsilio Ficino was translating the dialogues of Plato into Latin for an eager public. Cosimo asked him to interrupt his work on Plato and translate the *Corpus Hermeticum* first.[1]

Cosimo's request was no mere whim. Scholars in that era believed that these texts went back to the remotest antiquity and contained the summit of ancient wisdom. The cathedral at Siena, Italy, has an inlay dating from 1488 that shows this legendary sage and calls him *Hermes Trismegistus, contemporaneus Moysi,* "Hermes Trismegistus, the contemporary of Moses." This reflects the accepted belief of the time, which reckoned Hermes Trismegistus to be the Egyptian sage par excellence. Some believed that Moses, who the Bible said was "learned in all the wisdom of the Egyptians" (Acts 7:22), had gained his knowledge from him. Ficino said at one point that Hermes Trismegistus was the first link of the *aurea catena*, the "Golden Chain" of adepts that included the mythical Greek poet Orpheus, Pythagoras, and Plato. Ficino's translation of these texts into Latin, published in 1471, gave birth to the occult philosophy of the Renaissance (which I discuss in chapter 6).

The truth about these texts turned out to be more prosaic. In 1614, the classicist Isaac Casaubon proved that the *Corpus Hermeticum* didn't go back to the time of Moses (who, according to tradition, lived around 1300 B.C.) but was much later. Casaubon dated them to the late first century A.D., although scholars today believe they were written from the first through the third centuries A.D.[2] Casaubon reached his conclusions chiefly on linguistic grounds: the Greek of these texts is nothing like the Greek of 1300 B.C. It would be as if someone had claimed the book you are reading now had been written in 800 A.D. Anyone at all familiar with the English of that era could take one look at it and know it was not.

The Mind of Authority

Casaubon brought upon the *Corpus Hermeticum* a decline in prestige from which it's never entirely recovered. Since his time, the Hermetic writings have been relegated to second-class status by academic scholars, who often describe them as containing a confused mixture of Greek philosophy (especially Platonism) with Jewish, Zoroastrian, and Gnostic elements. They are regarded as holding some interest for the study of late classical religion but little else.

In recent years, however, scholarly opinion has begun to see some truth in the claim of Egyptian origins for these texts. To explore this argument, consider the title of the first and longest treatise in this collection: the *Poimandres*. The origin of this word is obscure. Many scholars have tried to connect it to the Greek *poimen*, or "shepherd," but this hasn't always satisfied even those who have proposed it. Some scholars have set forth another possibility.

The *Poimandres* begins with a mystical experience. The first-person narrator tells of a time when "my thinking soared high and my bodily senses were restrained." He encounters "an enormous being completely unbounded in size," who introduces himself by saying, "I am Poimandres, mind of authority."

It is this expression — "mind of authority" — that evokes an Egyptian background, because it's probably a translation of the Egyptian *p-eime-n-re*, which actually means "mind of authority."[3] Thus *Poimandres* is a grecized version of *p-eime-n-re*, with the literal meaning put alongside it. And the word translated as "authority" is *Re*, which is also the name of the Egyptian sun god.

The texts have other Egyptian echoes as well. A number of them are addressed to "Tat." This name evokes Thoth, or Tehouti, the Egyptian god of communication and learning corresponding to the Greek Hermes. But the most haunting mention of Egypt comes in a text called the *Asclepius*:

> O Egypt, Egypt, of your reverent deeds only stories will survive, and
> they will be incredible to your children! Only words cut in stone will
> survive to tell your faithful works, and the Scythian or Indian or
> some such neighbor barbarian will dwell in Egypt. For divinity goes
> back to heaven, and all the people will die, deserted, as Egypt will be
> widowed and deserted by god and human.[4]

This passage sheds an intriguing light on the purpose of these texts. Written in late antiquity, when the religion of Egypt was in advanced decay, they may be an attempt to capture the essence of its spiritual knowledge and pass it on to another civilization. The Greek language and Greek philosophic terms suggest that the Egyptian sages realized that their esoteric knowledge could only live by taking on a new guise and a new manner of speaking. The *Corpus Hermeticum* may have been part of an effort to do just that.

Some claim the Hermetic treatises contain traces of Jewish influence; although they are right, the echo is a faint one. Here's one example: "Mind, the father of all, who is life and light, gave birth to a man like himself whom he loved as his own child. The man was most fair: he had the father's image."[5] This has some affinity with the famous verse in Genesis: "So God created man in his own image, in the image of God created he him; male and female created he them" (Gen. 1:27). The God of Genesis is both male and female — another point of similarity with the *Poimandres*, which goes on to say: "He [man] is androgyne because he comes from an androgyne father."[6]

But these details are an exception. The cosmogony of the *Poimandres* is not like that of the Hebrew Bible, at least not in any literal sense.[7] According to the *Poimandres*, God the Father begins creating the universe by engendering a second god: a "craftsman" very much like the Gnostic demiurge or the creator in Plato's *Timaeus*. This "craftsman" then produces "seven governors: they encompass the world in circles, and their government is called fate. . . . The craftsman-mind, together with the word, encompassing the circles and whirling them about with a rush, turned his craftworks about." Out of this whirling arise the physical elements and "living things without reason" — the animals.

At this point God the Father creates man in his own image. The Father loves the son because he sees his own image in him. The son wants to create as well, but as he descends into the realm of lower nature to do this, he sees his own image and falls in love with it. This impulse brings about cosmic disaster. Like Narcissus, "when the man saw in the water the form like himself as it was in nature, he loved it and wished to inhabit it: wish and action came in the same moment, and he inhabited the unreasoning form. Nature took hold of her beloved, hugged him all about and embraced him, for they were lovers." Through this passionate romance with his own reflection, man falls into the realm of material nature and becomes subject to the "seven governors" — the seven planets that govern fate and destiny.

It's clear how much this myth resembles those of the Gnostics. In both cases we have a notion of two Gods, one benign but remote, the other evil or at any rate ambiguous; a descent into the realm of matter that becomes an imprisonment; and spiritual powers that bar the way between humanity and liberation. But the two visions also differ in some key respects. To begin with, the Hermetic hierarchy of seven "governors" forms a clearer and more elegant system than the cumbersome Gnostic networks of archons. And the Hermetic vision is not negative or paranoid, but genuinely tragic. Man falls in love with his own image as reflected in Nature, and Nature in turn falls in love with him — but by this love man is shackled to the physical world with its restrictions and sufferings. "Unlike any other living being on earth, mankind is twofold — in the body mortal but immortal in the essential man. Even though he is immortal and has authority over all things, mankind is affected by mortality because he is subject to fate; thus, although man is above the cosmic framework, he became a slave within it."[8]

To become free from this enmeshment, man must retrace his steps through the seven spheres of the "governors." At each stage he sheds one of the noxious traits imparted to him by these planetary rulers:

> Then the human being rushes up through the cosmic framework,
> at the first zone [the moon] surrendering the energy of increase and
> decrease; at the second [Mercury], evil machination, a device now
> inactive; at the third [Venus] the illusion of longing, now inactive;
> at the fourth [the sun] the ruler's arrogance, now freed from excess;
> at the fifth [Mars] unholy presumption and daring recklessness; at

the sixth [Jupiter] the evils that come from wealth, now inactive; at
the seventh zone [Saturn] the deceit that lies in ambush. And then,
stripped of the effects of the cosmic framework, the human enters
the region of the ogdoad; he has his own proper power, and along
with the blessed, he hymns the father.[9]

As the Greek philosopher Heraclitus said, "Character is fate." Esoteric philosophy teaches that the planets create our fate as much by shaping our natures as by dictating future events. The only way to liberate ourselves from
these planetary "governors" is to rise through these spheres, stripping ourselves of their associated vices — rendering them "inactive," as the *Poimandres*
puts it — through spiritual practice. This may be what it means to have
"seven devils" cast out of you, as Mary Magdalene did.

The Lost Egyptian Religion

Although the myth in the *Poimandres* is strange and exotic, in some ways it's
also quite familiar. There is a divine father who begets a son whom he loves;
the son comes down into a world of matter where he is ensnared, and he must
do battle with inimical cosmic forces in order to be freed. These details suggest that the *Poimandres* and the other Hermetic texts form a bridge between
the religion of ancient Egypt on the one hand and Gnosticism and esoteric
Christianity on the other.

Admittedly, this theory has its problems. The biggest one is that the teachings of the *Corpus Hermeticum* bear only a dim resemblance to the religion
known to Egyptologists — a religion of meticulous embalming of corpses; of
gods that are half-human, half-beast; of rites performed to ensure that the
Nile flooded regularly each year. Archaeological evidence spanning over three
thousand years suggests that it was these teachings, and not the Hermetic doctrines, that underlay Egypt's "reverent deeds."

Was there really an Egyptian esoteric doctrine, otherwise unknown, that
we see presented in the *Corpus Hermeticum*? One piece of evidence suggests
there was. The Hermetic texts speak of reincarnation (sometimes known as
metempsychosis, or the transmigration of souls). The *Asclepius* says that "those
who live faithfully under god" will ascend to become divine beings, but "for the
unfaithful it goes differently: return to heaven is denied them, and a vile migra-
tion unworthy of a holy soul puts them in other bodies." Another Hermetic

treatise tells us that a person who dies childless "is sentenced to a body that has neither a man's nature nor a woman's — a thing accursed under the sun."[10] Both these passages point toward reincarnation.

Now it's generally accepted that the ancient Egyptian religion did not teach reincarnation, and there is little if any archaeological evidence that it did. But the Greek historian Herodotus, who visited Egypt in the fifth century B.C., says, "The Egyptians were the first to teach that the human soul is immortal, and at the death of the body enters into some other living thing then coming to birth; and after passing through all creatures of land, sea, and air (which cycle it completes in three thousand years) it enters once more into a human body at birth."[11] This idea is very much like what we have seen in the Hermetic texts above.

Herodotus's testimony is sometimes dismissed out of hand, but could he have known of a secret Egyptian tradition that left no archaeological traces? The evidence grows more intriguing in that Herodotus goes on to say, "Some of the Greeks, early and late, have used this doctrine as if it were their own; I know their names, but do not here record them."

Herodotus probably means Pythagoras, the Greek sage of the fifth century B.C. who is best known for the Pythagorean theorem in geometry. This theorem was previously known in Egypt. In fact it's likely that Pythagoras learned it there and then brought it back to Greece along with other teachings, some of which were rather strange. One of the oddest details about Pythagoras is that he forbade his followers to eat beans. This is so peculiar that the theories concocted to explain it range from the flimsy to the hilarious, but the simplest explanation again appears in Herodotus: "The Egyptians sow no beans in their country; if any grow, they will not eat them either raw or cooked; the priests cannot endure even to see them, considering beans an unclean kind of pulse."[12] If indeed Pythagoras studied in Egypt, he might have picked up this food taboo, much as an American today who studies spirituality in India or Japan may become a vegetarian. Among the ideas that Pythagoras passed on to his Greek followers appears to have been the doctrine of reincarnation, which, as Herodotus implies, Pythagoras taught as if it were his own. (Reincarnation also appears in Plato, who bears many marks of Pythagoras's influence.)

We can see the doctrine of reincarnation in the Hermetic texts, but where do we find it in Christianity? Although most Christians assume that the teaching is totally foreign to their religion, the truth is a bit more complex. The third-century Church Father Origen, whom I discuss in detail later in this chapter, expounded views very much like those of the Hermetic texts. He wrote: "So long as a soul continues to abide in the good it has no experience of union with a body. [——] But by some inclination toward evil these souls lose their wings and come into bodies, first of men; then through their association with the irrational passions, after the allotted span of human life they are changed into beasts." Eventually "even the gracious gift of sensation is withdrawn" and the soul comes to inhabit a plant. From this point it begins its ascent again.[13]

Astonishingly enough, the doctrine of reincarnation has never been explicitly repudiated by the church, although many Christian theologians have dismissed or derided it. Today it is often claimed that the doctrine was rejected either by the First Council of Nicaea in 325 A.D. or by the Second Council of Constantinople in 553, but as a matter of fact neither of these dealt with the topic; instead they were concerned with the nature of Christ. One source of this misconception is Shirley MacLaine, the actress and New Age author, who introduced these ideas in her highly popular books, adding further to the confusion by mixing up the two councils.[14]

Reincarnation sits ambiguously on the edge of the Christian tradition. Valentin Tomberg (1900–73), a Baltic German convert to Roman Catholicism whose *Meditations on the Tarot*, published anonymously, remains one of the great modern classics of esoteric Christianity, observes, "The Church was hostile to the *doctrine* of reincarnation, although the *fact* of repeated incarnations was known — and could not remain unknown — to a large number of people faithful to the Church with authentic spiritual experience."[15] Tomberg's views are intricate and differ in some key respects from those of Origen and the Hermetic writings, but his comments serve as a reminder that to this day Christian esotericists often accept the possibility of reincarnation even though conventional Christianity does not.

In any case, the ancient sources suggest that something like the following happened: There was in Egypt an esoteric doctrine that spoke of reincarnation, the immortality of the soul, and the descent of the soul into matter as a form of bondage. This doctrine was not written down but was taught orally, and this is perhaps how Pythagoras learned it. He brought these ideas to Greece in the sixth century B.C., just in time to feed and inspire the discipline of philosophy that was just being born. Pythagoras's ideas went on to influence Plato (remember that Ficino specifically mentions both Pythagoras and Plato as part of the *aurea catena*, or Golden Chain). The following centuries would see these ideas recirculate from the Greeks back to the Egyptians to form a kind of esoteric common currency in the world of the eastern Mediterranean. In Egypt they would come into a final flowering in the Hermetic teachings, which in turn poured their wisdom into Christianity, particularly in its esoteric and Gnostic forms.

The Inoculation of Christianity

How, then, did these ideas actually influence Christianity? Partly through Gnosticism, whose affinity with the Hermetic teachings should be fairly obvious by now. But these ideas made their way into orthodox Christianity as well, chiefly thanks to two great fathers of the church who repudiated Gnosticism but embraced gnosis — along with many esoteric doctrines.

The first of these figures was Clement of Alexandria. As with most of the Church Fathers of that era, we know only skeletal details of his life.[16] He was born around 150 A.D., possibly in Athens, though he spent most of his life in Alexandria. Allusions in his written works indicate that he could have been an initiate of the pagan mystery religions, about which he seems unusually well informed. He sought spiritual knowledge from a number of sources, and makes reference to six "blessed and memorable men" whom he does not name but who, he says, spoke in "plain and living words." The last of these, who was "first in power," is usually identified as Pantaenus, head of the catechetical school in Alexandria. Clement became a Christian and eventually succeeded Pantaenus as head of the school. He apparently left Alexandria in 202 A.D. during the persecution by the Roman emperor Septimius Severus. Our last glimpse of him comes from 211, when he appears as bearer of a letter from Alexander, afterward bishop of Jerusalem, to the church of Antioch. Clement's death is generally placed around 215 A.D.

Clement is the author of a number of surviving works, including *The Instructor*, a guide to daily life for Christians; *Who Is the Rich Man That Shall Be Saved?* — a short treatise reassuring wealthy converts that Christ's criticisms of the rich did not mean they would have to give up their fortunes; and the compendious *Stromateis* (or *Stromata*, meaning "Patchworks" or "Miscellanies"), which deals in great detail with the relation of gnosis to Christian faith.

One of the most curious recent discoveries in New Testament studies is a previously unknown fragment of a letter ascribed to Clement. The scholar Morton Smith discovered it in 1958 at Mar Saba, an Eastern Orthodox monastery near Jerusalem. In this letter, Clement says the Evangelist Mark, after writing the familiar version of his Gospel in Rome, wrote a "more spiritual Gospel for the use of those who were being perfected." This "more spiritual Gospel," which Clement said was preserved in the church at Alexandria up to his own time, is otherwise unknown to us. It differed from the familiar version of Mark's Gospel, containing additional stories of Jesus's acts as well as "certain sayings of which . . . the interpretation would . . . lead the hearers into the innermost sanctuary of that truth hidden by seven [veils]." (The seven veils may have the same meaning as the "seven devils" and the "seven governors" that I've already discussed.) Clement's letter quotes some lines of this Gospel, including a story of the raising of a young man from the dead, rather like Lazarus. After raising him from the dead, "Jesus taught him the mystery of the kingdom of God."[17] Smith analyzed this letter and found that stylistically it resembles Clement's other writings enough to make a strong case for its authenticity.

Most intriguing, perhaps, Clement says that the "hierophantic teaching of the Lord" was not revealed in the familiar versions of the Gospel; it was reserved for initiates. Clement adds that the doctrines of the libertine Gnostic sect known as the Carpocratians sprang from a misinterpretation of Mark's secret text.

I don't have the space here to explore all the issues raised by this intriguing fragment. But remember that in chapter 1, I pointed out the almost universally accepted fact that the original ending of Mark, which deals with the aftermath of the Resurrection, was lost. Furthermore, scholars have long been struck by the extreme abruptness of Mark's Gospel in its transitions from one story or scene to the next. These facts may indicate that the actual situation was the opposite of what Clement claims: perhaps Mark initially wrote a text that included many secret teachings but was later edited — by Mark himself or by someone else — for general consumption. This at any rate would explain both the omissions and the Gospel's abruptness.

Whatever conclusions we may want to draw from this fragmentary letter, Clement's better-known writings reveal a man of tremendous learning and irenic temperament. While he heaped contempt upon the more superstitious elements of Greek religion — its orgiastic rites and the misbehavior of its gods — he admired Greek philosophy and tried to integrate it into the emerging Christian orthodoxy. His writings are full of citations, not only from the Bible and well-known pagan authors such as Homer and Plato, but from numerous others whose fragments only survive because Clement quoted them at one point or another. And although he has sharp words for the Gnostics, he grants a place to gnosis in his theological system and argues that it is compatible with — indeed the essence of — Christian faith.

Clement's thought is like that of the classical Gnostic schools in many ways. He frequently stresses the need to conceal the true meaning of Christian doctrine in symbols and allegories. He describes three tiers of humanity, the "heathen," the "believer," and the gnostic, who roughly correspond to the Gnostic division of humanity into the carnal, the psychic, and pneumatic. Most of all, Clement is lavish with praise for the true (that is, the orthodox Christian) gnostic — "the one who knows God." The gnostic is an imitator of God, patient and self-restrained, indifferent to pain and poverty, and willing to offer up his life in martyrdom if it is called for. Above all, the gnostic is a man of *faith*. "The gnostic is . . . fixed by faith." Moreover, "faith is something superior to knowledge."[18]

Like the other Church Fathers, Clement repudiates the "false gnosis," which, he claims, has brought true gnosis into disrepute. Theologically, the greatest sticking point was the Gnostics' refusal to identify the God of the Old Testament with the loving Father described by Jesus. But Clement also condemns their sexual mores (which, from his point of view, are either too lax or too strict, depending on the sect in question); their contempt for the body; and their repudiation of certain scriptures, such as the Epistles to Timothy.[19] (Actually, modern scholars agree with the Gnostics that these letters were falsely attributed to Paul.)

Yet underneath it all there seems to lie a deeper tension, a far more fundamental cause of division than any mere matters of doctrine or practice. I have alluded to it already in saying that for Clement, faith is above knowledge. This is the essential point at which orthodox Christianity and Gnosticism diverge. For Clement, as for practically all orthodox Christians, faith is the prerequisite: believe first and then you will know. For the Gnostic, faith is secondary; it is only a stopgap until you have knowledge — the direct experiential knowledge that is the essence of gnosis.

This no doubt accounts for the much-reviled arrogance of the Gnostics. They were not willing to put faith before knowledge; for them, either you knew or you didn't, and faith was only a way station, possibly a detour. To ordinary believers, such an attitude must have seemed extremely condescending. It also explains much about the Gnostic schools and their fate. Since the Gnostics trusted ultimately only in their own experience, each one saw the cosmos in slightly different terms; no two Gnostic teachers taught exactly the same doctrine. For much the same reason, an organized hierarchy was not only unnecessary but more or less impossible. Because they were unwilling to place their trust in ecclesiastical powers or theological party lines, they could not establish any institutions to compete with the emerging Catholic Church. So in the end they vanished.

Despite his affinities with the Gnostics, Clement ultimately chose the route of faith. Or was Clement playing a double game, making such assertions in his public writings but speaking quite differently among initiates? After all, he sometimes hints that what you should say in public may be the opposite of what you should say in private. We're not likely ever to find out. In any case, he was never repudiated by the hierarchy. He was canonized, and from his own time to the present, he has always remained among the most esteemed of the Church Fathers, particularly in Eastern Orthodoxy.

The Repudiation of Origen

Origen, another great Church Father from Alexandria, did not enjoy the same good fortune. In fact Origen has the peculiar distinction of being perhaps the greatest Christian philosopher to be disowned after his own time. There are a large number — including Meister Eckhart, Catherine of Siena, and Jacob Boehme — who were regarded with suspicion or hostility while they were alive, only to be rehabilitated after their deaths. But there are few who, like Origen, who were regarded as orthodox in their own time and disowned later. For this reason it's sometimes hard to discern exactly what Origen taught: not only have many of his works vanished, but some of them survive only in Latin versions by translators who watered down his meaning in order to make him more acceptable in their own day.[20]

Origen was born around 185 A.D. and was raised in Alexandria — the epi-center, as we have seen, of Gnostic currents.[21] He was raised in a Christian family. His father gave him a superb education, teaching him not only the Christian scriptures but the pagan classics as well, making Origen the most formidably learned of all the Church Fathers. His father died in the persecu-tion under Septimius Severus in 202 (the same one that caused Clement to flee Alexandria), leaving Origen, the eldest son, with the duty of providing for a large family. Fortunately, a wealthy Christian woman became his patron, en-abling him to finish his education so that he could work as a *grammateus*, a professor of Greek literature. In his youth Origen also studied under Ammonius Saccas, a Platonist who also taught the celebrated Neoplatonist philosopher Plotinus. Most scholars assume he studied under Clement, who was in Alexandria during Origen's youth, although the latter never mentions Clement by name in his surviving works.

From an early age, Origen showed not only remarkable intellectual gifts but a fiery passion for his faith. He took Christ's remark about "eunuchs which have made themselves eunuchs for the kingdom of heaven's sake" (Matt. 19:12) too literally and castrated himself in an attempt to follow it — an act he later regretted.

As Origen matured as a teacher, he encountered a formidable opponent — Demetrius, bishop of Alexandria. Origen began teaching at a time when bishops were expanding their already considerable powers. Because Origen did not allow a mere bishop who was very likely inferior to himself in learning and intelligence to dictate what he taught, his position in Alexandria became more and more untenable, and he went to Rome around 215. He returned to Alexandria, where he was condemned by the church in 231 (we do not know why, although apparently it was not over doctrinal issues). Around 234 he settled in Caesarea on the coast of Palestine, where he would stay for the rest of his life.

In 249, the emperor Decius inaugurated the most intense and systematic persecution of the Christians up to that time, requiring everyone in the empire (except Jews) to worship the pagan gods and to have papers certifying they had done so. Origen was arrested, cast into prison, and tortured. Decius's reign was short, and Origen was released after the emperor's death in 251. But his health was broken from his ordeals, and he died a year or so later.

Both in his lifetime and afterward, Origen won renown for extraordinary learning and phenomenal output. One ancient source numbered his works at six thousand, though the Church Father Jerome argues for the more cautious figure of two thousand. This is not as preposterous as it may sound, since it probably includes letters and sermons; moreover, a "book" in antiquity was the amount of material that could fit on a single scroll — considerably less than a modern printed book. Even by the most conservative estimates, Origen was a prolific author. His works include commentaries on numerous books of the Bible; *On First Principles*, the most significant of his surviving theological treatises; *Contra Celsum* (Against Celsus), a reply to a now-lost polemic against Christianity; and the compendious *Hexapla*, a parallel text of six different versions of the Bible in Hebrew and Greek.

Like Clement, Origen was not a Gnostic, and also like Clement, he treated many Gnostic teachings with contempt. One of the most interesting of these has to do with the nature of the Old Testament God. As we've seen, the Gnostics made a sharp distinction between the true, good God and the inferior demiurge; they often equated the latter with the deity portrayed in the Hebrew scriptures. Origen did not agree with these ideas. Why?

At one point in *Contra Celsum*, Origen turns to a claim made by the pagan philosopher Celsus that each nation has its own governing spirit, a kind of middle-level administrator in the cosmic hierarchy.[22] This, according to Celsus, is why customs and mores — even the very notion of what is pious and holy — vary from nation to nation. The Jews are no exception; they too have their own governing "angel."

This idea resonates with the Gnostic idea, suggested by Gal. 3:19, that the law "was ordained by angels in the hands of a mediator," but Origen rejects it. He says it is ridiculous, because it collapses the truth of what is actually holy and pious into a meaningless relativism: "If, then, religion, and piety, and righteousness belong to those things which are so only by comparison, so that the same act may be both pious and impious, according to different relations and different laws, see whether it will not follow that temperance also is a thing of comparison, and courage as well, and prudence, and the other virtues, than which nothing could be more absurd!"[23]

Origen justifies his views with an esoteric explanation of the Tower of Babel. He says this story speaks of a time when all nations spoke one "divine language": that is, they all worshipped the same God in the same way. But when they desired "to gather together material things, and to join to heaven what had no natural affinity for it," they fell away from true worship. They were punished by having their "language" confounded. That is, each nation was handed over "to angels of character more or less severe, and of a nature more or less stern, until they had paid the penalty of their daring deeds; and they were conducted by those angels, who imprinted on each his native language, to the different parts of the earth according to their deserts."[24] The one exception was "the portion of the Lord, and His people who were called Jacob, and Israel the cord of His inheritance; and these alone were governed by a ruler who did not receive those who were placed under him for the purpose of punishment" — that is, by God himself (5.31).

Essentially Origen is saying that while all the other nations are governed by some subordinate angel, the nation of Israel is not; they were "the portion of the Lord." They were the ancestors of the Christian religion, which also worships the one true God. Thus the God of the Old Testament is, as orthodox Christianity insists, the one true God.

What's especially fascinating about Origen's views is that they are exactly the same as those of the Jewish Kabbalah, which equates the one true God with the divine name YHVH, or Yahweh. The thirteenth-century Kabbalist Joseph Gikatilla explains, "The ministers [i.e., angels] of these other nations . . . cannot touch the name YHVH. . . .The Name YHVH . . . is only for Israel."[25] Even more strikingly, Gikatilla goes on to explain his views with an allegorical exposition of the Tower of Babel story that is much like Origen's. It's unlikely that Gikatilla knew of Origen's works or would have used them in his own interpretation of scripture. Rather, the similarity of these ideas in authors of such different periods and orientations suggests that it was part of the esoteric tradition that was carried on in both Judaism and Christianity. Later still, the idea would reenter Christian tradition through the Kabbalah itself. Giovanni Pico della Mirandola, a Christian Kabbalist of the fifteenth century (whom we look at in chapter 6), would write, "No king of the earth is punished on earth unless his heavenly militia is humiliated first."[26] This statement, written in the cryptic language of the Kabbalists, probably means that the fates of nations are dictated by those of their governing spirits.

Despite his universally admitted learning and piety, Origen's reputation suffered over succeeding generations. In the late fourth century, a Church Father named Epiphanius of Salamis attacked him as the source of the Arian heresy (explained below). In 553, almost three hundred years exactly after Origen's death, he was anathematized — that is, officially condemned — by the Second Ecumenical Council of Constantinople, and the Byzantine emperor Justinian ordered his works destroyed. This effectively put an end to Origen's authority in Orthodox Christianity, although Justinian's ruling had less weight in the Western than in the Eastern church, and Origen continued to be respected in the Western church into medieval times. The 1913 edition of *The Catholic Encyclopedia* emphasizes that "he does not deserve to be ranked among the promoters of heresy.[27]

Why was Origen anathematized? His teaching of reincarnation no doubt gave rise to suspicion, although it was never specifically rejected by the church. The main cause of his condemnation lay in his alleged inspiration of the Arian heresy in the fourth century. The Arian heresy — if it in fact deserves that name — was the doctrine espoused by the fourth-century theologian Arius that Jesus Christ, being the Son of God, was the first of God's creations and as such was not equal to the Father. Because the relation of the Father and the Son had been only vaguely spelled out up to that point, this controversy split the church apart.

It can be hard for a modern reader to grasp the intensity and viciousness of these ancient theological disputes. Yet they occupied the attention of a population that extended far beyond bishops and priests. Among his other talents, Arius knew how to write catchy songs, and it discomfited orthodox churchmen to hear tunes expounding his heresies sung by men in the street. As the Roman Empire became officially Christian (a process that took place over the fourth century) and the emperors began to involve themselves with the church hierarchy, these issues also became matters of high state.

In fact it was Constantine, the first Christian emperor, who brought the Arian controversy to a head by convening the First Council of Nicaea in 325 A.D. The council ruled that the Father and Son were both fully divine, formulated the doctrine of the Trinity now held by much of Christendom, and condemned Arius.

Origen didn't actually teach Arianism, but he did hold an emanationist view of the relation between the Father and the Son. This is sometimes called "subordination of the divine Persons." According to Origen, the Father "eternally generates" the Son, even though the Son was not created in time: "Would someone be so bold as to say that the Son began to exist after having not existed previously?" Origen asks. "When did . . . the Word who knows the Father not exist?"[28] Nonetheless, to later theologians, Origen's emanationism sounded enough like Arius's teaching that it was condemned by association.

This "subordination of the divine Persons" isn't the only reason Origen fell out of favor. Another teaching of his that later generations would condemn was what has since come to be called "universalism" — the doctrine that all souls can be saved (at least potentially), even those in hell. He cites such verses as 1 Cor. 15:28: "When all things shall be subdued unto him, then shall the Son also himself be subject unto him that put all things under him, that God may be all in all." Origen comments: "Just as when the Son is said to be subjected to the Father, the perfect restoration of the entire creation is announced, so when his enemies are said to be subjected to the Son of God, we are to understand this to involve the salvation of those subjected and the restoration of those that had been lost" — that is, damned.[29]

Universal salvation arises out of Origen's view of divine chastisement, which has more to do with correction than with punishment or retribution: "And so it happens that some in the first, others in the second, and others even in the last times, through their endurance of greater and more severe punishments of long duration, extending, if I may say so, over many ages, are by these very stern methods of correction renewed and restored."[30] For Origen, even the devil can be redeemed.

For churchmen more comfortable with the idea of "the lake of fire and brimstone" where the wicked "shall be tormented day and night for ever and ever" (Rev. 20:10), Origen's benign view of the Last Judgment was not to be tolerated. This, too, would count against him.

The final stroke against him had to do with his interpretation of scripture. Of all the Church Fathers, Origen was the least attached to the idea that the Bible is literally true in all respects. Perhaps his early experience with self-mutilation made him chary of taking even Christ's words totally at face value. At any rate, his compendious commentaries on the Bible were largely efforts to draw out its allegorical and symbolic meaning. Origen did not invent this approach — it can be traced back to Philo of Alexandria, a Jewish philosopher who lived around the same time as Christ — but Origen applied it more fully than any other theologian has before or since.

Origen held that scripture had three levels of meaning, corresponding to the body, soul, and spirit — the three-part division of the human entity according to the esoteric doctrine. He even denied that scripture was always true at the literal level:

> Now what man of intelligence will believe that the first and the
> second and the third day, and the evening and the morning existed
> without the sun and moon and stars? And that the first day, if we may
> so call it, was even without a heaven? And who is so silly as to believe
> that God, after the manner of a farmer, "planted a paradise eastward
> in Eden," and set in it a visible and palpable "tree of life," of such a
> sort that anyone who tasted its fruit with his bodily teeth would gain
> life: and again that one could partake of "good and evil" by masticat-
> ing the fruit taken from the tree of that name? And when God is said
> to "walk in the paradise in the cool of the day" and Adam to hide
> himself behind a tree, I do not think anyone will doubt that these
> are figurative expressions which indicate certain mysteries through
> a semblance of history and not through actual events.[31]

At this point it might be useful to step back and see what the condemnation of Origen means for us now. The relation of the Father and the Son is rather far removed from modern concerns; few even among theologians would be willing to come to blows over such issues. But when we come to Origen's notions of universal salvation and his allegorical interpretation of scripture, we can see how, if there had been more room for them in later theology, they might have forestalled many of the sharpest assaults on Christianity today. At present, two of the greatest sticking points with Christian teachings have to do with issues Origen directly addressed. In the first place, there's the incredible viciousness and injustice of infinite torment in hell for what, after all, are finite offenses on earth. By granting the possibility that everyone may be saved in the end, Origen blunts the harshness of an endless divine wrath. In the second place, Origen's allegorism frees us from taking the Bible literally. Without such an interpretation, we must either, like fundamentalists, insist that it's all to be taken at face value no matter how absurd this seems or, like modernists, admit that while the Bible was *meant* to be literally true, it's really nothing more than a collection of old fables dressed up as fact. Had the church not turned away from Origen in the sixth century, he might have been able to help it with its critics today.

The Exteriorization of Christianity

Yet the church *did* turn away from Origen. Appreciating his brilliance, the Catholic Church in particular has been careful not to denounce him fully, but to all intents he has been left on the sidelines. More broadly, in the first five hundred years of its life, the church, both Catholic and Orthodox (they would not split completely until 1054), worked hard to push out esoteric or Gnostic viewpoints. Such approaches were, it is true, never totally discarded. They've always been found in isolated sectors of the mainstream churches, and the monastic tradition, particularly in Eastern Orthodoxy, has often provided some haven for them. But over the centuries they have become increasingly marginalized. By the twentieth century, the impulse toward gnosis was all but forgotten in organized religion.

All this leads one to ask how this transformation of Christianity happened, and why. Most scholars view this question in light of the long power struggle among competing sects in the early centuries of Christian history. The triumph of Christianity itself is usually regarded as the result of imperial pressure. As

Edward Gibbon writes in his *Decline and Fall of the Roman Empire*, after the conversion of Constantine "every motive of authority and fashion, of interest and reason, now militated on the side of Christianity." Furthermore, this triumphant Christian church regarded itself not as subject to the state but as superior to it. To quote Gibbon again, "The emperor might be saluted as the father of his people, but he owed a filial duty and reverence to the fathers of the Church."[32] This newfound temporal power enabled the church to enforce its doctrinal decrees with the full might of the state.

This view makes sense in light of the struggles for power and control that dominate the pages of secular history. But one is led to wonder, can spiritual history be explained totally in terms of secular events? Those with a religious orientation have frequently said it cannot. Orthodox theologians, for example, have sometimes portrayed the history of church doctrine as a progressive series of triumphs of the Holy Spirit over the devil and his minions, the heretics. Conventional history dismisses explanations of this kind, if only because they lend themselves poorly to such key historiographical concerns as documentation and evidence. Nonetheless, taken with some caution, such perspectives can prove refreshing and enlightening, particularly if they are comparatively free from dogmatic prejudice.

One such perspective comes from René Guénon (1886–1951). Although he's little known in the English-speaking world, Guénon was one of the most influential esoteric philosophers of the last century; his disciples include such figures as the well-known Islamic scholar S. H. Nasr and Huston Smith, author of *The World's Religions*. A difficult and rebarbative thinker who despised modernity, Guénon nevertheless has a great deal to say about esotericism in world religions.

In an essay called "Christianisme et initiation" ("Christianity and Initiation"), Guénon says that at the outset Christianity *was* in many ways an esoteric teaching, but that it more or less consciously divested itself of these elements in order to make itself more popular. This was not merely a marketing ploy. The Greco-Roman religion was in an advanced state of decay, and something was needed to take its place. Had Christianity not made this sacrifice, as it were, Western civilization would have been destroyed entirely. Guénon writes:

> If we consider the state of the Western world — that is, the collection of nations included under the Roman Empire — at the time in question, we can easily recognize that, if Christianity had not

"descended" into the exoteric domain, this world as a whole would have been entirely deprived of any tradition, since those that had existed up to that point, especially the Greco-Roman tradition that had naturally become predominant, had come to a state of extreme degeneracy that indicated that their cycle of existence was at an end. This "descent," we must once again insist, was in no way an accident or a deviation. On the contrary, one should consider it as having a veritably "providential" character, since it kept the West in that age from falling into a state comparable to the one in which it finds itself now.[33]

Here we have a situation somewhat like that of the Egyptian religion, whose death was foreseen in the Hermetic texts. In this case, however, Greco-Roman religion — whose degeneracy was frequently lamented by the pagans themselves — did not even have enough living matter to be transmuted into another form. It was simply supplanted by a tradition that was still young and vibrant. Guénon adds that this "descent" was in all probability complete by the time of the First Council of Nicaea in 325 A.D.

Throughout his works, Guénon argues that there are two aspects of any authentic spiritual tradition: the "inner," or esoteric, and the "outer," or exoteric. Most religions have some fairly well-defined esoteric teaching at their core. Judaism has the Kabbalah; Islam has Sufism; Guénon even claims that in China, Taoism is not, strictly speaking, a different religion from Confucianism but its "inner" aspect. However this may be, when we come to Christianity, we don't find any obvious esoteric center. According to Guénon, this is because in those early centuries, Christianity took its "inner" rites and rituals, such as baptism and the Eucharist, and turned them into external religious forms.

This "descent" into externality has left the Christian tradition with a hole at the center. Christianity has never entirely lost its esoteric connection: that would be its demise, since esotericism is the living pith of a religion. But the inner aspect of the tradition has mostly been denied, ignored, or downplayed. As the Benedictine monk Brother David Steindl-Rast said in a 1992 interview, "The best way of hiding something is to put it out in the open, where nobody who looks for hidden things will find it. So the hidden teaching is right out front, but you have to have eyes to see. What does that mean in our context, having eyes to see? It means that you will get at it by committing yourself."[34] And yet there are many who seem to have committed themselves and have still come away wanting. Commitment, like faith, may not be enough on its own.

These considerations say a great deal about why Western civilization developed as it did. Christianity came more and more to deny its own interior, especially after the Middle Ages, when it gave primacy to reason over spiritual insight. The civilization that is its daughter has followed its example. The West is the civilization of the exterior par excellence. Our science, politics, economics, philosophy are all based on externalities, on what Guénon called "the reign of quantity." By reducing our thoughts and feelings to electrochemical reactions, modern neurology and biochemistry have even exteriorized our inmost depths.

I am not decrying these developments or holding out the image of some long-past age to draw forth nostalgia. In all likelihood the situation had to develop as it did; could it have done otherwise, it no doubt would have; and as Guénon suggests, it may even have been providential, at least at the start. In the end, whether this exteriorization, led at first by Christianity itself and then by the sciences that shunted it aside, will prove of benefit or of harm to the human race — even at the dawn of the twenty-first century it is too early to tell.

CHAPTER 3

The Lost Religion of Light

There are, as we know, many world religions. But of these, only a few truly claim to be universal — to be applicable to all nations and races — and have tried to spread themselves all around the world. The others have either consciously limited themselves to a specific nation, such as Judaism and Hinduism, or else have not moved far past their countries of origin, such as Taoism, Shinto, and the many indigenous traditions.

In fact, there are only four major religions that have tried to be universal in the sense I've described above.[1] Three of these — Buddhism, Christianity, and Islam — are well known. The fourth has become extinct. It's no longer practiced anywhere. If it's known to the public, it is only as a name.

This lost religion is Manichaeism. At its height, it claimed followers in regions from the Atlantic to the China Sea. It competed vigorously with Christianity, Islam, and Buddhism and only died out toward the end of the Middle Ages. Even since then, in a shadowy way it has managed to survive in a particular mindset that's very much alive today. For these reasons and for others that I'll soon approach, Manichaeism remains a crucial part of the Gnostic legacy.

Its founder was a man named Mani, who was born in Babylonia — present-day Iraq — on April 14, 216 A.D.[2] He was well born, being distantly related to the Arsacid dynasty that ruled the Persian Empire at the time. His father belonged to an obscure Judeo-Christian sect called the Elchasaites. Founded by the mysterious prophet Elchasai, who lived in the early second century A.D., the sect may have had some Gnostic influences but for the most part tried to live by the Law of Moses. They abstained from meat and wine. Purity was important to them, and they cleansed themselves often with ritual baths.

This issue was to mark Mani's first break with his native religion. Inspired by revelations from his *Syzygus*, or "Divine Twin" (in modern parlance, his "higher Self"), at the age of twenty-four Mani began to preach a doctrine that clashed with Elchasaism, as it would with most of the religions it would encounter. Mani contended that the body was by nature impure; mere baths were of no use in trying to cleanse it. The only true purification, he said, lay in a kind of gnosis that would enable the seeker to separate the primordial Light from the Darkness.

In a text called the *Kephalaia*, Mani described what he learned from his Divine Twin (also called "the Living Paraclete"):

> He revealed to me the hidden mystery that was hidden from the
> worlds and the generations: the mystery of the Depth and the
> Height: he revealed to me the mystery of the Light and the Darkness,
> the mystery of the conflict and the great war which the Darkness
> stirred up. He revealed to me how the Light [turned back? over-
> came?] the Darkness by their intermingling and how [in conse-
> quence] was set up this world.[3]

Mani soon broke with the Elchasaites, as much because of their isolationism as because of their insistence on ritual baths. Accompanied by his father and a small number of disciples, Mani traveled throughout Persia, Afghanistan, and India, proclaiming his message as the "Apostle of Light." He claimed that he "moved the whole land of India." Certainly he had some success in gaining the ear of Indian rulers. This in turn led to his invitation to the court of the Sassanid dynasty, which had recently seized control of the Persian Empire from Mani's relations, the Arsacids. Nevertheless, the Sassanid monarch, Shapur I, listened to Mani's teaching appreciatively and granted him patronage. Two of Shapur's brothers even converted to Mani's faith. Possibly Shapur saw Mani's religion, which freely and consciously borrowed elements from Christianity, Zoroastrianism, Buddhism, and Hinduism, as a way of unifying his far-flung realm.

Endorsed by the monarch, Mani's religion spread throughout the Sassanid Empire for the next several decades. Unfortunately, in 273 a new king, Bahram I, ascended the throne, and Mani's fortunes changed overnight. Bahram gave ear to the hierarchs of the dominant Zoroastrian religion, who naturally felt threatened by Mani's new faith, and Mani was thrown in jail. Bound with seven fetters, he continued to teach in prison, but he died there in 276. A burning torch was thrust into his body to make sure he was dead. Many of his followers were forced to flee eastward to Sogdiana (present-day Uzbekistan), and Mani's successor, Sisinus, was crucified some ten years later.

The Zoroastrian Background

The hostility of the Zoroastrian priests may have been partly inspired by Mani's use of their own teachings. Manichaeism is usually described as Gnostic, and in many ways it was, but his doctrine differed from the classic Gnostic systems in one crucial respect. The Gnostics believed that in essence there is one true, good God; the demiurge is an imitator. But Mani taught that the principles of Light and Darkness had coexisted from the beginning and were of more or less equal power. In this respect, his teaching draws on that of Zoroaster, or Zarathustra, the great Persian prophet who preached "the Good Religion of Ahura Mazda," the God of Light who struggled against Angra Mainyu, or Ahriman, the God of Darkness.

Zoroaster sits so marginally on the pages of history that current estimates for the dates of his life vary by a thousand years; scholarly opinion currently favors a birth date sometime around 1000 B.C. He probably lived in Bactria, in what is now Afghanistan, and his faith took root most strongly in Persia, where in Mani's time it was the established religion. Today it is all but unknown there. The vast majority of the world's Zoroastrians now live in the Indian province of Gujarat, where they are known as Parsis.

Zoroaster's view of the world as a battleground between good and evil has shaped all the great Western faiths. Originally Judaism, for example, had no concept of the devil as such. Yahweh was the source of all good and evil, and Satan, the "adversary," was seen as merely an accusing spirit — a kind of celestial district attorney, as in the prologue of Job. But after the Jewish exile in Babylonia in the sixth century B.C. (during which time Babylon itself was conquered by Persia), Judaism was imbued with the concept of a devil as an adversary not only of man but of God himself. Judaism in turn would pass this idea on to its offspring, Christianity and Islam.

Just as Mani differed from the classical Gnostics in saying that the forces of good and evil are more or less evenly balanced, he departed from Zoroaster in contending that the material world is itself essentially the product of darkness.

Zoroaster had taught that while the world has been infected by the presence of evil, it's not fundamentally bad in itself. Zoroastrianism does not repudiate the body or regard it as essentially defiled — which Mani did. In essence, Mani combined the Gnostic idea of the innate depravity of the material world with the Zoroastrian notion of two countervailing forces of Light and Darkness, of good and evil. This constitutes the heart of his contribution to world religion.

The War with the Body

If the physical world is innately depraved, it follows that the physical body must be depraved as well. This, too, forms a central theme of Mani's doctrine, although it's a theme that continually weaves in and out of the Gnostic legacy. Today many people point to Christianity as the source of the vilification of the body that has wreaked so much damage on the Western psyche. While Christianity has contributed a great deal to this often pathological tendency — witness the bizarre and masochistic self-mortifications of so many of the saints — it's not accurate to say this idea originated with the Christian tradition. It is much more ancient and universal.

The idea of the physical body as an impediment to the freedom of the spirit is widespread in the East, as it is in many parts of the world. After all, the *Tibetan Book of the Dead* — one of the most popular Buddhist texts for the past generation — is essentially a step-by-step manual showing the recently deceased person how to avoid incarnating into another body (human or otherwise). And the great Hindu saint Sri Ramakrishna once observed, "One cannot obtain Knowledge unless one gets rid of the feeling that one is the body."[4]

It would take a book longer than the present one to trace the history of this idea in world civilization, but let me at least say that in the West, this kind of contempt for the body appeared for the first time among the Greeks. It was probably introduced by Orphism, a mystery religion allegedly founded by the mythical poet Orpheus. Making a pun in Greek, the Orphics proclaimed that "the body is a tomb" (*soma sema*).[5] Plato took up this idea, which resonates often in his writing — most hauntingly in the *Phaedo*, which narrates the last hours of Socrates' life. At the end of a long discussion on the immortality of the soul, Socrates drinks a cup of poisonous hemlock (a fate decreed by the

Athenian court, which had convicted him of corrupting the city's youth). As the poison takes effect, Socrates turns to one of his disciples and says, "Crito, we owe a cock to Asclepius" before he dies.[6] This utterance is usually interpreted in light of Asclepius's role as the god of healing. One offered a cock to the god in thanks for a successful healing — meaning that Socrates was being cured of the disease of life.

Although it's so universal, the idea that the body is an impediment or a prison or a tomb — the feeling that, as W. B. Yeats put it, the human spirit is "fastened to a dying animal" — is extremely peculiar. Since to a great degree we *are* bodies, how could we have ever come to think the body is a nuisance?

Much of the answer lies in one often overlooked but crucial fact. *Human beings are creatures that are capable of viewing the body as an "other."* This is an astonishing part of our makeup. It may even be the main thing that distinguishes us from the animals (some of whom use language, toolmaking, and other faculties that we tend to regard as uniquely human). This capacity gives us tremendous advantages. It makes us far better able to suppress our immediate impulses than most (if not all) other creatures, and it in large part explains our ability to carry out the complex tasks and achievements on which we as a species pride ourselves. Feeling itself to be separate from the body, the mind can direct it more efficiently.

On the other hand, this ability also creates some problems. Despite its remarkable abilities, the body has very definite limits. It's frequently unwilling or unable to carry out the projects the mind concocts for it — or it may want to do something of which the mind disapproves. The mind then experiences the body as a recalcitrant slave, setting the stage for the inner conflict that also characterizes the human species. The mind feels imprisoned in a sullen and hostile lump of flesh.

I'm not proposing a facile solution to the profound philosophical issue of the relation between body and mind, but these considerations suggest why we could even begin to conceive of the body as an impediment. All the same, the body is not easily eluded. Even if we grant that consciousness may survive apart from physical embodiment (an idea that is practically universal), we still have to take our material form into account, to make use of it somehow. How can we do this without becoming totally submerged in physical drives, which seem to shackle us to mortality? To understand Mani's answer to this question, we will have to take a look at his cosmology in more detail.

The War between Light and Dark

In the beginning, Mani taught, there were two initial powers: the Light and the Dark. He apparently didn't say how these two powers came to be or whether they might be the products of some unseen God who had generated them both. (Some of his later followers speculated on this topic and reached varying conclusions.)

The Father of Light, the God of the Realm of Light, has a number of "limbs" or emanations: Reason, Mind, Intelligence, Thought, and Understanding. In addition, there are countless "Aeons" and "Aeons of Aeons" — divine beings — surrounding him.

Mani also taught that the infinite Realm of Light has a mirror image in the Realm of Darkness. Just as there is a Father of Light, there's a Father of Darkness, with his corresponding attributes of "Dark Reason," "Dark Mind," and so on. He is named Satan or Ahriman (Mani was extremely skillful in adapting his concepts to the terms of already existing religions).

Originally the two realms were totally separate. But at some point the Darkness had some experience of the Light and began to crave it. This started the great cosmic drama in which Mani saw himself and his disciples as key players. When the realm of the Dark began to invade the Light, the latter created the First Man in response. This cosmic figure went into battle with the Darkness, which tore him apart and devoured the particles of Light he contained.

To remedy this situation, the Father of Light sent a divine "Call" to awaken the fallen First Man. The Father also produced another emanation, the "Living Spirit," who created the world we know. Although this creator comes from the realm of the good, he has to make use of mixed materials to make the universe. As a result, the universe is a combination of Light and Dark. Its purpose is to separate out the particles of Light from the Darkness that engulfs them. When these particles have been extracted from their bondage, the world will end.

For Mani, the entire cosmos is an enormous filtration system that will collapse when it has finished its task. The Milky Way, the embodiment of the Perfect Man, is a path for the liberated particles of Light to ascend to the Father; the moon waxes because it is a ship of Light that is filling up with particles on their way home. When the moon wanes, it means that these elements of Light have been transferred to the sun, the next stage on their journey. As Mani expressed it:

Then he [God] created the sun and the moon for sifting out whatever there was of light in the world. The sun sifted out the light which was mixed with the devils of heat, while the moon sifted out the light which was mixed with the devils of cold. This rises up on a column of praise, together with what there are of magnificats, sanctifyings, good words, and deeds of righteousness. . . .This is thrust into the sun, then the sun thrusts it to the light above it, in the world of praise, in which world it proceeds to the highest unsullied light.[7]

The drama does not end here. The Forces of Darkness counterattacked by creating the human race. Although man has Light within him, the Darkness made sure that he would perpetuate his enslavement by desire — particularly the desire for reproduction, which would keep the Light in bondage for endless generations.

The forces of good responded by sending a number of divine messengers to waken humanity from this painful slumber so that the Light in them could return to its native realm. These included Zoroaster, the Buddha, and Jesus, all of whom were invoked as precursors by Mani himself. According to Mani, his predecessors preached a true doctrine, but this was later corrupted by their followers. Mani had come to set things right; he styled himself "the Seal of the Prophets" (a title later assumed by Muhammad).

According to Mani, salvation requires two things. A individual must recognize the truth of his situation — a form of gnosis — and he must follow certain practices that will enable him to rescue the lost shards of Light and effect his own return. These practices constituted the main forms of religious observance in Manichaeism.

The Hearers and the Elect

Manichaeans faced a double duty regarding the sparks of Light. They not only had to liberate as many of these particles as possible, but they also had to avoid harming them. Since they believed these particles dwell in all things — plants, stones, and dirt, as well as animals and humans — this was not an easy task. As a result, truly observant Manichaeans were surrounded by a stockade of taboos. Sexual intercourse was forbidden (because it perpetuated the imprisonment of the Light in matter); they could not eat meat or drink alcohol. They could not engage in agriculture, because the acts of plowing and reaping were believed to injure the tiny sparks of Light that were embedded in the soil and plants. Even bathing was forbidden, on the grounds that it would hurt the Light imprisoned in the water.

Obviously these strictures made ordinary life almost impossible, and in practice only a small part of the Manichaean community followed them. They were known as the "Elect." They constituted the elite of the faith, and bishops of the Manichaean church (which roughly resembled the orthodox Christian church in structure) could be chosen only from among them, as was Mani's successor, the chief hierarch at the see in Babylon. Women were admitted to the company of the Elect, although they could not serve in positions of leadership.

Because the life of the Elect was so constrained, few Manichaeans wanted to join this exalted company. Most of the community consisted of Auditors, people who "heard" Mani's message and devoted themselves to providing the Elect with the necessities of life in the form of alms. This "soul-service," as it was called, bestowed merit upon the Auditors, so the two levels of believers were linked by mutual advantage.

Religious rituals took fairly familiar forms, including prayers, fasts, and weekly confession of sins (since it was clear that no Manichaean would be able to entirely avoid transgressing the long list of offenses). But perhaps the most interesting form of observance was the ritual meal, a service that brought Auditors and Elect together on a daily basis. It was the only meal the Elect ate.

Here is a description of part of this service, given by a Manichaean apostate named Turbo:

> And when they [the Elect] are about to eat bread, they pray first, speaking thus to the bread: "I have neither reaped thee, nor ground, nor pressed thee, nor cast thee into an oven; but another has done these things, and brought to me; I am eating without fault." And when he has uttered these things to himself, he says to the Catechumen [i.e., Auditor], "I have prayed for thee" and thus that person departs.[8]

Evidently Turbo thought these addresses were rather disingenuous, as if the Elect were placing the blame on the Auditors in silence and then reassuring the same Auditors that they had been praying for them.

The ritual meal consisted of eating, of course, preceded by some prayers and prostrations. Auditors evidently left before the eating began; the Church

Father Augustine, who at one time had been a Manichaean Auditor, said he had never actually watched the Elect eat the ritual meal.[9]

What is most interesting about this central rite of the Manichaeans is the rationale behind it. It was meant to liberate the elements of Light through being eaten by the Elect. Thus the entire religion was centered on a rite that both imitated and helped advance the purpose of the universe itself: enabling the Light to return to its source. The Manichaean ritual meal was conceived as Mani believed the universe was — as a purification device.

The Auditors, who produced the food for the Elect, were an essential part of the system. For this service they were promised, if not full liberation after death, at any rate a more favorable incarnation the next time around. Regarding this issue Augustine writes (with the customary contempt shown by the Church Fathers for religions they disliked):

> All you promise (the Auditors) is not a resurrection, but a change
> to another mortal existence, in which they shall live the life of your
> Elect, the life you live yourself, and are so much praised for; or if they
> are worthy of the better, they shall enter into melons and cucumbers,
> or some food which will be chewed, that they may be quickly puri-
> fied by your belches.[10]

The jibe about "melons and cucumbers" refers to foods that, the Manichaeans felt, contained unusually high quantities of Light.

Consciousness and Light

This account may make Mani's teaching look somewhat ridiculous. A modern reader is likely to think that Augustine's contempt is well justified. Consider the space you're in right now. It's easy to recognize that there are countless particles — or, if you like, waves — of light that fill the atmosphere around you. They're what make it possible for you to see. But what point could there be in "liberating" them by separating them all out to one side? Even if it were feasible in some bizarre way, it would be as pointless as one of the tasks in the fable of Cupid and Psyche. Angry at Psyche for having won her son's love, Venus orders her to sort an enormous heap of mixed seeds and grains into separate piles. In the story, Psyche is magically aided by an army of ants, but we can't count on similar assistance. And anyway, what purpose would it serve?

On the other hand, it may not be wise to jump to conclusions based on surface appearances. After all, it would be extremely easy to sneer at the Christian Eucharist in much the same way. The idea of consuming the body and blood of a man who has been dead for two thousand years is at least as absurd as the Manichaeans' idea of purification by eating. Becoming fixated on the literal meaning may blind us to deeper truths.

What, then, is this primordial Light? Mani held that it dwells in everything, not only in plants, but in minerals and the earth. It's hard to make sense of this in regard to physical light; how does a rock or a clod of earth have any physical light embedded in it?

The most likely answer lies in the fact that for millennia, light has served as a metaphor for consciousness. The resemblance is obvious enough: on different levels they are what enable us to see. Consciousness, or mind, differs from physical light only in that it is what *sees* as well as what we *see by*. The mind does not need external illumination; it has its own. (This may explain why Tibetan Buddhism calls it the "Clear Light.") Moreover, there has long been an esoteric teaching that consciousness exists in all things, both the animate and the apparently inanimate. Swami Vivekananda, the Hindu sage who brought the tradition of Advaita Vedanta to the West at the end of the nineteenth century, put it this way in an 1896 lecture:

> He [the Atman, or Self], the One, who vibrates more quickly than
> the mind, who attains more speed than the mind can ever attain,
> whom even the gods reach not, nor thought grasps — He moving,
> everything moves. In Him all exists. He is moving; He is also im-
> movable. He is near and He is far. He is inside everything, He is out-
> side everything — interpenetrating everything. Whoever sees in
> every being that same Atman, and whoever sees everything in that
> Atman, he never goes far from that Atman. When a man sees all life
> and the whole universe in this Atman, . . . there is no more delusion
> for him. Where is any more misery for him who sees the Oneness in
> the universe?

Elsewhere Vivekananda defines this principle as "Pure Consciousness."[11] Christ in the *Gospel of Thomas* alludes to a similar truth: "It is I who am the light which is above them all. It is I who am the All. From Me did the All come forth, and unto me did the All extend. Split a piece of wood, and I am there. Lift up the stone, and you will find Me there" (*Thomas*, 77). Again, in a literal sense this utterance is nonsensical. If you hack a piece of wood apart, you are not going to find a tiny Jesus hiding inside. In all likelihood Christ is not speaking of himself either personally or theologically. He is speaking of this primordial mind or consciousness, which is that in us — and in all things — which says "I am." Although rocks and stones are not conscious beings as we are, to some degree this primal awareness dwells in them also.

When Mani's Light is understood in this sense, a whole new vista opens up on his thought. It is not physical light that is liberated in the bodies of the Elect, but the light of consciousness. By becoming part of an awakened human body, the consciousness that has become stuck in simple forms of life, or in apparently inanimate matter, can be set free.

Even so, this theory may still seem fanciful. The central insight behind it is best grasped from a cognitive point of view — one that reflects a process that goes on countless times per second in the human mind, and of which we are normally unaware.

If you look around the space you are in, you will see a whole array of objects that you can immediately recognize and identify. This is so basic to perception that we take it utterly for granted. But the instant this recognition happens, a subtle though rather complex process takes place. Say there is something in front of you. You recognize it as a book. By this very act of perception, you bring two opposing things into being. On one end, there is an "I" that sees the book. On the other end, there is the book that is seen. So there is that which *sees* and that which *is seen* — a seer and a seen. That which sees is, in Manichaean terminology, the "Light," or *pneuma*, which is Greek for "spirit." That which is seen is, again in Manichaean terms, the "Darkness" or *hyle*, which is Greek for "matter."[12] It has no Light, or consciousness, of its own.

In the process, the seer — that is, the subject — suffers a loss of identity. You become fixated upon the objects you see; you take them for real. The Light that is your consciousness becomes lost and buried in them. Mind is distracted by its own experience, pulled here and there, and has nothing stable to rest upon, because it has lost or forgotten the only stable thing there is — its own awareness. It becomes enmeshed in the Darkness of the objects it perceives, fearing or craving them.

The only way out of this impasse is for the Light of consciousness to detach itself from its enslavement to its own experience. In one way or another this is the goal of many different types of meditative practice. Nor is this basic theory limited to Mani's system; it is the essential meaning of a number of dualistic philosophies.

Dualism is a curious word, and some explanation of it is necessary. Originally coined in 1700, it was soon used to characterize Descartes' philosophy, which posited a radical distinction between body and mind.[13] Descartes believed that the body and mind essentially have little to do with one another; they run on parallel tracks, and the connection between them is tenuous. This view is dualism in the modern philosophical sense. Because it arose so much later than Mani's teachings or other traditional dualistic systems that we're looking at in this book, I won't discuss it any further here.

In another sense of the word, *dualism* is often applied to certain traditional teachings, particularly of India. Perhaps the most distinguished of these is the philosophical system known as the Samkhya. It is extremely ancient, tracing its origins back to the Hindu *Vedas* and *Upanishads*; the *Katha Upanishad*, which has been dated as far back as the fourth century B.C., is the text that contains the first clear references to Samkhya teachings.[14] The Samkhya holds views very much like the one I've sketched out above. What I have called "consciousness" or the "Light" it calls *purusha*; what I have called "that which is seen" or the "Darkness" is known to the Samkhya as *prakrti*. These two primordial forces essentially (or ideally) have nothing to do with one another; it is only when *purusha* becomes enmeshed in *prakrti* that the world of suffering and illusion is born. Spiritual practice is meant to restore the pristine separation of the two. The universe itself has the same purpose. In the words of a classical Samkhya text, "This creation, brought about by *prakrti* . . . is for the purpose of the release of every *purusha*."[15]

All of this helps clarify Mani's dualism. He, too, saw the cosmos as an enormous system for filtering out Light from Darkness. Individual human beings, notably the Elect, could serve this purpose, first by their own inner illumination, and then by purifying the sparks of Light through observances like the ritual meal. These processes symbolize the truth that the awakened individual herself becomes a cosmic savior.

While I can't definitively prove that the Samkhya influenced Manichaeism, it remains possible and even likely. Mani spent time in India, and he was unusually apt at incorporating ideas from other religions into his own. (One Manichaean text describes the faith as being like an ocean into which the rivers of all previous religions flow.) At the very least, the resemblances between Samkhya and Manichaeism suggest that they arose from the same fundamental insight.

I've made every effort to explain the meaning of the Light and the Darkness in plain and understandable language, but even so it remains subtle and elusive. This is not so much because these ideas are conceptually difficult, but because they require one to view one's own subjective experience from an un-accustomed angle. This is one reason that many of the Gnostics insisted that their doctrines were not for the many.

In fact, the essential elusiveness of these truths helps us understand why Gnosticism did not catch on in the long run and why Manichaeism also went into decline. There is no substitute for gnosis. Either you are awake or you are not. But this awakening may not be possible for all or even for most people. It seems to come in its own time into a mind that has been prepared to receive it. Mani dealt with this problem by having his Auditors participate in "soul-service," which would at least help them acquire merit so they could be liberated the next time around. Many forms of Buddhism have adopted a similar strategy.

Nonetheless, Manichaeism had a natural propensity to view this radical opposition between Light and Darkness in another and far more obvious way — as a struggle between good and evil. This kind of thinking comes much more readily to the human mind than do the insights I've been dis-cussing above. In earthly life, the human mind is primarily oriented toward survival and to a great degree sorts its experience into two categories: those things that aid survival and those that don't. Hence our powerful drive to view things as either good or bad in a radically simplistic way. This is the point of view that is now commonly equated with Manichaeism, and when people today describe something as "Manichaean," this is usually what they have in mind. Frequently it's also what they mean when they speak of "dual-ism." Although Mani's fundamental insight probably probed more deeply into cognitive experience than this, it seems likely that as the centuries pro-gressed, his teachings came to be viewed even by his own followers in this more external sense. It is a pattern into which practically all religions have fallen: an original insight of great profundity deteriorates more and more into outward observances. Gnosis is supplanted by the eating of ritual meals.

Decline and Disappearance

Mani's religion was not destined to triumph in the long run. It put up a valiant fight for survival and managed to keep a place for itself in the religious life of the world for about a thousand years after its founder's death. But it eventually perished — at least in institutional form.

The foremost cause of its fate was persecution. In 302 A.D. the Roman emperor Diocletian, the persecutor of Christianity, issued a harsh edict against the Manichaeans as well, evidently regarding them as a fifth column for the Persians, Rome's archenemies.

This ban was lifted by Constantine's Edict of Milan in 312, which proclaimed universal religious freedom in the empire. After this point, Manichaeism spread rapidly through the Roman domains. The Church Father Augustine was an Auditor from 373 to 382. In the end, however, the increasing unification of Roman imperial might with Catholic/Orthodox Christianity would doom Mani's religion in Roman lands. The Christian emperor Theodosius (who reigned from 379 to 395) forbade Manichaean gatherings, and in the sixth century the Byzantine emperor Justinian intensified the persecution, making a concerted effort to search out and eliminate any adherents of Mani's faith in the imperial bureaucracy. These acts of official suppression, along with the disruption caused by the barbarian invasions, doomed Manichaeism in Europe.

In the Persian Empire, the persecution that carried off Mani himself was eventually relaxed, and Manichaeism flourished there until the empire collapsed in the early seventh century. Under the Muslim Arab conquerors, Manichaeism continued to be tolerated for a while, but eventually the Abbasid caliphate in Baghdad took to violent persecution of the sect. Even so, Manichaeism continued to survive in Mesopotamia until the tenth century.

It was in Central Asia that Manichaeism established itself most successfully. Manichaean missionaries traveled along the silk routes, competed vigorously with Nestorian Christianity and Buddhism, and eventually reached as far as China. In 762 the Turkic Uighurs, then the dominant power of Central Asia, adopted Manichaeism as their official religion. They even forced their subjects to convert to Mani's faith and pressured the Chinese to establish two Manichaean temples in their own realm.

This state of affairs did not last long. When the Uighur empire collapsed in 840, Manichaeism lost its official support. The Chinese launched a persecution of the Manichaeans, who were derided as vegetarians and devil worshippers. Yet Manichaeism continued to exist in China, especially in the coastal area around Fukien. Indeed this is the last area in which traces of the religion have been found. Stray elements of Manichaeism continued to function under the guise of secret societies up to the seventeenth century.

Thus in all its history, Mani's religion managed to gain some measure of secular power for only a brief time in Central Asia. Indeed the fate of this ambitious but ill-starred faith underlines the importance of political sponsorship for the advance of any religion. What would Christianity have become had the Roman state not come to its aid in the fourth century? How far would Islam have reached had its adherents not spread it with the sword? Religions as diverse as Judaism, Buddhism, Taoism, and Confucianism have all benefited from the support of the secular arm at crucial points in their history. Mani's faith was not so lucky.

Of course other factors came into play as well. One of these was the intense competition for religious allegiance in western Asia, the region of its birth. Moreover, one can't help feeling that the fundamental attitude of Mani's religion toward the world also had a decisive impact on its destiny. Manichaeism must have been a somewhat chilly faith; its adherents would not give food to beggars because this would perpetuate the imprisonment of the sparks of Light in the bodies of inferior beings. Attitudes such as this must have given the Manichaeans an air of aloofness that hindered their success in the long run. In order to establish itself, a religion must strike a careful balance between pointing toward another reality and showing too much contempt for this one. If a faith becomes too unworldly, it runs the risk of perishing in the world.

Manichaean Survivals

And yet Mani's religion has left many traces. In the East, there is evidence of its influence on such traditions as Taoism and Tibetan religions.[16] In the West, Augustine repudiated Manichaeism but never rid himself entirely of its radical dualism, which he helped pass on to Catholicism in such forms as the idea of original sin. This doctrine, first formulated by Augustine, was not held in the early centuries of Christianity; to this day, the Eastern Orthodox Church has never adopted it.

More elusively but more pervasively, Manichaeism continues to survive as a mindset. The late Frederic Spiegelberg, professor of religion at Stanford University, was fond of saying that most people are Manichaeans without knowing it. In his book *Living Religions of the World*, Spiegelberg writes:

> Today Manichaeism exists nowhere as a confessed or practiced
> religion or cult, but it has conquered the subconscious of modern

man. . . . [H]ow much of Puritan, rigorous ethic is Christian; based
upon the doctrines of Jesus Christ, and how much is based upon
Mani; upon a fear of the body, the instincts, and the natural inclina-
tions of Man[?] . . . [A]re we Christians with a Manichaean subconscious, or Manichaeans with a Christian subconscious?[17]

Of course, Mani cannot be blamed for all of the dualistic thinking that has
gone on in history. The habit of dividing the world sharply into good and bad,
black and white seems to be ingrained into the very structure of our brains. But
Spiegelberg's comments remind us how pervasive this mindset is. Even many
sophisticated thinkers seem to struggle to avoid falling into it. And yet, because
the lost religion of light perfected and refined this point of view, the dualism of
good and evil, black and white has come to be characterized as "Manichaean."

Mani's theology has been echoed in subsequent forms of spiritual thought.
One of the most intriguing of these appears in the Kabbalistic doctrines of the
sixteenth-century Jewish mystic Isaac Luria, whose intricate cosmology bears
some resemblance to Mani's. Luria taught that at the beginning, God created
vessels to hold the divine Light that he was about to pour into the manifest
world. But the vessels could not hold their contents. They shattered, sending
sparks of Light in all directions. The duty of the Kabbalist is to liberate these
trapped sparks by performing conscious and intentional acts of righteousness. While there are many Kabbalistic systems — indeed it would be no ex-
aggeration to say that there are as many systems as there are Kabbalists —
Luria's is by far the most widespread and influential within Judaism today.
The entire Hasidic movement, for example, grew out of Lurianic Kabbalah in
the eighteenth century.[18]

On the other hand, there is little if any evidence that links Luria's thought
directly to Mani's. Luria lived in Palestine, which has always been a major
crossroads of spiritual traditions, but any remnants of Manichaeism had long
since vanished in that region by Luria's time. It's probably safer to suppose
that these two great religious visionaries came upon their insights indepen-
dently, although, as we will see in chapter 6, there were Kabbalists before Luria
who had similar ideas.

There are other, more plausible claimants to Mani's heritage. They flourished in such remote regions as the Caucasus and the Balkans, away from the
centers of imperial power, both Christian and Muslim. These movements
were to culminate in the great heresy of the Middle Ages, one that would
change Western Christianity forever.

CHAPTER 4

The War against the Cathars

By any conceivable account, Christianity represents one of the great success stories of history. A sect founded among an oppressed people by a leader who was executed as a criminal, today it counts among its adherents a third of the world's population.

Despite these triumphs, the story of Christianity can be strangely depressing, often amounting to a tale of unsavory compromises with tyranny combined with vicious suppression of rivals. The writings of many Church Fathers are almost unreadable, not because of their abstruseness, but because of their arrogance and hostility. Much of this polemic concerned obscure doctrinal issues that the evidence of scripture itself left vague. At the same time, Christ's essential teachings of love and forgiveness were frequently neglected or ignored. In its ceaseless combat over creeds and dogmas — about which you can always find cause for dispute if you're looking for it — the Christian church has often flouted the central truths stressed by Christ himself.

As a result, a modern reader looks back on many of these controversies with more than a little misgiving. Did the right side really win? And what was the right side anyway? Did the truth of the Holy Spirit prevail within Christ's church against the onslaught of error and deceit? If so, the Holy Spirit often chose savage methods to achieve his end.

Nowhere in the bleak chronicles of heresy does the modern reader feel this tension so acutely as when encountering the Cathars. They appeared in the south of France and northern Italy around the twelfth century, where their presence coincided with a flowering of art, literature, and culture that the Middle Ages had never before seen. The Cathar preachers displayed such charity and continence that they were nicknamed *les bonshommes* — the "good men." Unlike the Catholics, they remained on good terms with one another even when they disagreed on matters of doctrine. And they so threatened the Catholic power structure that the Inquisition itself was founded to deal with them. In the end, they would be eradicated with a meticulous brutality that might arouse envy even among modern practitioners of genocide. To explore their saga is to confront the strange possibility that the Cathars may have been right: by that time the established church no longer had anything to do with Christ or with the "good God," but had been taken over by the forces of darkness.

Who were the Cathars, and where did they come from? Their Catholic contemporaries had no doubts on this matter: they were offspring of the detestable heresy of Mani that had mutated from its oriental form and made its way to the western Mediterranean. Modern scholars are not quite so sure. The more cautious among them tend to doubt the continuity of the "great heresy," as it came to be called, and focus instead on the breaks and discontinuities in this much-reviled tradition. Nevertheless, there do seem to be connections between the Religion of Light in Babylonia and the *bonshommes* of Provence. These threads formed around the edges of the great religious empires of Christianity and Islam, which were marking their territories in the early medieval period.

Armenia, the Balkans, and the Bogomils

The first of these regions was Armenia. Armenia prides itself on being the first Christian nation, having adopted the faith as its sole religion in 301 A.D., over ten years before Christianity was even legalized in the Roman Empire. In the early centuries of the Common Era, Armenia maintained its independence by the sort of astute political balancing act that is frequently necessary for smaller nations living in the shadow of large ones. Finally, however, in 387 A.D., Armenia was partitioned between the Byzantine Empire and Sassanid Persia. But even in succeeding centuries, its place as a borderland between great powers enabled it to offer haven to heretics and schismatics of every type.

Two such groups have interest in the present context.[1] The first were the Massalians, "the praying people," an anticlerical sect about whose teachings little is known. Their dualistic beliefs apparently included the idea that each human being is possessed by a personal devil. This devil could only be cast out by a sacrament called the "baptism by fire," after which the individual was supposed to be free from evil influences and could do as he or she liked. This led to charges of immorality from the Orthodox clergy.

The second group were the Paulicians, so called because of their special reverence for the apostle Paul. They, too, seem to have held some kind of dualistic teaching that distinguished between the wicked creator god of this world and the hidden God of the world to come. They became renowned as formidable warriors and presented serious military problems for the Byzantine state.

It's not certain how much either of these sects was directly influenced by Mani's religion. The Byzantine Orthodox polemicists often referred to the Paulicians and Massalians as Manichaeans, but this may simply have been a handy tag to place on them. Some — probably most — scholars believe there was at least some connection between the Manichaeans and the two Armenian sects. Others prefer to trace the Paulicians' and Massalians' heritage to Marcionic and other types of Gnostic Christianity that held on for centuries in Syria and Mesopotamia. In either case, these two Armenian sects represented a continuation of the Gnostic legacy into the early Middle Ages.

In 759 the Byzantine emperor Constantine V resettled some Paulicians in the Balkans in the hope that they could be pacified and converted to Orthodoxy. This move proved disastrous for the Byzantines in the long run. Instead of meekly converting to Orthodoxy, the Paulicians spread their heterodox ideas. This was all the easier to do because the Byzantines soon lost control of the region to the Bulgars, a pagan Turkic people who swept through the Balkans and established an empire of their own.

This uneasy time gave rise to yet another heresy. Its origins are also disputed, but most scholars see it as a descendant of Paulicianism. (Other possible influences include Massalianism, Manichaeism transmitted directly across the steppes from Central Asia, and even remnants of the old Orphic and Dionysian mysteries that were still practiced on the edges of Greece as late as the seventh century A.D.). This new sect was called the Bogomils after its semilegendary founder, Bogomil. Practically nothing is known about him other than his name, which in Slavonic means "beloved of God" or "worthy of God's mercy." He is alleged to have lived during the reign of the Bulgarian tsar Peter (927–68). Associated with Bogomil was another heterodox prophet named Jeremiah, whose identity is obscure; in fact he is sometimes thought to have been the same person as Bogomil.

The known facts about the rise of the Bogomils are so few and their sources are so dubious that in the end most scholars seem content to say that the movement arose in tenth-century Bulgaria and leave it at that. In any event, it's hard to avoid the conclusion that the Bogomils had some connection with the Manichaeans. The two sects shared many crucial features, including a dualistic vision of a world divided between good and evil gods, with this world being in the possession of the latter; a two-tier hierarchy of believers, the Auditors and the Elect; an allegorical interpretation of scripture; and a rigorous asceticism, in which the Elect abstained from meat, wine, and marriage.

Another detail that will echo later on in this narrative is that, according to one Byzantine source, the Bogomils reviled the Virgin Mary with "offensive words." This attitude sprang out of a theological doctrine called Docetism (from the Greek *dokein*, "to appear"), which said that Christ only *appeared* to be born in the flesh but was actually a kind of materialization or spirit body. Docetism can be traced back to very early times in Christianity, and it's generally linked to Gnostic currents. The assertion that Christ was born of the Virgin Mary and suffered under Pontius Pilate was inserted in the Apostles' and Nicene Creeds to combat Docetism.

To return to the Bogomils, their story from their founding in the tenth century to their disappearance in the fifteenth is marked by hardship and persecution — one of the countless tragic episodes in the grim chronicles of the Balkans. The Byzantine state made a concerted effort to eradicate the heresy in its territories, which during the twelfth century, under the reign of Emperor Manuel Comnenus, briefly included the Balkans again. After Manuel's death in 1180, the Orthodox Serbs became the dominant force and drove the Bogomils westward to Dalmatia and Bosnia. The Bogomils did not regain power in the region until the mid-fourteenth century, shortly before it was conquered in turn by the Ottoman Turks. At this point many Bogomils converted to Islam, and some of them became more vehement adherents of their new faith than their conquerors were. This helps explain why so many Bosnians are Muslims to this day, and why the religious conflicts in the area are still so grievous. They are the legacy of hatreds a thousand years old.

Bogomilism in another form may have survived into the twentieth century. The Bulgarian mystic Omraam Mikhaël Aïvanhov (1900–86) claimed that both he and his spiritual master, Peter Deunov (1864–1944), were spiritual descendants of the Bogomils. Over 150 books of Deunov's teachings have been published in Bulgarian, and at the time of his death he had over forty thousand followers.[2] Most of Aïvanhov's pupils live in the south of France, where he settled in 1938 and lived the rest of his life, but there are groups of pupils in other locations, including Canada and the United States.

The teachings of these latter-day sages do not, it is true, superficially resemble those of the Bogomils. Aïvanhov, for example, taught an eclectic mix of Kabbalah, Gnosticism, and Hindu spirituality. One of his chief spiritual practices was what he called *Surya Yoga*, or "sun yoga," which involves certain meditative rites designed to imbue the devotee with solar energies (the practices are performed at sunrise). Is this just another example of New Age syncretism? Possibly not. Nita de Pierrefeu, a French scholar of Catharism, notes that the Cathars rose at dawn to greet the sun, the "weaver of light," a practice they inherited from the Bogomils.[3] Hence Aïvanhov and Deunov may represent a more direct continuation of this legacy than it might seem on the surface. In any case, it's a striking coincidence that their centers of operation were Provence and Bulgaria — precisely the regions where the Bogomils and Cathars thrived so long ago.

The Great Heresy in the West

Although Catharism would eventually come to be centered in Provence, the earliest glimmers of its arrival in western Europe are found farther to the north. In 991, one Gerbert d'Aurillac was consecrated as archbishop of Rheims. During the ceremony he was required to profess belief in the sanctity of both the Old and New Testaments and in an evil spirit that existed by choice rather than by origin. These rather curious professions suggest that Gerbert may have been suspected of some dualist heresy then current in the region. Whatever suspicions may have hung over him did not hinder him in his career: he became Pope Sylvester II in 999 (a post that some said he gained through sorcery).[4]

Despite isolated instances of heretical preachers and rumblings of Manichaeism throughout the eleventh century, the first certain instance of what would become known as Catharism can be traced back only to 1143–44. It appeared in Cologne, in the Rhineland, and was led by the local archbishop. Their teachings and practices will by now have a familiar ring. A Believer was admitted to the Elect by means of a "baptism by fire" administered by the laying on of hands. The Cologne sectarians abstained from meat and wine and admitted marriage only between virgins. They claimed that their religion had adherents throughout the world, and that they had received their teachings from Greece (that is, Byzantium), where these doctrines of true Christianity had been preserved from the earliest times.

The archbishop of Cologne was burned along with his followers, who refused to recant, but this would not be the last Western Europe would see of these teachings. A similar group of sectarians would meet a similar fate in Cologne in 1163. In 1145, Bernard of Clairvaux, founder of the Cistercian Order, went to Languedoc, in the south of France, to combat heresies there. Around the same time, the clergy of Liège (in present-day Belgium) informed the pope that "a new heresy had arisen in various parts of France, a heresy so varied and manifold that it seems impossible to characterize it under one single name."[5]

Despite the opposition of the Catholic clergy, the Cathar heresy spread rapidly in Languedoc, no doubt because the region was open to many different religious currents. Jews were tolerated and even appointed to public office. Indeed the Jews in the area were experiencing a mystical revival of their own. The Kabbalah first made its appearance there. (Although the Jewish esoteric heritage was already ancient at this time, this was when the name *Kabbalah*, or "tradition," began to be applied to it.) The Kabbalists of twelfth-century Provence produced a cryptic work called the *Sefer ha-Bahir*, or "Book of Illumination," one of the earliest treatises that can be properly called Kabbalistic.

Other factors were at play in Languedoc. The Catholic clergy were known for their laxity and corruption, making the abstemious Cathar preachers look saintly by comparison. Greek monks, some of whom had been influenced by Bogomilism, came to settle in French monasteries. And the two crusades that had been launched by that point, the first successful, the second disastrous, opened up communications with the eastern Mediterranean, with its vast array of divergent sects.

Interestingly, the heretics in France were first known as "Publicans." This word is familiar from the New Testament, where it means "tax collector." But in this case it's probably a corruption of *Paulicians* (the Greek equivalent was pronounced *Pavlikianoi*), indicating that the Paulician heresy, in name at least, had spread this far from its original home in Armenia. Later the sectarians became known as Cathars, from the Greek *katharos*, or "pure" (a term applied to the Elect), and as Albigenses, because the first Cathar bishopric in southern France was established in the town of Albi.

Catharism spread so rapidly that sometime between 1166 and 1176 the leaders of the sect decided to convene a sort of ecumenical council at the town of St.-Félix-de-Caraman near Toulouse. Presiding over the council was an individual named Nicetas, the bishop of the dualist church in Constantinople, who was known as Papa ("Pope") Nicetas.

One of the chief goals of this conference was to convert the Cathars from their previously held doctrine, known as "mitigated" or "monarchical dualism." In this view, the evil god initially derived his power and authority from the good God, as in the classic Gnostic systems. The new view, adopted by most of the Cathars in the West at that time, is called "absolute dualism": the good and evil principles exist in opposition from eternity, as Mani taught. These conflicting views represented schisms in the Balkan dualist churches at the time. While these interactions are too complex to be treated here, it's important to note that despite their differences, the two sects of the Cathars remained on good terms with each other.[6] Perhaps this was a manifestation of genuine goodwill; perhaps the threat of their enemies encouraged them to stick together. In any event, this concord contrasts sharply with mainstream Christianity, whose history is replete with anathemas hurled over doctrinal disputes that were often far more trivial.

By the end of the twelfth century, the Cathar faith was well established in the south of France. It permeated the aristocratic courts, where the ladies were often administered the *consolamentum*, the rite that admitted them to ranks of the Cathar *parfaits* (this term, meaning "perfect," was the equivalent of the Manichaean "Elect"). The men, like most Cathar Believers, preferred to wait until their death was very near at hand, as this rite committed them to various austerities, among the more inconvenient of which was total abstention from violence.

The *Consolamentum*

What exactly was the Cathar *consolamentum*? Above I mentioned a "baptism of fire" allegedly practiced by the Cologne sectarians, and it's reasonable to suppose that this rite corresponded to the *consolamentum*. To understand the meaning of this practice, it may be helpful to turn to the Gospel of John, the most important book in the Bible for the Cathars. In John 3:5, Christ tells Nicodemus, "Except a man be born of water and the spirit, he cannot enter into the kingdom of God." Mainstream Christianity equates this rebirth with the rite of baptism by water, which is believed to confer (or to mark) this dual rebirth.

The Cathars and their Gnostic predecessors didn't quite see things that way. For them, water baptism merely admitted the aspirant into the outer circle of the faith, that of the "psychics," or, in Cathar terms, Believers. It was the *consolamentum* that enabled one to be reborn of the "spirit," to enter the ranks of pneumatic Christians, or the Elect. Only at this level could a member of the sect be considered truly *katharos,* or "pure." Some accounts of this rite survive, so it's possible to piece together how it proceeded.

The initiate was rarely, if ever, admitted upon first joining the faith. Indeed the evidence suggests that recruits were at first exposed to teachings that were very much like those of orthodox Christianity. Only after a year or two of probation were they initiated "into the whole heresy and madness," to use the words of one heresiologist.[7] Even then they might wait a long time before having the *consolamentum* administered. The typical Believer would not receive it until he or she was very close to death, since, as with the Manichaeans, admission to the Elect enforced strict austerities upon the initiate.

For the small elite (estimates suggest that there were only a thousand to fifteen hundred Cathar *parfaits* in Languedoc at the beginning of the thirteenth century, when the movement was at its height), the *consolamentum* was given earlier on in life. It was generally preceded by the *endura,* a fast of forty days, in imitation of Christ's retreat into the desert after his own baptism.

The ritual itself was not secret — Believers were permitted to be present — and was comparatively simple in form.[8] The aspirant was brought in silence to the place of initiation. A number of lighted torches were arranged along the length of the room, probably to symbolize the "baptism by fire." In the midst of the room was a table covered with a cloth, which served as an altar. A copy of the New Testament rested upon it.

The assemblage arranged itself in a circle; the aspirant stood in the middle. The Lord's Prayer was recited, and the aspirant received addresses and admonitions suitable for the occasion. He was told, "The Church signifies union, and wherever true Christians are, there are the Father, the Son, and the Holy Spirit, as the Holy Scriptures show." Passages from scripture were read that described how the Father, the Son, and the Holy Spirit manifested in the human being. One verse that was frequently used was 1 Cor. 3:16–17: "Know ye not that ye are the temple of God, and that the Spirit of God dwelleth in you?"

The elder presiding over the rite then admonished the aspirant to repent of all his faults and to forgive those of everyone else, an obligation he was to keep for the rest of his life.

The *consolamentum* included further texts and readings that proved the superiority of this baptism by the spirit, for example Acts 1:5: "For John truly baptized with water: but ye shall be baptized with the Holy Ghost not many days hence." The ritual went on to say: "This holy baptism, by which the Holy Spirit is given, has been preserved by the Holy Church from the Apostles until now, and it has passed from 'good men' to 'good men' up to this point, and it will till the end of time."

After the aspirant made his repentance and was pardoned by the assembly, the *consolamentum* proper was administered. The elder took the New Testament and placed it upon the candidate's head, while the other members of the Elect present placed their right hands on him. The elder then said, "Holy Father, accept this thy servant into thy justice, and bestow thy grace and Holy Spirit upon him." At this point, according to Déodat Roché, one of the twentieth century's leading scholars of Catharism, "the soul rediscovered the spirit from which it had been separated (or, as we would say, of which it had lost consciousness)."[9]

The rite concluded in the primitive Christian manner, with the kiss of peace. To safeguard purity, however, the "kiss" was communicated between the sexes only by placing the New Testament upon the recipient's shoulder.

As we can see, the *consolamentum* was a simple rite, and there are few details in it that would seem totally out of place in a modern Christian church; indeed one Catholic scholar admitted that it contains no statement that could not have been uttered in perfect faith by an Inquisitor.[10] Obviously its meaning and power cannot be reduced to any of its parts, or even to all of them taken together, but were due to the candidate's intense preparation and the depth of feeling in the community. And this raises a crucial question: can gnosis, which is, after all, a state of inner illumination, be conferred by a mere ritual, no matter how profound?

This issue leads us to the nature of initiation, which in its many forms is a universal phenomenon. Initiation marks an individual's transition from one phase of life to another. But does it merely *mark* this transition, or does it somehow make the transition happen? In a puberty ritual, by which primitive tribes admit a young man or woman to full adult responsibility, it is clearly both. The individual must be of the proper age, but the rite is more than a glorified birthday party: he or she is traditionally taken aside and taught the wisdom of the tribe, often after a preparation period that includes seclusion, fasting, and other rigors.

While the *consolamentum* was no puberty ritual, in broad outlines the process was the same. The aspirant prepared for it by the forty-day fast, or *endura*, which was so rigorous that it sometimes proved fatal. After this probationary period — which in itself would weed out all but the most serious candidates — the individual was received into the circle of the Elect, and the Word of illumination descended upon him, symbolized by the act of placing the New Testament upon his head.

But did this automatically confer gnosis upon the initiate? To answer this question definitively is impossible, since it would require a knowledge of the inner states of people who have been dead for centuries. But there are a number of traditions in which spiritual power is transferred directly by initiation. The Hindu concept of *shaktipat* refers to a palpable spiritual force that can be transmitted from master to pupil; the Sufis, the mystics of Islam, have a very similar concept, called *baraka* (which literally means "blessing"). For the Cathars, whether or not their *consolamentum* conferred true inner illumination, it's at least safe to say that the rigors of preparation and the intensity of feeling present must have made it a life-changing event for practically all the Elect.

Some scholars have contended that the *consolamentum* required the aspirant to renounce the conventional Christian baptism, but Déodat Roché disagrees: "The number of Catholic priests and monks who were won over to Catharism appears to have been significant, and this alleged renunciation of their baptism would have forced them to leave the Roman church, which they did not do." Roché cites a fragment of a Florentine Cathar ritual: "Do not imagine that in receiving this baptism [of the Spirit], you must despise the other baptism, or anything that you have done or said that is truly Christian and good, but you must understand that it is important to receive this holy ordination of Christ as a supplement to the one that did not suffice for your salvation."[11] This fact is curious in light of the Cathar view that the Roman church was little more than an emissary of darkness. While it could have been a tactical move to stave off persecution, this seems unlikely. As even their enemies admitted, the Cathars were neither impostors nor hypocrites.

This detail suggests that the Cathars' purpose may have been different than is generally supposed. They did not intend to start a new religion; possibly they did not intend even to start a new church. What they may have wanted to do was to restore an inner level of Christianity that had been stifled in the centuries of struggle against heresies and striving for temporal power. The Cathar division of members into Believers and Elect parallels the inner and outer levels of religious teaching, which I discussed in chapter 2.

Catharism may have been an attempt to reintroduce this inner level of Christianity into a church that had become stuck on the level of the exterior. This is a perennial problem in religion, as we can see from this verse in the Gospels: "Woe unto you, scribes and Pharisees, hypocrites! for ye shut up the kingdom of heaven against men: for ye neither go in yourselves, neither suffer ye them that are entering to go in" (Matt. 23:13). The "scribes and Pharisees" represent those guardians of doctrine at the outer level who become obsessed with preserving the letter of the doctrine but refuse to experience it inwardly for themselves or to let anyone else do so. It's ironic, of course, that a church that is based on Christ's teaching would have fallen into a trap that he warned against so explicitly.

If this is true, it would explain why the Cathars were so successful and why the hierarchy found them so threatening. Strictly speaking, the Cathars were not doing anything that was outside the bounds of Christianity. As one Catholic scholar noted, "The Cathar rites of the thirteenth century remind us of those of the primitive Church to a degree that is more and more striking the closer we come to the apostolic age."[12] But the Cathars were casting doubt on one of the central pillars of Catholic teaching: that its doctrines and practices are both necessary and sufficient for salvation. In the *consolamentum*, initiates were told that their baptism by water had not been sufficient at all.

This leads us to ask whether salvation, as traditionally conceived, and gnosis are the same thing. By this point it should be clear that they are not. Salvation is generally understood to be a promise made by God of aid at the time of one's death: the soul will be rescued from straying into undesirable dimensions of reality — in a word, from hell. It is freely given for the asking. Gnosis is a state of cognitive awakening that is vouchsafed to a very small number of people (mostly because only a very small number seek it out). Salvation is the goal of external Christianity; gnosis is the goal of the inner circle. In biblical symbolism, salvation is represented by the water baptism of John the Baptist; gnosis is represented by Christ's baptism of the spirit.[13]

Stated in this way, the distinction is easy enough to see, but it was not always understood, probably at even a very early stage of Christianity. Perhaps this was the main cause of dissension between the Gnostics and the proto–orthodox Christians in the first and second centuries. The Gnostics were concerned with inner illumination; deliverance at the hour of death may have seemed to them a diversion from the real heart of the spiritual quest. To the proto-Catholics, on the other hand, this preoccupation with gnosis was a dangerous detour from what *they* regarded as the only issue of importance. A thousand years later, this controversy (or misunderstanding) was still being played out, with the Catholics regarding the Cathars as dangerous heretics with their specious *consolamentum* — clearly worthless when the sacraments of the Church were necessary and sufficient for salvation — and with the Cathars telling their followers that mere baptism by water was not sufficient for true awakening.

Courtly Love

Another phenomenon associated with the Cathars is *l'amour courtois*, or courtly love, made famous by the poetry of the troubadours, the medieval Provençal poets of love. The connection may seem strange. It's not quite obvious what this version of romantic love had to do with Catharism, which was so adamant about its contempt for earthly things. In his classic study *Love in the Western World*, Denis de Rougemont describes the issue thus:

> On the one hand, the Catharist heresy and courtly love developed
> simultaneously in the twelfth century and also coincided spatially in
> the south of France. How suppose [*sic*] that the two movements were
> entirely unconnected? For them not to have entered into relations
> would surely be the strangest thing of all! But on the other hand, and
> weighting the opposite side of the scales, how could there be a con-
> nexion between those sombre Cathars, whose asceticism compelled
> them to shun all contact with the opposite sex, and the bright trou-
> badours, joyful and up to any folly, who turned love, the spring,
> dawn, flowery gardens, and the Lady, all into song?[14]

The name *courtly love* would lead us to suppose that it sprang up in the noble courts of the era. But the word "court" (*cour* in French; the adjective is *courtois*) may be pointing, not to the court of a king, but to the twelfth-century "courts of love," which handed down rulings and adjudications on the matters of the heart. They were presided over by women of high birth.

Eleanor of Aquitaine, wife of King Louis VII of France and later of King Henry II of England, held one. So did the Countess of Champagne, whose court produced a remarkable ruling in 1174:

> We declare and affirm . . . that love cannot extend its rights over two married persons. For indeed lovers grant one another all things mutually and freely, without being impelled by any motive of necessity, whereas husband and wife are held by their duty to submit their wills to each other and to refuse each other nothing.
>
> May this judgement, which we have delivered with extreme caution, and after consulting with a great number of other ladies, be for you a constant and unassailable truth.[15]

Ermengarde, viscountess of Narbonne, delivered a similar opinion: "The affection between a married couple and the genuine love shared by lovers are shown by nature to be completely opposed and to have their sources in completely different movements [of the soul]."[16]

So far we know two things about courtly love: women laid down its laws, and it had nothing to do with marriage. Indeed it specifically *excluded* marriage. A third stipulation is just as important: the lovers were not to have sexual intercourse.

This is not to say that courtly love was always or totally free of carnality. In its classic form, it involved a progressive increase of intimacy that began with a glance, proceeding to conversation with the beloved, then to touching her hand, then to the kiss. In the end it might lead to the *assais,* or "test," which was not exactly chaste. The lover could look at his lady naked, hold her, embrace her, and caress her — the contact could well lead to orgasm for both parties. But actual penetration was not allowed. (No doubt this rule was violated on more than one occasion, as rules often are.)[17]

These facts, however bewildering, bring this curious phenomenon into sharper focus. Courtly love was the opposite of marriage. The obligations between the partners were those of the heart: they were freely chosen, not the result of a contract that society would enforce. Because intercourse was forbidden, the love would produce no children. Consequently it would not threaten the essential basis for marriage: that the couple provide a stable home for their offspring, where the woman is guaranteed some support from her husband and the husband knows that the children are his own. Finally, unlike marriage, where in medieval times the husband had the upper hand, in

courtly love the man was the humble suppliant of *la dame de ses pensées* —
"the lady of his thoughts." One of the precepts of *De arte amandi* (On the Art
of Love), a fourteenth-century treatise on courtly love, admonishes male
lovers, "Be ever mindful of all the commands of the ladies."[18]

But how is courtly love connected to de Rougemont's "sombre Cathars,
whose asceticism compelled them to shun all contact with the opposite sex"?
In the first place, courtly love is the exact opposite of the sexuality permitted
by the Catholic Church, which condoned sex only for procreation (hence its
prohibitions of abortion and birth control). As Frederic Spiegelberg observes,
"The Catholic tradition that sex is permissible if the chance of procreation exists, but otherwise is not permissible, was turned around by the Manichaean
prophets to say that sex is permissible as long as procreation is prevented."[19]

The *bonshommes* may also have had something else in mind. The poetry of
the troubadours abounds with praises of the "Lady," whose frustrating un-
availability evokes all manner of longing. Sometimes the homage verges on
the sacrilegious. "By her alone shall I be saved!" cries William of Poitiers, the
first of the troubadours.[20] In other verses, the poet promises to keep the Lady's
secret, as if it were a matter of religious faith. The troubadours' verses are suffused with a delicious ambiguity about the nature of this Lady — whether she
is a flesh-and-blood woman to whom the swain has vowed himself or
whether she stands for something higher.

To see what the Lady may have symbolized, let us return to Déodat Roché's
observation that the *consolamentum* was meant to unite the soul with the
spirit. In essence, the rite was a mystical marriage between the psyche and the
transcendent Self, or the true "I," from which the psyche, the ordinary level of
consciousness, had previously been cut off. The troubadours, in their laments
for this lost Lady, may have been speaking allegorically of a longing for this
higher Self.

This idea points to an extremely important fact about the spiritual path. In
the previous chapter, I suggested that human beings are creatures who are capable of viewing the body as an *other*. What is even more peculiar is that we
are capable of viewing the self as an *other* as well. Paradoxically, we experience
that which is most essential to ourselves, that which alone has the right to say
"I," as tenuous, remote, even nonexistent. In Christ's parable, it is the master
that is away (Matt. 24:45–51). For the Gnostics, it is the pearl at the bottom of
the sea; for the troubadours, it is *la dame de ses pensées*, beguiling, distant, yet
drawing the aspirant ever upward toward his higher nature.

Courtly love, then, involved what modern psychology calls *projection*. The lover's imagination mingles or confuses his own higher nature with the distant Lady, whose mere glance sends him into paroxysms of rapture. The distinction may not have been clear even to all of the devotees of this enigmatic form of love. No doubt the Cathar adepts and the greatest of the troubadours understood the symbolic meaning of this Lady, but it's equally likely that many lovers equated her with their ladies of flesh and blood.

If the troubadours were evasive about the exact nature of the Lady, their poetic heirs, most famously Dante, brought the matter into the open. Indeed we could see Dante's entire literary career as a movement from his love of Beatrice the actual woman, whom he first espies at the age of nine, to his personification of her as the divine Wisdom who guides him through the spheres of heaven in the *Paradiso*. But these two aspects of Beatrice are indissolubly linked from the start. In the *Vita Nuova*, Dante recalls:

> The moment I saw her I say in all truth that the vital spirit, which dwells in the inmost depths of the heart, began to tremble so violently that I felt the vibration alarmingly in all my pulses, even the weakest of them. As it trembled, it uttered these words: *Ecce deus fortior me, qui veniens dominabitur mihi* ["Behold, a god more powerful than I, who comes to rule over me"].[21]

Dante and Beatrice never come together. Like a troubadour, Dante contents himself with admiring her from a distance, and she dies at an early age. And yet there is something delectable in the flashes of love he experiences simply from greeting her in the street:

> Whenever and wherever she appeared, in the hope of receiving her miraculous salutation I felt I had not an enemy in the world. Indeed, I glowed with a flame of charity which moved me to forgive all who had ever injured me; and if at that moment someone had asked me a question, about anything, my only reply would have been: "Love," with a countenance clothed with humility.[22]

Notice that Dante does not complain that he cannot enjoy Beatrice's favors; instead, the briefest glimpse of her launches him into a joy bordering on religious ecstasy. Something within him has transformed lust into adoration. This, too, was essential to courtly love. While it did not always exclude physical contact, it emphasized transmutation rather than consummation. Nor was this a matter of mere technique. The sublimation of the sexual drive into a higher emotional force was meant to happen spontaneously, through the natural operation of the heart.

If the quest for such transmutation seems odd to us today, we must remember the religious backdrop of the time. The Cathars and the Catholics didn't agree about much, but their views on sexuality were remarkably similar: they thought it was bad. For the Cathars, with their Manichaean heritage, sex imprisoned the sparks of light in the darkness of matter, while for the Catholics it was a regrettable necessity so that the human race could perpetuate itself in this fallen realm. For their different reasons, both sects were entirely happy to embrace an ideal that sacrificed sexual expression to a higher, purer counterpart.

In *Love in the Western World*, Denis de Rougemont argues that courtly love was the ancestor of romantic love as we know it today. Courtly love, rooted in the inaccessibility of the beloved, inspired the tragic tales of Tristan and Iseult and of Lancelot and Guinevere in the Arthurian romances. Later on, the same impulse would find expression in the tragedies of Shakespeare, Corneille, and Racine, and would culminate in the Romantic exaltation of doomed passion. "From desire to death via *passion* — such has been the road taken by European romanticism; and we are all taking this road to the extent that we accept — unconsciously of course — a whole set of manners and customs for which the symbols were devised in courtly mysticism," de Rougemont writes.[23]

De Rougemont is undoubtedly overstating his case. Romantic love seems to be universal. Many cultures apart from the West have dwelt upon the melancholy intertwining of love and fatality. Nonetheless, de Rougemont does seem to be right in one respect. The greatest love stories of the West are those of doomed love. Tristan and Iseult do not settle down; neither do Heloïse and Abelard, Romeo and Juliet, Zhivago and Lara, or any of the other great lovers of history and literature. De Rougemont argues that this exultation of the tragic has encouraged discontent with the more humdrum but more stable attachments of domestic life, which, he says, is why marriage stands on such a shaky footing today.

It's unlikely that the perplexities of modern love can all be laid at the door of the troubadours or their literary heirs. Our modern anguishes, like the ones of old, seem to point to something deeper in the reaches of human nature — a discontent that stirs in us at the most unpredictable times and for the most arbitrary reasons, urging us to despise the familiar and pine after the faraway. It is an old predicament, and it has inspired much of the best and the worst in human life, as it has in love itself.

The Albigensian Crusade

The Cathar impulse in the West reached its high-water mark around the beginning of the thirteenth century. The beginning of its decline can be dated to the accession of Innocent III to the papacy in 1198. More than any pope before or after him, Innocent was obsessed with consolidating temporal as well as the spiritual power: his entire papacy was an attempt to assert his authority over mere earthly monarchs. As part of his effort to create a universal theocracy, he was determined to destroy the dualist heresies that threatened the religious unity of Europe.

In 1199, Innocent sent a mission of Cistercian monks to Languedoc to preach against Catharism; this envoy would be followed in later years by missions led by clerics, including Dominic Guzmán, founder of the Dominican Order. Indeed the origin of the order can be traced to Dominic's efforts to convert the heretics of Languedoc in those years. Innocent also urged the French nobility to suppress the Cathars, but many nobles of Languedoc, especially Raymond VI, count of Toulouse, refused to oblige. In 1207, Innocent excommunicated Raymond. The next year, when a papal legate was murdered in Languedoc, Innocent launched a crusade against the Cathars, usually called the Albigensian Crusade (since the Cathars were also known as Albigenses).

It would be too lengthy and tedious to go into the intricacies and reversals of this war, in which various monarchs and nobles, including Raymond himself, often found it expedient to switch sides at crucial moments. But in essence two major forces were at play. The Catholic Church was determined to stamp out a religious rival, and the nobles of northern France were eager to use this pretext to gain possession of Languedoc. Naturally, the crusade soon surpassed its initial mandate in savagery and cruelty, and Innocent himself had to remind the crusaders of the true purpose of their warfare. The struggle continued on and off until 1229, when it was concluded by the Peace of Paris between Raymond VII (son of Raymond VI, who had died in 1222) and King Louis IX of France. By this agreement Raymond had to cede much of his territories to Louis and the church. Furthermore, his daughter was obliged to marry one of the king's brothers; upon their deaths, their territories would become part of the French kingdom. From a political point of view, the chief result of the Albigensian Crusade was the consolidation of the French kingdom under the Capet dynasty.

The crusade did not succeed in destroying the heresy itself. Large numbers of the *parfaits* were captured and burned, but the persecutions were not systematic enough to eliminate them. In the years between 1227 and 1235, however, Pope Gregory IX issued a number of decrees that established the Inquisition, to be staffed chiefly by two new monastic orders, the Franciscans and the Dominicans. Unlike earlier tribunals, which were haphazardly administered by local bishops, the Inquisition was directed *ab apostolica sede*, "from the apostolic see," that is, by the papacy. This move would lead to a tremendous increase in efficiency and centralization for the persecutions.

The climactic moment in the fall of the Cathars was the capture of the stronghold of Montségur in the foothills of the Pyrenees. After the Peace of Paris, the Cathar bishops had found it expedient to withdraw here, farther from Italy and northern France. In May 1242, after two visiting Inquisitors were murdered at Montségur, French forces assaulted the citadel.

Montségur's almost impregnable position made the siege lengthy and difficult, and the attackers were unable to cut off the castle completely from the rest of the world. But as the months progressed, the position of the Cathars and their protectors continued to worsen, and the nobles defending the castle began to negotiate with their attackers. As part of the terms, the *parfaits* at Montségur were offered the choice of recanting or being burned at the stake. They chose martyrdom, and in March 1244 over two hundred of the Cathar Elect went to the flames singing. Before the capitulation, however, three or four *parfaits* made a daring escape. Legend says they took with them a mysterious "Cathar treasure," which has never been found. It is not even clear whether this treasure consisted of gold and jewels or texts and teachings. Rumors about the Cathar treasure continue to surface in the occult lore of Europe.

The fall of Montségur did not, in and of itself, end the Cathar movement, which then moved its headquarters to Lombardy in northern Italy, where struggles between the pope and the Holy Roman Emperor made it difficult for the church to attack the heretics. But the long decades of persecution had broken the back of Catharism, and the increasing efficiency of the Inquisition further hastened, its demise. Catharism continued to survive into the fourteenth century, but at that point it disappears from the face of history.

The Secret Heresy of Hieronymus Bosch

Did the Cathars leave any heirs in the succeeding centuries? There is not much evidence that they did — but that is to be expected, given that this hunted sect had a dire need to cover its tracks. The most fascinating case for a Cathar survival into the Renaissance appears in a recent book by Lynda Harris entitled *The Secret Heresy of Hieronymus Bosch*.[24]

Bosch's strange, lurid, but compelling paintings are familiar to anyone who has taken a basic art history course. Scholars today usually regard his images as the products of his own imagination and characterize him as a distant ancestor of twentieth-century surrealism. But it is possible that another purpose lay behind his bizarre imagery.

In Bosch's time — the early Renaissance — the tradition of European painting employed a rich and intricate symbolic vocabulary. A dog symbolized fidelity; a lute with a broken string symbolized mortality. Like any other form of language, this network of images was generally understandable but still allowed for a great deal of individual expression. Harris contends that Bosch's symbolic language expressed his allegiance to the Cathar heresy.

Bosch was born sometime between 1450 and 1460 in the town of s'Hertogenbosch in the Brabant, a district of the present-day Netherlands near the Belgian border; he would live there for his entire life. He came from a family of artists and outwardly lived a conventional bourgeois existence. He was a respected citizen and was considered to be a Catholic in good standing; in fact he was a member of a pious association called the Brotherhood of Our Lady. His only departure from the ordinary — apart from his paintings themselves — was a visit he made to Venice sometime around 1500, where he may have met such artists as Giorgione and Leonardo da Vinci, both of whose works show some traces of Bosch's influence (as his do of theirs). He died around 1520.

What evidence do we have for his connection to the Cathars? The artist we know by that name *Bosch* (from *s'Hertogenbosch*) did not use the surname until around 1500. Before then, he used his hereditary surname, *van Aken*, which suggests that the family came from Aachen in Germany. Aachen was near Cologne, which, as we have seen, was the site of the first known Cathar community. Moreover, the earliest reference to an ancestor of Bosch's dates from 1271, when the records of s'Hertogenbosch show a wool merchant named van Aken doing business with England. Cathars were often members of the cloth trade. It is possible, then, that the van Aken family left Germany in the mid-thirteenth century to avoid the increasing persecution of Cathars, the Netherlands being more tolerant. Here, Harris suggests, the family may have continued to practice Catharism in secret for the next two hundred years.

All this evidence is, of course, circumstantial. The most powerful argument for Bosch's secret heresy comes from the symbolism of his paintings, which is bizarre and inexplicable from the perspective of Catholic doctrine but quite comprehensible from the Cathar point of view. While Harris goes into great detail about Bosch's symbolism, here two fairly simple examples will have to suffice.

In the background of the central panel of Bosch's *Adoration of the Magi* at the Prado, we see a tiny figure of a man leading a donkey with an ape riding on it. Nearby is a statue of what looks like a Greek god on a column atop a small mound.

Harris argues that this is a subtle but deliberate jeer at the traditional imagery of the Flight into Egypt. Most representations of this episode from Matthew's Gospel show Joseph leading Mary with the infant Jesus on a donkey. Frequently they are depicted passing by the fallen idols of Egypt, which have toppled in the presence of the true God. Bosch's imagery shows the opposite. It is an ape, and not the Virgin, that is riding on the donkey, and the idol stands undisturbed on its column.

Such imagery is difficult to explain coming from the hand of a pious Catholic, particularly a member of the Brotherhood of Our Lady. But remember that the Bogomils and their successors, repudiating the doctrine of Christ's humanity, mocked the Blessed Virgin. Bosch's tiny detail fits in with these dualist beliefs.

There are other features in this painting that support such a view, and there are other details in other paintings that point still more clearly to a Cathar influence. In one strange work, called *The Stone Operation*, an oafish peasant is having the top of his head cut open by a man dressed in clerical attire and wearing a funnel on his head. Next to this figure is a monk in a black robe holding a pitcher. Off to the side is a woman with a book on her head, watching the scene with a look of distant melancholy.

By the standard symbolism of the time, this scene would speak of the removal of the stone of folly, but here it is not a stone that is being extracted from the man's head; it is a flower. By Harris's interpretation, the two performing the operation are members of the Catholic clergy, and what they are extracting is not folly but the flower of the man's spiritual potential. Both the funnel and the pitcher held by the two quacks allude to the false Catholic baptism by water. But it's the book on the woman's head that is most striking, since, as we've seen, the *consolamentum* was conferred by placing a copy of the New Testament on the initiate's head. This would make her a Cathar adept watching the folly of two quacks — the Catholic clergy — destroying the spiritual potential of an unsuspecting lout.

Harris's interpretations of these and other paintings makes a great deal of sense out of what otherwise seem to be whimsical and arbitrary details. But could Bosch's family have kept the Cathar faith for two centuries without being detected, and could Bosch himself have held beliefs that were diametrically opposed to his outward practice without giving himself away?

In both cases, the answer is yes. Family traditions can hand down heterodox religious beliefs over a long period of time, as we see in the Marranos, the Jews of Renaissance Spain who practiced their religion in secret for generations while pretending outwardly to be Catholics. More controversially, there are forms of paganism and the "Old Religion" that were allegedly kept up in family contexts during long centuries of persecution.

As for Bosch's ability to live so duplicitous an existence, this becomes more comprehensible if we recollect that he lived in what Paul Johnson, in his *History of Christianity*, characterized as a "total society."[25] Recent instances of totalitarian societies show that people who live in them often go to extremes of deceit and concealment to protect themselves. And given the range of its influence, the technological limitations of the era, and the political disunion of Europe, the Christendom of Bosch's time was not only a totalitarian society, but a remarkably successful one. No fascist or communist state in the twentieth century was able to keep such extensive control — and for centuries rather than decades. It is hard for a modern American to imagine what it must have been like to pay lip service for a lifetime to values that were totally opposed to those of one's heart, but it has often been done. In many parts of the world it still has to be done today.

Even if Bosch and others like him did continue to practice Catharism in secret, they were the last heirs of a dying tradition. The great dualist heresy, begun with Mani over a thousand years before, finally expired at the beginning of the modern era. We know this from the simple fact that when the European nations introduced religious toleration in the sixteenth and seventeenth centuries, no hidden Cathars came to the surface. By then they had all vanished, most likely absorbed either into Catholicism or into the dozens of Protestant sects that sprang up after the Reformation.

And yet the Cathar legacy has perpetuated itself in memory and legend. The *parfaits* burned at Montségur, formerly reviled as heretics, are now hailed as martyrs to the cause of religious freedom. The troubadours are honored as revivers of the tradition of the Divine Feminine in an age of male domination. Cathar influences may even have survived in ordinary language. The French often speak of *le bon Dieu,* "the good God." Did this phrase, now taken entirely for granted, originate long ago in the idea that there is a "good God" who has to be distinguished from another God, who is evil? Perhaps this commonplace expression is a fossil of Cathar theology preserved in the amber of day-to-day speech.

CHAPTER 5

Gnosis in the Medieval Church

N ow that we've traced the history of the great dualist heresy from its birth to its death, it's reasonable to ask how much of the Gnostic impulse survived within mainstream Christianity during the same period. The answer is, surprisingly, a great deal. The Catholic and Orthodox churches had no patience for some of the central ideas of the old Gnostics, especially that the God of the Old Testament was an inferior deity and that the world was his misshapen spawn. And yet some of the main Gnostic themes persisted — sometimes as direct survivals of the Gnostic schools, but also as elements of the universal esoteric doctrine without which no religion can long survive.

Prime among these was the idea of a hierarchy of unseen entities that stand between corporeal reality and the absoluteness of God himself. Many spiritual works characterize these figures as equivocal and possibly hostile toward humanity. An early text known as the *First Book of Enoch* expands upon the Genesis account that speaks of "the sons of God" who married "the daughters of men" (Gen. 6:2). In *1 Enoch*, these sons of God, or "angels," are highly ambiguous. They do teach the human race useful arts, but they are motivated by lust for the "beautiful and comely daughters" of men, and when they marry them, they beget "great giants, . . . who consumed all the acquisitions of men."[1] Inspired in part by such texts, the Gnostics saw these dark angels as the archons — the forces of spiritual bondage that bar the way to illumination. Catholic and Orthodox Christianity often retained very similar systems, but they transmuted the archons from evil cosmic overlords into angels and archangels who held their appointed places in the heavenly hierarchy.

The Celestial Order of Dionysius

Among the most influential portraits of the heavenly hierarchy was the *Celestial Hierarchy* of Dionysius the Areopagite. The original Dionysius was a convert of Paul's (Acts 17:34), but Paul's Dionysius did not write this treatise, which was probably the work of an anonymous sixth-century Greek theologian. Nonetheless, I shall call him by this name, since we know him by no other. Dionysius portrays nine orders of heavenly beings, arranged in three triads: the Thrones, Cherubim, and Seraphim at the top; the Powers, Virtues, and Dominions in the middle; and the Angels, Archangels, and Principalities at the bottom.

It's not clear where Dionysius got this system, which he himself seems to understand only imperfectly at times. But he does in his way represent a continuation of the Gnostic legacy as it would be digested by orthodox Christianity. His use of this legacy did much to shape the medieval Christian worldview.

To take a reasonably simple example, Dionysius lists two orders of these divine beings as Principalities and Powers. This echoes a verse I've already quoted, Eph. 6:12: "For we wrestle not against flesh and blood, but against principalities, against powers, against the rulers of the darkness of this world, against spiritual wickedness in high places" (cf. Rom. 8:38; Eph. 3:10; Col. 1:16, 2:15). But there is a big difference between this verse and Dionysius's system. In Ephesians, the "principalities and powers" are by no means friendly to the Christian. They are equated with "spiritual wickedness in high places."

Dionysius sees them in a far more positive light. "The name of the celestial Principalities signifies their Godlike princeliness and authoritativeness in an Order which is holy and most fitting." Similarly, the Powers are so called because they lead those below "to the Supreme Power which is the Source of Power."[2] For Dionysius, the orders of angels do not oppose spiritual ascent but facilitate it.

Ephesians describes "principalities and powers" in a way that helped inspire the Gnostic idea of the archons. But for Dionysius, these orders are holy and beneficent and lead the soul toward God. In this case, the heretics may have been closer to the meaning of scripture than the orthodox. This is not the only case in which orthodox Christianity would adopt a teaching that is more or less explicitly contradicted by its own sacred scripture.

Dionysius's celestial schema would be copied down through the centuries in Christianity. The most famous use of it appears in Dante's *Paradiso*, which describes heaven as a series of concentric spheres surrounding the earth. Each sphere is governed by a planet, and each is associated with a particular one of Dionysius's orders (the Principalities are in the sphere of Venus, the Powers in the sphere of the sun). Dante pays tribute to Dionysius by putting these words into the mouth of Beatrice, his guide to heaven:

> And Dionysius with such desire
> Set himself to contemplating these orders
> That he named and distinguished them as I do.[3]

Following Dionysius, Dante has transformed the forces of spiritual wickedness into guardians of the divine cosmos.

Gnosis and the Celts

If Dionysius was able to take the equivocal or malevolent spiritual powers of Paul and transform them into heavenly choirs, the Christianity of the Celts is often credited with doing the same for the natural realm. Anyone who has wandered through the British Isles has undoubtedly been struck by the terrain's elusive magic. The restful yet startling greens of the verdure and the cold, dreamy grays of the skies and rocks all seem to hint at an eerie otherworld concealed behind the façade of substantiality. It's easy to see how this land could inspire rich fancies of the imagination.

Among the most vibrant products of this imagination is the history of these isles. The Irish spoke of the Tuátha De' Danann, a mysterious race of supernatural beings who inhabited their country before the Celts. The Irish, Welsh, and Gauls devised intricate genealogies for their kings and nobles, whose ancestry they traced to a strange mélange of biblical patriarchs and Greek and Roman heroes. The medieval era produced the great Arthurian romances, which painted an idealized yet tragic picture around a legendary Romano-British chieftain. More recently, this powerful force of imagination has conjured up a past for Celtic Christianity that has more to do with fantasy than with reality.

By this view, Celtic Christianity was originally independent of the Church of Rome. This native-born Celtic Christianity fostered a holistic worldview that combined Christian teachings of love and compassion with reverence and awe for nature. Rather than exterminating the old pagan religion, this Celtic Christianity made a home for it, and even absorbed much of the wisdom of the Druids, the pre-Christian sages of the Celtic world. Only with the Synod of Whitby in 664, an assembly of churchmen from Northumbria, was the Roman hierarchy able to put its foot on the neck of this indigenous Christianity.

How much of this portrait of Celtic Christianity is accurate? To find out in more detail, a brief historical sketch is in order. Britain was conquered by the Roman Empire in 43 A.D., and Christianity came to the island over the next few centuries along with the other accouterments of Roman civilization. A legend dating at least as far back as the thirteenth century says that Joseph of Arimathea, who in the Gospels gave his tomb over for the use of Christ's body, came to Glastonbury in 63 A.D. and founded the first Christian church in Britain. But as the Western Roman Empire collapsed at the beginning of the fifth century, Rome had to withdraw its legions. Britain was overrun by the pagan Angles, Saxons, and Jutes, who would not be converted to Christianity till the seventh century.

Ireland's acceptance of Christianity is generally dated from 431 A.D., with the coming of one Palladius as the "first bishop of the Irish believing in Christ." Patrick, a Romano-British missionary who would become the island's patron saint, arrived soon thereafter. The process of conversion, which took place over the next two centuries, was long, slow, and mainly peaceful. The Christian faith was not imposed on Ireland by the Roman Empire, which never ruled the island. As a result, the Irish were able to create a much more serene and eclectic merger of their new faith with the old ways than we see in much of Europe. As John Carey, a scholar of Old Irish, points out:

> Exactly how, and by what stages, the old beliefs gave way to the new is probably something we shall never know. But we can at least see the outcome in the literature of the eighth century and later: a culture whose Christian faith found room for a keen interest in the pagan past, and was able to tolerate survivals that would elsewhere have been viewed with suspicion if not rejected out of hand.[4]

The Irish culture of the Dark Ages — ages that were dark everywhere in Western Europe except for Ireland — displayed an unusual thirst for learning. In addition to collecting the lore of their own rich pre-Christian heritage, the Irish monks amassed manuscripts from all over Europe, including texts that were elsewhere neglected or destroyed as heretical. In the words of a recent bestseller, this is "how the Irish saved civilization."

This omnivorous love of knowledge fertilized Irish Christianity in sometimes unusual ways. John Carey analyzes a ninth-century Irish treatise, *In Tenga Bithnua* (The Ever-New Tongue), in which the apostle Philip describes "twelve plains beneath the edges of the world" that the sun illumines every night in its journey under the earth. Remarkably, the closest parallels to this passage are found in Egyptian funerary texts from the New Kingdom (1570–1070 B.C.), which give similar descriptions of the twelve chambers the sun visits in its nightly journey. Carey suggests that this motif may have come to Ireland through the intermediary of a now-lost *Apocalypse of Philip*, written in Egypt and read in Gnostic circles. (Philip was, along with Thomas, the apostle most often associated with Gnosticism.) The text would have been brought to Ireland by way of Spain in the seventh century.[5]

None of this, of course, implies that Irish Christianity was ultimately Gnostic, or even particularly heterodox. In fact, as Ian Bradley points out in *Celtic Christianity*, the "romantic view of Celtic Christianity as a gentle, anarchic, deeply spiritual movement crushed by the authoritarian weight of Roman bureaucracy and imperialism" is undoubtedly exaggerated.[6] Bradley goes on to note that the importance of the Synod of Whitby, at which this crushing supposedly took place, is also overblown. The synod was convened to regularize liturgical practice in the British church, especially the method for calculating the date of Easter, which the Celtic churches had been doing differently from Rome. Carey offers a similar opinion: at Whitby, "what was at stake was not a matter of doctrine so much as a conflict between local tradition on the one hand and a push for uniformity of practice on the other." Some thirty years earlier, a convention of Irish bishops had already voted to use the Roman method of dating.[7]

There is something in the Celtic world that seems to evoke the wistful side of human nature. As early as the seventh and eighth centuries, Irish monks were pining for the Golden Age of the saints who had brought the faith to their shores. In later centuries, this half-hidden Celtic heritage would be invoked again and again by people who wished for a return to a simpler, purer, more mystical faith, for a greater sense of the wonder of God's creation and a more vivid experience of the other dimensions that lie beyond our mundane realm. That the world that embodied these ideals existed partly in the past, partly in the imagination should not blind us to their sublimity.

The Orthodox Science of Consciousness

The leitmotif of Egypt continues to recur throughout this narrative, some-times as the dominant note, sometimes as a faint echo. This is not because of any special pleading on my part. It is simply because so many mystical cur-rents in Christianity can be traced back to this memorious country.

Of these, by far the greatest is the hesychast tradition in Eastern Orthodoxy. The word *hesychast* derives from the Greek *hesychia,* or "stillness," referring to the state of inner silence that was the goal of this practice. Hesychasm, which is still practiced today, is one of the few forms of esoteric Christianity that can rival the great systems of Hinduism and Buddhism in subtlety and depth.

Hesychasm has its roots in the spiritual practice of the Desert Fathers, a col-lection of seekers and hermits who began to repair to the wilderness of Egypt in the third century. The founder of the movement is reputed to have been a holy man named Antony, who was born about the middle of the third century and withdrew from the world around 270. His devotion and asceticism soon became a matter of legend. He was also the founder of semieremetic monasti-cism, in which the monks dwelled separately in huts and were generally left to their own devices, meeting only for common worship. (Cenobitic monasti-cism, in which monks live and pray in communities, dates from slightly later.)

Antony's ascetic practices attracted the attention of the Evil One. Accord-ing to the *Life of St. Antony* by the Church Father Athanasius, the devil first sought to derail him from his spiritual practice by various blandishments. One night "the devil, unhappy wight, even took upon him the shape of a woman and imitated all her acts simply to beguile Antony." Antony resisted, so the devil made another assault: "Coming one night with a multitude of demons, he so cut him with stripes that he lay on the ground speechless from the excessive pain. For he affirmed that the torture had been so excessive that no blows inflicted by man could ever have caused him such torment."[8] In the end, of course, Antony is victorious, and his legend proved to be extremely fertile ground for artistic inspiration. Countless paintings and prints have de-picted his sufferings at the hands of infernal spirits, and it even furnished the theme for Gustave Flaubert's novel *The Temptation of St. Anthony.*

Athanasius's account, though written soon after Antony's death around 356–57 (Antony apparently lived to age 105), partakes enough of hagiography to raise doubts about its truth. But whether or not Antony really had to suffer the demonic assaults so luridly described by Athanasius, his story came to symbolize a major theme of the hesychastic tradition — the liberation of human consciousness from its own desires and terrors.

This tradition began to coalesce in Egypt and Palestine in Antony's time and thereafter, when monks such as Evagrius the Solitary began to set down teachings of practical mysticism. In the fifth century, John Cassian, a disciple of Evagrius, brought some of these teachings to the West. Here they would inspire the formation of the great monasteries that served as the bedrock of medieval civilization.

When Egypt and Palestine fell to the Arabs in the seventh century, the center of Orthodox spirituality shifted to the Byzantine Empire, then consisting chiefly of Greece and present-day Turkey. By the ninth century, monks were settling on Mount Athos, a rocky offshoot of the Chalcidice (Halhidiki) Peninsula in northern Greece. In 1060, the Byzantine emperor issued an edict prohibiting women from the Holy Mountain, as it came to be called. Even female animals were forbidden (except for cats, which were useful for controlling the rat population). To this day Athos, an all-male enclave of monks (now numbering around 1,400) remains the center of Orthodox monastic life.

In the eighteenth century, a monk named Nicodimos of the Holy Mountain, along with another monk named Makarios, compiled an extensive anthology of hesychast spirituality called the *Philokalia* (the name means "love of the good" or "love of the beautiful" in Greek). It includes texts dating from the fourth to the fifteenth centuries. Its five volumes (in modern editions) provide a succinct but comprehensive summary of the hesychastic way.

The spirituality of the *Philokalia* focuses on the liberation of something called the *nous* from passions and distractions. The exact nature of this *nous* has often been obscured by the words chosen to translate the term. The standard — indeed only — English version of the *Philokalia* renders it as "intellect." But the *nous* has very little to do with the intellect in the modern sense. The translators admit as much. Their glossary defines the term as "the highest faculty in man, through which — provided it is purified — he knows God. . . . The intellect . . . understands divine truth by means of immediate experience, intuition or 'simple cognition.'"[9] But this isn't terribly helpful either. If the intellect "understands divine truth by means of immediate experience," why does it need to be purified?

In fact the spirituality of the *Philokalia* is much easier to understand if we translate the Greek *nous* as "consciousness" — a use that is perfectly congruent with the meaning of this word in other Greek authors, including Plato and his school. This translation enables us to see the hesychastic path much more clearly. The *nous* is the consciousness that dwells "in the depths of the soul"; it is the "eye of the heart."[10] (People in those times experienced consciousness as residing in the heart rather than in the head.) It can be identified with what I have called the Self or the "true I." In its unpurified — that is, its ordinary — state, this consciousness is pulled and torn by any number of conflicting desires, thoughts, and emotions. The task of the spiritual aspirant is to liberate the *nous* from these "passions" so that it can rest in *hesychia,* or serenity. At that point it can experience the "Uncreated Light" that is of the essence of God himself. As Evagrius the Solitary writes, "He who loves God is always communing with Him as his Father, repulsing every impassioned thought."[11]

The authors of the *Philokalia* emphasize that this path is not an easy one. The "enemy" — the devil — is constantly lying in wait to ensnare the monk. The latter must maintain a constant inner watchfulness against the wiles of the enemy and his demonic minions. This watchfulness cannot be allowed to slip for even a short time, for a respite from the assault simply means that the enemy has temporarily withdrawn in order to regroup his forces.

The *Philokalia* mitigates this dismal outlook by reminding aspirants of the delights of spiritual knowledge, but at first one cannot entirely trust even in joy. "Initiatory joy is one thing, the joy of perfection another. The first is not exempt from fantasy, while the second has the strength of humility. Between the two joys comes a 'godly sorrow' (1 Cor. 7:10) and active tears."[12]

For all its austerity, the *Philokalia* displays a profound understanding of human psychology. In its ordinary state, the mind, constantly pulled in many directions by all sorts of desires and grievances, knows no peace. It can never come to peace merely by satisfying its urges, because this is never going to be entirely feasible; and even if one urge is satisfied, another will soon come to take its place. Peace of mind comes from detaching oneself from these passions and unifying the consciousness by centering it on God. This is the "unceasing prayer" of which the hesychasts speak.

One striking aspect of hesychast psychology is that it constantly portrays as *external* what we usually regard as *internal*. Thoughts, feelings, and desires are impulses sent by the devil. Even those that are self-created (the technical term for such creations is *logismoi,* "thoughts") often have a quasi-autonomous life of their own. The story of the demonic attacks on Antony suggests that they can even have palpable physical effects.

In enumerating the sins of which the monk should beware, the authors of the *Philokalia* provide a compendious list of the weaknesses and vices of humankind. Above them all is the demon of sexual desire, which "begins to trouble man from the time of his youth," as John Cassian writes. "This harsh struggle has to be fought in both body and soul, and not simply in the soul, as is the case with other faults."[13]

It stands to reason that if one is holding out a life of perfect chastity — in thought as well as in deed — as an ideal for oneself, such a goal would be resisted by a large and powerful part of one's own nature. But why should sexuality be so bad? As we have seen, this is a view that was as predominant in heterodox as in orthodox Christianity. Why does the tradition in all its forms so often regard even sexuality in marriage as a regrettable concession to human weakness?

This question is rarely addressed in any kind of serious way, even today. Critics of the Christian attitude customarily dismiss it merely as a case of compulsive guilt or hatred of the body. But this does not take us much closer to understanding.

The almost automatic hatred of sexuality present in Christianity and in certain other traditions (many forms of Hinduism and Buddhism, for example) may stem from a misunderstanding of the human sexual impulse. By this view, sex is meant for reproduction; any other use of it is aberrant and sinful. But this overlooks the fact that sexuality seems to have a broader role in human life than it does in many species.[14] Humans do not rut, they do not have mating seasons, women do not go into heat. Such biological strategies would suffice if sex were merely necessary for reproduction. But humans seem to live naturally, or at any rate ordinarily, in a state of low-grade sexual arousal and find it necessary to channel this energy into any number of interests, both sexual and nonsexual. While even those who aren't monks may often find this inconvenient, it seems to be deeply built into our natures. If one is unaware of this fact — or regards it as a consequence of fallenness and sin — one could easily regard sexuality as a snare laid in one's path by the devil.

While it's apparently possible to cut off one's sexual urges, the testimony of monks from all sects and eras indicates that this is a long, difficult, and unpleasant process. Even if it does end in the unutterable experience of the Uncreated Light, it may not be feasible for most people. And this is a key fact to remember about hesychasm. Above all, it is a way for monks. The directions in these texts — which are specific, detailed, and insightful — are meant not for people living in the maelstrom of ordinary life but for recluses sequestered in the deserts of Egypt or on the Holy Mountain. Quite possibly many masters of hesychasm would have said these practices are not even to be attempted while one is immersed in this world.

The reader may wonder why such a long discussion of hesychasm should appear in a work about the Gnostic heritage. Certainly the authors of the *Philokalia* — who were all strictly Orthodox — would have repudiated the slightest suggestion that their work smacked of Gnosticism. Nevertheless, some of the most prominent aspects of this tradition bear a strong resemblance to Gnostic thought and practice. In the first place, there is the emphasis on gnosis — here described as a turning of the *nous* toward the Uncreated Light — as the central focus of the spiritual path. In the second place, the hesychast mystics sometimes seem to resemble the Gnostics in their disgust with the world. While the hesychasts follow Orthodox teaching in denying that the body and the physical world are the handiwork of a degenerate god, in practice their attitude often comes very close. The devil is, after all, the "god of this world."

Did the Gnostics — who, as we have seen, were centered in Egypt — directly influence the Desert Fathers and their spiritual heirs? That would be extremely difficult to prove. Any evidence in favor of this view would have been destroyed long ago. Or is this curious similarity simply another instance of the maxim that we become what we oppose? Possibly. I myself lean toward a third option: that the Gnostics and the hesychasts both embodied a certain attitude toward reality. If one has a strong enough sense of a world beyond, a world that is finer and purer than our own, the world before our eyes will seem like a distraction or a trap. This insight may even point to the inner meaning of Christ's utterance: "The kingdom of heaven is like unto treasure hid in a field: the which when a man hath found, he hideth, and for joy thereof goeth and selleth all that he hath, and buyeth that field" (Matt. 13:44).

The Hesychast Controversy

Although they were never branded as heretics, at one point the hesychasts had to defend themselves in the court of ecclesiastical opinion. This occurred in the early fourteenth century, when Western theology made its way to Eastern Orthodoxy in the person of one Barlaam of Calabria. Although he was both Greek and Orthodox, Barlaam had studied in the West and had been influenced by Scholastic philosophy, which was beginning to dominate Catholic thought. In the 1330s, Barlaam was appointed to a post at the University of Constantinople. Apparently motivated by a mixture of careerism and an appetite for polemic, he decided to make a name for himself by pointing out the theological errors of the hesychasts. The chief of these, in Barlaam's view, had to do with the substance known as the Uncreated Light.

The Uncreated Light, also called the "Light of Tabor," holds a crucial place in Orthodox theology. It is considered to be an "energy" of God — that is to say, something that proceeds directly from his essence. It is an emanation of God rather than a creation; hence its name. By experiencing the Uncreated Light, the hesychasts seemed to be claiming to experience God himself.

This hit a sore spot, not only with the fastidious Barlaam, but with much of the Christian tradition. More, perhaps, than any other great world religion, Christianity has always insisted on the radical gulf that separates Creator from creature. A Hindu mystic, experiencing the ultimate ground of being, might be moved to exclaim, "I am that," but no Christian — in any event, no orthodox Christian — could permit herself to do this. The hesychasts were not making any such claim. But even their insistence that they were experiencing the Uncreated Light was too much for Barlaam.

Barlaam's training in the Scholasticism of the Western universities had taught him that God was not only radically different from the human creature but radically unknowable. Reason was the only means of knowledge, and reason could not give a mere human access to the divine dimensions. The only legitimate alternative was to learn about God indirectly, through rational investigation of his creation. For the hesychasts to claim experience of God through the Uncreated Light was, for Barlaam, a dangerous error.

To defend themselves against these charges, the Athonite monks chose the theologically ablest man among them: Gregory Palamas. Gregory wrote two works refuting Barlaam: the *Hagiorite Tome*, which was later incorporated into the *Philokalia*,[15] and *The Triads in Defense of the Holy Hesychasts*. Both are honored as central texts of Orthodox mysticism.

The dispute quickly grew into a matter of general interest, as church and state in the Byzantine Empire were inextricably intertwined. Gregory and Barlaam met in public debate in 1341, from which Gregory emerged as the victor, chiefly by drawing a deft distinction between the *essence* of God and the *energies* of God: the mystic can experience the latter but not the former, maintaining the rigid divide between Creator and creature.

The defeated Barlaam eventually returned to Italy, where he converted to Catholicism; we catch a last glimpse of him serving as tutor in Greek to the poet Petrarch. This would not be the end of the struggle — Barlaam's position would be taken up by a Bulgarian named Akindynus — and Gregory would be excommunicated and cast into prison in 1343. Eventually, however, the hesychast position won out. In 1347, Gregory was released and the charges of heresy dropped. Since 1351 his ideas have been accepted as part of the theology of the Orthodox Church.[16]

One more aspect of this controversy is worth mentioning, as it touches upon a central theme of the Gnostic heritage. Gregory's *Triads* are a defense not only of hesychast theology but of hesychast practice. Hesychast monks rely upon a technique called the Prayer of the Heart, also known as the Jesus Prayer. This consists of repeating a single prayer over and over again in obedience to Paul's injunction to "pray without ceasing" (1 Thess. 5:17). The earliest version of this prayer, cited by John Cassian, is taken from Ps. 70:1: "O God, make speed to save me; O Lord, make haste to help me."[17] A later version, which is the best known, is "Lord Jesus Christ, have mercy on me, a sinner."

In essence the practitioner repeats this prayer unceasingly as a form of meditation until it begins to root itself in the beating of the heart; hence its name. The hesychasts also used certain techniques of rhythmic breathing to aid them in their efforts. Their opponents argued that all this amounted to "introducing divine grace into themselves through their nostrils."[18] Moreover, rooting the prayer in the heart violated the essence of the spiritual path, which was to free the *nous*, the consciousness, from the body. As Gregory writes, "These people say, in effect, that we are wrong when we wish to enclose our nous within our body. Instead, they say, we must cast it out of our body. They strongly criticise some of our people, and write against them, under the pretext that our people encourage beginners to look into themselves and to introduce their nous into themselves by means of breathing practices."[19]

As outlined in *The Triads*, hesychasm consists of freeing the *nous* from the passions and turning it toward God. Thus purified, it turns back toward to the body to become the master of the household that is the human being. As Gregory describes it:

> This is how we turn against this "*law of sin*." We expel it from the
> body, and instead we introduce supervision by the nous, and by this
> authority we bring each power of the psyche, and every member of
> the body which will respond to it, under the rule of the nous.

For the senses, we determine the object and the limits of their ac-
tions. This work of the law is called "*self-control*."

For the passionate part of the psyche, we achieve the best state of
being, which bears the name of "*love*."

We also improve the rational part, by eliminating all that prevents
the thoughts from turning towards God. That part of the law we
name "*watchfulness*."[20]

Gregory's arguments reveal a crucial difference from the Gnostic impulse,
which, as we have seen, emphasizes freeing the consciousness from the body.
Hesychasm does not mean freeing the *nous* from the body as such, "since the
body is not evil"; rather, it aims at freeing the *nous* from the passions. Thus
cleansed and redeemed, the *nous* is capable of governing the psyche and the
body and sanctifying them in turn. As Gregory argues, this harmonizes with
Orthodox teaching, which has always stressed that Christ himself proved the
essential holiness of the flesh through the Incarnation. The Gnostics, by contrast, denied the holiness of the flesh. They also tended to deny the Incarnation through doctrines like Docetism.

And yet the emotional force of much Orthodox and Catholic mystical
writing, which stresses the defilement of the flesh and the need to detach the
mind from the world, often seems closer to the Gnostics than to Gregory. It's
paradoxical to consider that a quasi-Gnostic point of view — a radical refusal
to associate the body with the spirit — was embraced by Barlaam, a defender
of the Scholastic philosophy who eventually converted to Catholicism, while
at the same time the Catholic Church was persecuting the Cathars in the West
for holding remarkably similar opinions. But then the history of religion
often reveals conflicting trends even in the same institution.

Meister Eckhart's Defense

Hesychasm was saved for Orthodoxy not only by the theological genius of
Gregory Palamas but by the subtlety and flexibility of Greek thought. By the fourteenth century, the Greek world had had a more or less unbroken philosophical
tradition going back some nineteen hundred years. Much of this tradition, both
pagan and Christian, was illumined by mystical insight. The Greek mind was thus
well equipped to repel the assaults of the cumbrous Scholasticism of the West.

Mystics in the West were not so lucky, as we can see from the case of a man
who was perhaps the greatest spiritual visionary of his time: Meister Eckhart.[21]

Eckhart was born around 1260 in Tambach, Germany; his father was the steward of a knight's castle in the Thuringian forest. Around the age of fifteen, he entered a Dominican monastery and began the lengthy course of study required to join the order. He studied in Paris and Cologne, probably in the 1280s. We next hear of him in 1294, when he is described as "Brother Eckhart, Prior of Erfurt, Vicar of Thuringia." His brief work *The Talks of Instruction* dates to this period.

Around the same time, the Dominicans sent him to Paris — then the center of Western learning — to debate with their archrivals, the Franciscans. He acquitted himself well enough that he was granted advanced degrees by the College of Paris, and he continued to rise in the Dominican Order. He occupied the Dominican chair for theology at Paris in 1302–03, and was asked back again in 1311–13 (a rare honor). By the time he was sixty, he had been appointed to the highly eminent post of professor at the college at Cologne. Most of his sermons, which contain the essence of his teaching, probably date from this period.

It was at this late point in his life that Eckhart was charged with heresy. His accusers were fellow Dominicans who went through his writings and drew up a list of the theological errors they contained. Eckhart was sincerely indignant at these charges — "I may err but I may not be a heretic — for the first has to do with the mind and the second with the will!" he replied. He insisted that he had made no errors but that if he had, he would recant them. He appealed his case to the pope, as was his right, and traveled to Avignon (then the seat of the papacy) to defend himself.

The Inquisition took several years to proceed with the inquiry. In February 1327, Eckhart was notified that his appeal to Avignon had been denied. This is the last we hear of him alive. In a bull of 1329 condemning Eckhart's teaching, Pope John XXII speaks of him as dead. This was perhaps fortunate, because Eckhart would have been grieved to hear that he had been deceived "by the father of lies who often appears as an angel of light" into "sowing thorns and thistles among the faithful and even among the simple folk," as the bull put it.

Why did the church condemn Eckhart? Returning from his Paris debate, he said, "When I preached at Paris, I said — and I regard it well said — that with all their science, those people at Paris are not able to discern what God is in the least of creatures — not even in a fly!"[22] The statement is telling. In the first place, its tone reveals Eckhart's character — blunt, plainspoken, but with an immeasurable amount of spiritual depth. In the second place, his remark that the learned doctors of Paris could not have said what God was even in a fly strikes at the heart of the controversy he provoked. In a way it was not that different from the dispute that divided Barlaam and Gregory.

One aspect of Eckhart's theology that the churchmen found troubling was his tendency to speak of God as the being inherent in all living creatures (even, we may presume, a fly). At one point in his lengthy *Defense*, he has to explain the following statement: "My living is the being of God, or my life is the essence of God: whatever is God's is whatever is mine." Despite its profound mystical truth, such an utterance seemed to erase the line between creature and Creator that mainstream Christian theology has always taken such pains to maintain.

Similarly, Eckhart tended to blur the distinction between the Son of God in the sense of the unique Second Person of the Trinity and the Son of God that each of us, in our essence, truly is.

> The Father . . . begets me as his Son and the same Son. All that
> God does is one; therefore he begets me as his Son without distinc-
> tion. . . . For this reason, the heavenly Father is truly my Father, be-
> cause I am his Son and from him I have all that I have, and because
> I am the same Son and not another, because the Father does only
> one thing, therefore he makes me his one Son without distinction.
> We are transformed and changed into him even as in the sacrament
> the bread is changed into the body of Christ; and however many
> loaves there may be, yet they become one body of Christ.[23]

Here Eckhart is stating some of the central themes of esoteric Christianity. The Father is the transcendent aspect of the divine; the Son is the immanent aspect. This divine core, the true "I," exists in all of us equally. It is what unites us, for, as paradoxical as it may sound, this "I" is the same in all of us. To be "transformed and changed into the body of Christ" is to become aware — cognitively and experientially — of this profound unity with all the other Sons of God and with the Father.

Practically every esoteric Christian has said something like this in one way or another. And yet it was too much for the church in Eckhart's time, as it is often too much for the churches in our time. To say, as Eckhart does, "The Fa-ther ceaselessly begets his Son and, what is more, he begets me as his Son — the self-same Son!"[24] seems to erase the distinction between God and man. It threatens to make gods out of human beings — quite apart from the fact that

Christ himself said, "Ye are gods" (John 10:34). The irony is that much more acute in that Christ made this statement (quoting Ps. 82:6) to refute his Jewish opponents, who chided him for claiming to be a Son of God. Over 1,300 years later, Eckhart crossed the Pharisees of the Middle Ages by expressing the same insight. As both Christ and Eckhart learned, it can be dangerous for a man to realize he is one with God; it makes the authorities jealous. Mystics have generally dealt with this problem by adhering to codes of strict silence.

Eckhart's *Defense* is also revealing in its language. The terminology he uses — "essence," "predication," "equivocals," "univocals" — comes from the Aristotelian philosophy that had recently been adapted for Catholicism by Thomas Aquinas. In fact Eckhart also produced a number of Scholastic writings in Latin, which are less well known than his German sermons and treatises. Often the combination of Aristotelian logic and mystical illumination produces brilliant insights. And yet the Aristotelian terms and categories in Eckhart strike a strangely dissonant note. It is not that he does not understand them — his Dominican training gave him a great facility for such thought; Aquinas, too, was a Dominican — but rather they do not always lend themselves well to expressing mystical insight. The categories of Aristotle, with their relentless segregation of all things into genus and species, rarely do justice to a realm where contradictions are either resolved or transcended.

That the Catholic Church would come to rely on Aristotle and Aquinas to define its worldview has sometimes been lamented as a tragedy. So it may be. It is hard for us to say so, because, even today, some eight hundred years later, we are the products of this worldview. Even though Scholasticism has been increasingly discarded by the Catholic Church itself and is now regarded as a quaint antiquity in philosophical history, it has shaped our minds to an extraordinary degree. The Western capacity for creating extremely precise categories and superfine distinctions is a legacy of Aristotle. So is our interest in empirical inquiry and solid facts. To ask whether we would be better off without these things is like asking whether we would be better off if our parents had never met. We would not be here without them.

And yet Eckhart's fate suggests that Western civilization paid a high price for the brilliant mechanism of Aristotelian thought. Since that time, mainstream Western philosophy and theology have hardly known what to do with mystical insight — or indeed with any state of consciousness apart from the totally ordinary. Usually they have found it easier to act as if such things did not exist. And this has brought terrible suffering upon us who are the heirs of

European civilization. Our mastery of the physical world has not cured us of the wish for another one; our deft handling of materiality has not taken away our longing for the spirit. But we have been told too often that it is unrealistic to seek such things, so, persuading ourselves that they are childish fantasies, we displace our longings onto material objects. Such things cannot satisfy us, and we know they cannot satisfy us. But at this point they are the only things that we as a civilization can manage to believe are real.

CHAPTER 6

The Sages of
the Renaissance

If I were to turn the history of the Gnostic legacy into a drama, I would put it into two acts. The first would deal with the rise and fall of the great dualist heresy. The second would begin with the entrance of the Kabbalah into the general Western heritage.

The Kabbalah has already appeared in this narrative as part of the spiritual ferment in Languedoc in the days of the Cathars. As we saw, this was the period in which Jewish esoteric doctrine became known as the Kabbalah (which is Hebrew for "tradition"). But the Kabbalah's origins go back much further. Jewish legend traces them back to the expulsion of Adam from Eden, when the archangel Raziel gave him a book of teachings that would enable him to return. (As a matter of fact, an actual *Book of Raziel* does exist, though it's a collection of spells and incantations dating from medieval times.)[1] Adam passed this mysterious work on to his son Seth, who handed it down to Noah, who taught it in turn to his son Shem. Abraham learned it from Melchizedek, the mysterious "king of Salem" who was "priest of the most high God" (Gen. 14:18) and whom esoteric lore sometimes identifies with Shem. Abraham taught it to Isaac, who taught it to Jacob, who taught it to Levi. The wisdom continued in the tribe of Levi until Moses, a Levite, passed it on to Joshua.

In yet another version, the tradition began with Enoch, the first fully enlightened human being, who "walked with God" (Gen. 5:22) and was transformed into the angel Metatron, who directs the spiritual evolution of humanity. Metatron appeared to Abraham in the guise of Melchizedek and initiated him into the secret doctrine.[2]

Scholarly accounts trace the Kabbalah's origins in part to Gnostic and Neoplatonic influences on Judaism in the first centuries of the Common Era.

Gershom Scholem, the greatest modern scholar of the Kabbalah, noted that "it was Gnosticism, one of the last great manifestations of mythology in religious thought . . . which lent figures of speech to the Jewish mystic."³ The earliest known versions of the Kabbalah — in the first and second centuries A.D. — are connected with a movement known as *merkavah* mysticism. *Merkavah* is Hebrew for "chariot," and devotees of this tradition attempted to replicate the experience described in the first chapter of Ezekiel, where the prophet sets out an intricate vision involving four "living creatures" along with a kind of wheeled vehicle. "When the living creatures were lifted up from the earth, the wheels were lifted up" (Ezek. 1:19). While the exact nature of the *merkavah* mystics' practice is not clear, it probably involved a kind of visualization preceded by intense austerities and devotions.

Ezekiel's original vision came during the Babylonian Exile in the sixth century B.C., when the prophet "was among the captives by the river of Chebar" (Ezek. 1:1). This suggests that the vision of the chariot, and the mysticism that underlay it, may originally have had a Babylonian origin. Certainly during and after the Exile, the Jews were exposed to wide streams of esoteric thought from Babylon, Persia, and Greece, and this shaped much of their religious thought and literature, including the later books of the Bible. Some six hundred years later, Jewish currents would make their way back into the general pool of esoteric thought in the Mediterranean, helping to shape the schools of the Gnostics as well as those of proto–Catholic Christianity. These latter would in turn influence the subsequent Jewish mystics: cultural currents rarely, if ever, flow in one direction alone.

A view like this is the only one that really does justice to the complex interrelations among Judaism, Christianity, Greek philosophy, and Persian, Babylonian, and Egyptian religion during the early centuries after Christ. But all this happened hundreds of years before the emergence of the Kabbalah proper in the Middle Ages. In the intervening years, esoteric ideas were kept alive in small and secretive schools of Jewish adepts in settings as far apart as Babylonia and Germany. It was only in the twelfth century that the Kabbalah made its entrance onto a limited public stage with the appearance of a work called the *Sefer ha-Bahir*, or "Book of Illumination." Although it was probably written in Germany or the East, this extremely cryptic book made its appearance in Provence in the late twelfth century. (Because this was exactly the time and place when Catharism was at its height, scholars have tried to connect the Kabbalah with the teachings of the *bonshommes*, but for the most part in vain.)[4] In the twelfth and thirteenth centuries, the *Bahir* was followed by other texts, including the compendious *Zohar*, or "Splendor," which mostly consists of a long and discursive mystical commentary on the Pentateuch.

It would take us too far afield here to trace the history of the emergence of the Kabbalah, but it's worth noting the motives that lay behind it. In the eleventh and twelfth centuries, the Jewish world had been captivated by increasingly rationalistic views of its religion, inspired by the influence of Aristotle, whose works were read in Arabic. It was partly to counter this rationalism that the caretakers of the Jewish mystical heritage decided to give their ideas a wider airing.[5]

Pico's Condemned *Conclusions*

Kabbalah entered Christianity for very similar reasons. By the late fifteenth century, Aristotelian philosophy in the form of Scholasticism had established itself as the official teaching of the Catholic Church. Scholasticism involved an increasingly dry and pedantic approach, often deteriorating into mere hairsplitting. The old saw about theologians disputing about how many angels can fit on the head of a pin is attributed to this era. As we saw in the previous chapter, such a worldview did not fit well with mystical experience.

By the middle of the fifteenth century, the men of the nascent Renaissance were hungering for a fresher approach, intellectually as well as spiritually. Their appetites for knowledge were stimulated by the fall of Constantinople to the Turks in 1453, which caused many Greek scholars to flee westward to Italy, bringing with them their texts and (what was just as important) their ability to read them. The rediscovery of the Greek classics in the West dates to this period. It was speeded further by the invention of printing.

It was in this era that Marsilio Ficino translated the *Corpus Hermeticum* into Latin, creating a thirst for the *prisca theologia* — the "ancient theology" — of the sages of antiquity. Ficino found other evidence of this "ancient theology" in Plato and Pythagoras as well as in the Hermetic texts. As I mentioned in chapter 2, he saw the thread of this universal esoteric doctrine — the *aurea catena*, or "Golden Chain" — running through these philosophers and linking pagan wisdom with that of the Hebrews and Christians.

If Ficino set the stage, it was his pupil Giovanni Pico della Mirandola (1463–94), a nobleman from a small domain near Modena, who gave the Kabbalah its public debut in Christendom. Like many men of his era, Pico was omnivorous in his learning and avid in his love of life. In May 1486, at the age of twenty-three, he ran off with the wife of a gentleman from Arezzo, carrying her off on horseback. After the lady's husband fetched her back with the help of a company of riders, Pico spent his summer in more ethereal pursuits, immersing himself in Kabbalah.

Pico did not know much Hebrew at the time, and it is doubtful whether he ever learned enough to make his way through the recondite texts of the Kabbalah. For the most part he had to rely on the translations of a Jewish convert to Christianity named Samuel ben Nissim Abulfaraj, also known as Flavius Mithridates.[6]

Mithridates was a curious figure in a tradition that has produced many curious figures. Five years before, he had preached a sermon in the Vatican in which he had contended that secret Jewish evidence from a pre-Christian version of the Talmud proved the mysteries of Christ's Passion. Vain and self-aggrandizing, Mithridates nonetheless held to a high standard of intellectual honesty, steering his pupil away from spurious Kabbalistic texts written by other Jewish converts.

After a summer that must have included a breakneck pace of work for Mithridates (he translated an estimated three thousand folio pages during that time), Pico emerged in November 1486 with a groundbreaking collection of "900 conclusions, dialectic, moral, physical, mathematical, metaphysical, theological, magical, and Kabbalistic, elucidated partly according to his opinion and in the spirit of the wise men of the Chaldaeans, Arabs, Hebrews, Greeks, Egyptians, and Latins." These "conclusions," Pico goes on to say, are written in a style that "imitates, not the splendor of the Roman tongue, but the manner of speaking of the most renowned disputants of Paris" — that is, the Aristotelian jargon of the Scholastics.[7]

It's revealing to compare Pico's *Conclusions* with the *Defense* of Meister Eckhart. Where the latter uses the Scholastic language hesitantly and haltingly — knowing all too well how his ideas, stated in that form, will sound to his inquisitors — Pico's use of the same jargon is bold, enthusiastic, and audacious. It would be difficult to argue that this collection presents a coherent mystical or philosophical view. Pico himself says they are theses for discussion, and at the outset he offers to "dispute them publicly" with any comers.

Of all of the *Conclusions*, none, perhaps, is more fascinating than the 780th: "Nulla scientia, quae nos magis certificet de divinitate Christi, quam Magia et

Cabala," "There is no knowledge that convinces us more of the divinity of Christ than magic and the Kabbalah."[8] This was a bold move, not only because it cut against the Aristotelianism and Thomism that had already become dominant in the Catholic Church, but because it brought to the forefront an esoteric tradition that up to then had been little known outside the Jewish world.

Although Pico invited any and all scholars to come and debate these ideas with him, a papal commission found thirteen of his theses heretical, and Pope Innocent VIII forbade any such gathering. Pico recanted the problematic conclusions, but so equivocally that the pope went on to condemn all nine hundred. Pico fled to France, where he was eventually arrested. Through the intercession of King Charles VIII of France, he was given a papal dispensation and spent the rest of his short life in Florence, where he died at the age of thirty-one.

In his works, Pico introduced a theme that to this day continues to resonate among esotericists: the notion that "Moses on the mount received from God not only the Law, which he left to posterity written down in the first five books [of the Bible], but also a true and more occult explanation of the Law. It was, moreover, commanded him of God by all means to proclaim the Law to the people, but not to commit the interpretation of the Law to writing or to make it a matter of common knowledge."[9] This secret, oral Law was the Kabbalah.

Christianity, too, imparted a secret tradition hidden away from vulgar eyes, according to Pico: Jesus "preached to the masses in parables and separately to the few disciples to whom it was given plainly to understand the mysteries of the kingdom of heaven plainly without figures of speech."[10] Pico quotes Dionysius the Areopagite to the effect that "it was a prescribed and holy custom in the church not to communicate the most secret dogma in writing, but only by voice and to those who had been properly initiated."[11] We have seen similar teachings in the Gnostics, Clement, and Origen.

For his part, Pico did not believe that this secret knowledge was limited to the Jewish tradition or its heirs. Noting that "Moses was learned in all the wisdom of the Egyptians" (cf. Acts 7:22), Pico saw Egyptian wisdom as the fount and origin not only of the religion of the Hebrews but of the philosophy of the Greeks. "All the Greeks who have been considered superior — Pythagoras, Plato, Empedocles, Democritus — used the Egyptians as masters," he asserts.[12]

To say this esoteric doctrine was Egyptian in origin was a crucial step. By making Egypt the common spiritual ancestor of the Greeks and the Hebrews,

Pico and Ficino were claiming — contrary to the Jewish Kabbalists — that the esoteric doctrine did not belong to Israel alone but was the common heritage of humanity. And this is reasonable. If a doctrine of this kind is true, it must be universally true; and if it is universally true, it cannot be the possession of a single nation alone.

Much in the Kabbalah would have seemed familiar to an educated person of the time. One of the central doctrines of the Kabbalah is that of the ten *sefirot* — principles or emanations of God that span the enormous distance between the Absolute and the physical world.[13] The *sefirot* are sometimes shown as a series of ten concentric circles, making them look very much like the heavens as portrayed by Dante and his spiritual forebears.

The Kabbalah also speaks of four worlds — the divine, spiritual, psychological, and physical. Of these, the spiritual world, *Briah* in Hebrew, is what Pico calls the "intelligible" or "angelic" world. He equates it with the Platonic realm of Ideas.[14] The psychological world, whose Hebrew name is *Yetzirah*, or the world of "forms," Pico calls the "celestial." Like most Kabbalists, he equates it with the spheres of the planets.[15]

But there was also much in this Kabbalistic doctrine that would *not* have seemed familiar even to a well-read Christian intellectual. In 1527, over thirty years after Pico's death, one of his Kabbalistic teachers, named Dattilo, gave some lectures that were attended by a Christian orientalist named Johann Albert Widmanstadt. Here is Widmanstadt's account of one of Dattilo's theories:

> Certain living seeds lie hidden in the bowels of the earth and in the elements that surround it. In the course of this world's [that is, nature's] tireless efforts, and as result of the struggle of creation and decay, these living seeds travel through various [forms of] plants, bushes, fruit trees and living creatures, all the way to the human body, and through to the sentient soul. Indeed, after a heavenly soul has been poured into them, they are eventually admitted into eternal bliss, even though they are, by comparison to this [highest soul] inferior and subject to it, because they are of the earth.[16]

The horrified Widmanstadt goes on to denounce these "monstrous ideas," which "burst forth from the kabbalah of the Jews, to attack the Church of Christ."

Why this doctrine is so "monstrous" and why the Church of Christ should be so threatened by it is not entirely clear, but the doctrine itself should by this time have a familiar ring: Dattilo's teaching very much resembles the Manichaean concept of the sparks of light embedded in all things. Later in the sixteenth century, this same idea would form a central part of the thought of the renowned Kabbalist Isaac Luria (1534–72). Often it is portrayed as an original insight of Luria's, but this passage suggests that it goes back further in the Kabbalistic tradition. The idea that supposedly inanimate matter has a life and consciousness of its own is also a tenet of alchemy.[17]

Reuchlin and the Holy Names

One of Pico's most influential students was the German scholar Johannes Reuchlin (1455–1522), who met Pico in 1490 and was inspired by him to take up the study of Hebrew and Kabbalah. Although Pico's proficiency in Hebrew is open to question, there is no doubt about Reuchlin's. Adding this language to his command of Latin and Greek, he became what one colleague described as a *miraculum trilingue* — a "trilingual miracle" — and published a Hebrew grammar and dictionary in 1506. Unlike most Christian scholars of his day, he insisted that one could not properly understand the Old Testament without knowing Hebrew, and eventually became a defender of Jewish books and literature. Ironically, his chief opponent was a converted Jew named Johann Pfefferkorn, who launched a campaign to destroy all Hebrew books, including the Talmud. Reuchlin contended that these works had value in their own right and defended them against destruction.

One of the central points of Reuchlin's Christian Kabbalah — which he shared with Pico — had to do with the names of God, which has long been one of the chief preoccupations of the Kabbalists. The most important of these names is the Tetragrammaton, יהוה: YHWH, thought to have originally been pronounced "Yahweh."

Reuchlin believed that there were three principal names of God, each of which represented an age or dispensation of the human race. In this he harks back to the twelfth-century visionary Joachim of Flore, who divided human history into the pre-Christian Age of the Father, the Christian Age of the Son, and the coming Age of the Holy Spirit, which would be ruled by love (a sort of medieval antecedent of the New Age). In Reuchlin's scheme, the first was the era before the Mosaic Law, when God was known to the patriarchs as Shaddai, or שדי, often translated as the "Almighty" (cf. Exod. 6:3). The second was the Age of the Law, when God was known as YHWH, יהוה. The third was the

Christian period of grace and redemption, when God was known not through four letters but through five. Following Pico, Reuchlin placed the letter *shin*, or ש — which, he said, signified the Logos — in the middle of the Tetragrammaton and came up with the name יהשוה, YHSWH, *Yehoshua* or "Jesus."[18]

Unfortunately this was not how Jesus would have spelled his name in Hebrew. The actual spelling of *Yehoshua* is יהושע — the last letter is different from Reuchlin's version. For this reason if for no other, Reuchlin's mystical "completion" of the Tetragrammaton was unlikely to convince Jews. On the other hand, as Moshe Idel, a modern scholar of Kabbalah, points out, "Secret names are part and parcel of the Kabbalistic lore; from this point of view the Christian Kabbalists did not invent anything in principle. In the Jewish Kabbalah we can find formations of 'divine' names . . . which are as bizarre as the form YHSVH."[19]

What lay behind this preoccupation with the divine names? Jewish tradition tends to regard the word and the thing as inextricably linked: the Hebrew noun *davar* means both "word" and "thing." The sixteenth-century Kabbalist Moses Cordovero writes, "These names are the sefirot. It is not that these names are ascribed to the sefirot, God forbid. On the contrary, the [divine] names [themselves] are the sefirot."[20] If this is so, penetrating the structure of the divine names would enable the Kabbalist to enter the supernal garden of the divine realm and to glimpse the nature of God himself.

Kabbalistic practice with the divine names can take any number of forms. Some are meditative. In one method, the practitioner intones the letters of the Tetragrammaton with each of the Hebrew vowels in turn: each combination corresponds to one of the *sefirot*.[21] Other approaches involve intellectual speculation on the structure of the divine names such as Reuchlin attempted. Each Hebrew letter has its own mystical meaning. For Reuchlin, the letter ש (*shin*, denoting the sound *sh*) represented the Logos, but more commonly, Kabbalists link it with the element of fire, partly because of sound — the Hebrew word for fire is *esh* — partly because the letter's shape suggests flames.

Despite their evocative power, such practices can be used to prove almost anything. In any case, proof in any logical or factual sense is beside the point. In a way, the Kabbalah is the opposite of some forms of Zen, which use logical paradox (through mystical riddles or koans) to induce a kind of mental shock that may lead to enlightenment. By contrast, the Kabbalah works by constantly expanding the mind's network of associations so that everything becomes interconnected. Kabbalistic texts such as the *Zohar* are often couched in a kind of metalanguage that is not Hebrew or Aramaic as such, but an idiom made up of quotes and allusions to the Bible, Midrash, and Talmud. It's as if we are dealing with a language whose units of speech are not nouns or verbs, but tags and lines of scripture. Contemplating the letters of the divine names forms part of this process of constantly expanding the network of associations, but it is a portal to higher awareness, not a proof in any conventional sense.

Viewed in a broader light, two things seem to have beeen going on with Pico, Reuchlin, and the Christian Kabbalists who succeeded them. On the one hand, they were genuinely excited to find — or imagine they had found — Kabbalistic evidence for the truth of Christianity. And yet it's hard to believe that some of the finest minds of the Renaissance were burning with passion for what in the end was little more than a new missionary marketing technique. Something else must have been at work.

Joseph Dan, a modern scholar of Kabbalah, points toward this other dimension. He says of the Christian Kabbalah: "The message of this school of thought is not only that the Jews should change, but that Christianity itself has to be revitalized by a renewed understanding of its ancient origins that has become possible by the revelation of new sources."[22] But these sources and origins do not merely go back in time; they are also based in the hidden realities to which the Kabbalah points. The Christian Kabbalists were attempting to root the external truths of their religion in the esoteric doctrine that had become obscured by Scholasticism and heresy-hunting.

The Practical Kabbalah

The modern reader who sees the phrase "the practical Kabbalah" is apt to burst out laughing. What, after all, could be less practical than this arcane and confusing collection of mystical speculations?

Nevertheless, the practical Kabbalah, as it came to be called, forms an important part of the Western esoteric tradition. The principle behind it is reasonably easy to explain. The Kabbalah teaches that the four worlds interpenetrate in intricate ways, and they are connected by an elaborate network of correspondences. For example, the Kabbalistic *sefirah* known as Gevurah ("strength," also translated as "severity") corresponds on the Yetziratic level with Mars, the planet traditionally associated with war. On the physical level it is connected with iron, the strongest of the familiar metal elements. The name of God associated with Gevurah varies in different Kabbalistic systems: sometimes it is *Yah*, sometimes *Elohim*, sometimes *Elohim Gebor,* or "strong God." There are also perfumes, angel hierarchies, and geometric symbols associated with each *sefirah.*

By this premise, certain operations in the physical world could bring about shifts in the higher worlds. These in turn cause further alterations in the physical world — hence the term "practical Kabbalah." If, say, you are going to war, you might want to have a symbol associated with the *sefirah* Gevurah, or Mars, drawn on parchment, perhaps, or inscribed on a medallion. One magical text from the early modern era, the *Clavicula Salomonis* (The Key of Solomon the King), shows a pentacle, or magical symbol, of Mars that "is of great virtue and power in war, wherefore without doubt it will give thee victory." It consists of a circle within a circle containing Hebrew letters and words; above the circle is the astrological symbol of Mars. As the editor of the text describes it, "In the Centre is the great Name Agla; right and left, the letters of the name IHVH; above and below, El. Round it is the versicle from Psalm cx.5: 'The Lord at thy right hand shall wound even Kings in the day of His Wrath.'"[23] *Agla*, another divine name, is an acronym for *Atah Gedul le-Olam* — roughly translated, "Thou art great for ever and ever."

Magic of this sort was a subject of intense interest to all the Christian Kabbalists I have discussed so far. Ficino espoused a kind of "natural magic" that made use of the correspondences among such things as metals, fragrances, and planets. Pico and Reuchlin took this a step further in stressing the power of the divine names, thus integrating Kabbalah and natural magic. They did not, however, create Kabbalistic magic in any sense of the term — in one form or another, it had been used for centuries, going back to antiquity — but it was they who brought it to the attention of educated Christian Europe.

In the next generation, the most influential figure in the practical Kabbalah was Henry Cornelius Agrippa of Nettesheim (1486–1535), usually known as Cornelius Agrippa, as he styled himself in his writings.[24] Born in Cologne to a family of the minor nobility, in his boyhood Agrippa was possessed by the desire to serve the Holy Roman Emperor Maximilian I. Since his own family were courtiers, this ambition proved to be within reach. Agrippa would later write that he served the emperor first as a secretary, then as a soldier.

Like many of the ablest men of his time, Agrippa's was a versatile and restless temper, and, like Pico, he was something of a prodigy. In 1508, he masterminded a scheme to capture the impregnable fort at Tarragon in Spain on behalf of Maximilian. The capture was astonishingly successful, but the scheme as a whole did not fare so well. The fort was in turn besieged by a peasant army, and Agrippa and his cohorts had to flee under cover of night. Both the capture and the escape were popularly credited to the influence of magic, which would cement the young man's reputation as an occultist.

Indeed gaining access to hidden knowledge was another early ambition that Agrippa was able to achieve. By the time he was twenty-three, he had gathered many of the notes for his *Occult Philosophy*, and by 1510 he had written a draft of the first three books, which he sent to the abbot and occultist Johannes Trithemius for review. The published version of the *Occult Philosophy* is dedicated to Trithemius, who seems to have served as a mentor to Agrippa.

For the last twenty-five years of his life, Agrippa pitched back and forth between adulation and disgrace. In 1515, he delivered a series of lectures (now lost) at the University of Pavia on the *Poimandres* of Hermes Trismegistus. They met with such acclaim that the university awarded him doctorates in divinity, law, and medicine. In 1518, he settled in the town of Metz, where he had been hired as a lawyer. But by the next year, his occult interests had attracted the criticism of several local priests, exacerbated by his bold defense of a woman accused of witchcraft. In 1520, he had to leave town. The following years show Agrippa in occupations as diverse as physician — treating plague victims other doctors had abandoned — and engineer: he drew up several designs for siege engines, hoping to win the favor of a monarch. He married three times. His first wife died; his second cheated on him (Rabelais in his *Gargantua* mocks Agrippa's blindness to her infidelity); and he divorced the third in 1535, soon before his own death. Given the turbulence of his life, it's understandable that he entitled one of his later works *The Uncertainty and Vanity of Sciences*.

Agrippa's masterwork is the *Three Books of Occult Philosophy*, which he published in 1531.[25] It is one of the most influential books even written on the Western magical tradition and on the practical Kabbalah: one recent edition subtitles it "The Foundation Book of Western Occultism." Its voluminous contents include chapters on the orders of evil spirits, on "perfumes and suffugations," on magical sigils, even a brief discussion of how to raise the dead. There are very few magical treatises in the West that are not in some way indebted to Agrippa.

The practical Kabbalah thus takes its name from the fact that it produces practical results. Many of these results have to do with the usual run of human concerns: getting love or money, healing disease, and so on. Since these concerns are so universal, it's not surprising that the practical Kabbalah would enter the tradition of folk magic in later centuries. Often Kabbalistic techniques have been handed down through several generations, none of whom had a clear idea of Hebrew, so the terms are frequently garbled.

One example appears in a work called *The Sixth and Seventh Books of Moses, or Moses' Magical Spirit-Art*, dating probably from the nineteenth century (my edition lists no date or publisher). It tells of the use of the "semiphoras," which is a mangled version of *shem ha-meforash*, the "divided Name," created by permuting the Hebrew letters in three verses of the Bible (Exod. 14:19–21). Unfortunately, the discussion on the "semiphoras" is not about the actual *shem ha-meforash*, but on the uses of the names of God connected with the *sefirot* (in other words, a completely different set of divine names).

The text goes on to discuss the occult uses of various psalms. For Psalm 19, it instructs, "During a protracted and dangerous confinement take earth from a crossroads, write upon it the five first verses of this Psalm, and lay it upon the abdomen of the parturient." It would be easy to sneer at this primitive folk magic, but in an age when good medical care was a costly luxury — and even then the doctors often did not know what they were doing — writing a few lines of sacred verse might have done much to ease the nerves of the "parturient" and her family.

The Fortunes of John Dee

Because of the ambiguous role of the magus in Western civilization — who is seen sometimes as a sage, often as a charlatan — these figures have risen and fallen in the esteem of history, much as they did in their own day.

John Dee, court astrologer to Queen Elizabeth I, the inspiration for the character Prospero in Shakespeare's *Tempest*, and the man who, according to legend, conjured up the storm that sank the Spanish Armada, furnishes a vivid example. Dee (1527–1608) saw extremes of good and bad fortune in his life.[26] At one point a close adviser to Elizabeth, he ended his years in poverty and disgrace. He espoused a version of the Christian Kabbalah that sought to reform the church; he also sketched out the ideal of a universal British monarchy that inspired the beginnings of the British Empire. And yet he became most famous for a strange series of spirit encounters involving a medium named Edward Kelly (or Kelley). The record of these conversations with beings of the other world was published in 1659 under the title *A True and Faith-*

ful Relation of What Passed for Many Years Between Dr. John Dee and Some Spirits by a debunker named Meric Casaubon, who sought to discredit Dee's reputation posthumously and largely succeeded. Dee was generally regarded as a plain fraud until the twentieth century, when scholars began to see him as a key figure in the intellectual world of the Elizabethan Age.

Dee's seminal influence is apparent in a 1577 work entitled *General and Rare Memorials Pertaining to the Perfect Art of Navigation*. Here he invokes the supposed Arthurian ancestry of the Tudor dynasty and its mythical rights to foreign domains to encourage Elizabeth to lay claim to vast territories overseas. An allegorical engraving in this book shows Elizabeth seated in pomp on a ship named *Europa*, indicating Dee's vision for an England that would take leadership of the continent instead of the Catholic Hapsburg dynasty that was then its dominant power. It would be too much to claim that Dee was the guiding genius of nascent British imperialism, but it would not be amiss to say he sounded a note that would resonate for centuries.

In 1583 Dee, accompanied by Kelly and their families, embarked on a six-year sojourn in Central Europe, visiting Krakow as well as Prague. At that time Prague was the capital of the Holy Roman Empire, ruled by Emperor Rudolf II, known both for his religious tolerance and for his interest in occult philosophy. Dee apparently tried to preach a reform of Christianity that would be guided by esoteric principles. One contemporary account says that Dee "predicted that a miraculous reformation would presently come about in the Christian world and would prove the ruin not only of the city of Constantinople but of Rome also."[27] In other words, Dee was predicting that Protestantism would triumph decisively over both Catholicism and Islam (whose head was at that time the Turkish sultan). Although Dee met with Rudolf, he did not manage to inspire him with any great enthusiasm for his vision.

Like his contemporary Nostradamus, Dee was in many ways a failure as a prophet.[28] Unlike Nostradamus, who was held in high regard by the French court until his death in 1566, Dee would find himself pushed into the background when he returned to England in 1589. The court's mood had changed during his absence. Some of Dee's protectors, such as Elizabeth's favorite, the Earl of Leicester, had died. Moreover, suspicion of sorcerers and witches had grown. The public — and some of those in power — were not always able to distinguish a learned magus from a low sorcerer who trafficked with evil spirits. Indeed Christopher Marlowe's highly popular 1593 tragedy *Doctor Faustus* explicitly connected the two, turning sorcery hunting into a popular craze. As a result, the last two decades of Dee's life were a time of disappointment and impoverishment, made worse by the accession to the throne of James I in 1603. James was obsessed with witchcraft and had even written a tract against witches entitled *Demonologie*. Dee could expect no favors from him and did not receive any. In 1608, the old magus died in great poverty.

The Apostasy of Giordano Bruno

It would be possible to sketch out the equally fascinating, and equally tempestuous, careers of other great Renaissance magi. Some, like Doctor Faustus, are partly or mostly legendary, but the majority stand clearly enough in the light of history. Practically all of them fell afoul of the powers that be in one way or another, much as Pico, Agrippa, and Dee did. The last one I discuss in this chapter met an even harsher fate, partly because in some ways he was not really a Christian at all.

Giordano Bruno (1548–1600) was, it was true, a Dominican monk, although he got into trouble with the order in 1576 (for the usual reasons having to do with heresy) and left.[29] Like many other Renaissance mages, he had an irascible temperament and found it easier to get into trouble than out of it. In the end, this would lead to his arrest at the hands of the Inquisition in 1592; after eight years of imprisonment and interrogation, he was burned at the stake in Rome in 1600.

Bruno's intellectual interests were many and varied. He was a master of the Renaissance art of memory, which involved an elaborate process of visualization and association. One might, for example, construct a "memory palace" in one's mind, with rooms and furnishings visualized in detail. To memorize a speech, one would associate each point with one of these furnishings and thus be able to recall them as one took a stroll through this palace in the mind. Knowledge of this art made it possible to perform prodigious feats of memory, though it has sometimes been observed that one would already have to have a phenomenal memory to master it.

Bruno also expounded some views that were unconventional for their time. He held not only to the then-controversial heliocentric theory of Copernicus but went further, asserting that the universe was infinite in scope. This was a radical step in the context of a worldview that saw the universe as nine or ten concentric spheres surrounding the earth. Many have believed that Bruno was burned for these scientific theories, which would make him a martyr for the cause of scientific progress.

But as the British scholar Frances Yates suggests in her book *Giordano Bruno and the Hermetic Tradition*, Bruno was not executed for his scientific theories; in fact, she says, Bruno was not really a scientist. Instead, like the other figures I have discussed in this chapter, he was a magus — but he had a far more tenuous allegiance to Christianity than they did. He told the Inquisition that the Catholic religion "pleased him more than any other," but, he added, there was a great deal wrong with it — a rather lukewarm endorsement before a tribunal with the power of having him burned at the stake.

For Bruno, both Judaism and Christianity were later and inferior versions of the Egyptian mystery religion that he sought to revive. He regarded the Jews with contempt, asserting, "No one could ever pretend with any degree of probability that the Egyptians borrowed any principle, good or bad, from the Hebrews." He went further and contended that the cross of Christ was a degenerate version of the Egyptian cross, known as the *ankh,* or *crux ansata.*

Bruno's Egyptian religion has little to do with the Egyptian religion exhumed by archaeologists in the last two centuries. Rather it is the doctrine of the *Corpus Hermeticum,* which in Bruno's time was still believed to date back to the great age of Egypt. That Bruno wanted to revive the Egyptian religion wholesale may have been eccentric, but it's quite understandable in the light of the history of the seventeenth century, with its appalling religious warfare. For Bruno, Egyptian Hermeticism was a means of rising above these petty conflicts, a means of fostering tolerance and awakening a higher awareness.

There is another, perhaps even more important, sense in which Bruno departed from Christianity. Almost from its inception, the Christian religion was obsessed with distinguishing good spirits from bad. "Brethren, believe not every spirit, but try the spirits whether they are of God," says the First Epistle of John (4:1). For centuries, Christian mystics have followed this advice. From the *Philokalia* to Teresa of Avila and later, there has been a rich and sophisticated literature attempting to show how to distinguish false from true inner voices so that one will not fall prey to demons.

Bruno had no use for any of this. In fact his magic involved consciously invoking demons, which in his system are as much a part of the cosmic ecosystem as the stars, planets, and elements. "Bruno wants to reach the demons," Yates tells us; "it is essential for his magic to do so; nor are there any Christian angels within call in his scheme to keep them in check. Bruno, of course, like all good magicians, regards his magic as good magic; only other people's magics are ever bad to the magician."

This suggests that Bruno was a precursor, not of hard-headed scientific positivists, but of figures like C.G. Jung, the British occultist Aleister Crowley, and more recently, the archetypal psychologist James Hillman. These twentieth-century visionaries, in their wildly different ways, emphasize that the inner voices, demons, and angels that are evoked through magic or imagination are really parts of one's own character. You may or may not like them, but you ignore them at your peril. This drive toward a radical self-knowledge even of the most loathsome and dissociated parts of one's character goes beyond conventional moral imperatives. "I would rather be whole than good," Jung once said.

Like many heretics, Bruno was ahead of his time. He had few direct followers, though both Galileo and the utopian visionary Tommasso Campanella were familiar with his work. More importantly, Bruno's Egyptian Hermeticism, which strove to rise above the sectarianism of Judaism and Christianity and restore the tolerance of pagan antiquity, may have eventually borne fruit in Freemasonry, as we shall see in the next chapter.

If anyone deserves the title of "Renaissance man," it is these figures: Ficino, Pico, Reuchlin, Agrippa, and Bruno, all possessed of a far-reaching intelligence that they could apply to any number of disciplines. And yet we rarely ask what made it possible to be a Renaissance man. Although a person of our time would be appalled by the bigotry and superstition of the early modern era, it must have seemed like an age of dizzying freedom compared to what had gone before. The advances in learning spurred by the invention of printing (among other developments) immeasurably widened the intellectual vistas of Western Europe. At the same time, the body of knowledge was still small enough that a single individual could master most major fields.

None of this, however, entirely explains the phenomenon. It would have been difficult to absorb all this knowledge without a comprehensive worldview that could integrate it into a coherent whole. And the worldview that served this purpose was the esoteric doctrine that men like Ficino, Pico, Reuchlin, and Agrippa brought into public awareness. In its harmony and coherence, the Renaissance worldview was similar to medieval thought, but it had a sense of possibilities that the Middle Ages had lacked. In its freedom and openness, it resembled our own time, but unlike our time, it was not confused and hamstrung by an excess of information. In a sense the Renaissance represented a superb balance between structure and possibility that comes along only rarely in the history of a civilization.

None of this is meant to foster nostalgia for the Renaissance or to argue that we should return to its worldview. It *is* to suggest that our age has something to learn from that one. The early twenty-first century, for all its grandiose talk of globalization and technological wonders, is not so different from the late Middle Ages. Materialism in all its forms — scientism, commercialism, the "reign of quantity" — has become vacuous and petrified. Mere technological progress no longer seems to provide meaning for our civilization, and more and more people are coming to doubt the value of progress in its own right. Moreover, if the Middle Ages showed how vicious religion could become when corrupted by almost absolute power, our own time shows how vicious it can be when it is cast out like an abused stepchild. It is far from clear where the next step is to be taken or where it will bring us. But it will undoubtedly require the kind of moral and intellectual courage that we see in the proud and valiant sages of the Renaissance.

CHAPTER 7

Rosicrucianism and the Great Lodges

"The history of the world," wrote the novelist Ishmael Reed, "is the history of warfare between secret societies."

A fascinating statement, although an unprovable one. If these societies are really secret, how can we know anything about them, much less the influence they have had over history?

And yet there are secret societies, and they occasionally make an appearance on the stage of world events. Among the most famous were the Rosicrucians, an elusive order of adepts that caused a brief but intense furor among the savants of Europe in the early seventeenth century.

That is, if the Rosicrucians ever really existed — a subject that remains a matter of debate. We know next to nothing substantial about them. Much of what we *do* know comes from two short treatises that began to circulate in manuscript form around 1610 and were published in 1614, in western Germany. They are entitled the *Fama Fraternitatis* (The Rumor of the Brotherhood) and the *Confessio Fraternitatis* (The Confession of the Brotherhood). They were anonymously published, and we don't know who wrote them.

Nevertheless, the two Rosicrucian manifestoes created a myth that has exercised an intense allure among spiritual seekers right up to the present. They tell the story of a man named Christian Rosenkreutz (literally "Rose Cross"), who was born in Germany in 1378. Although of noble birth, Rosenkreutz was poor and was early in life apprenticed to a man named "Brother P.A.L.," who was determined to visit the Holy Land.

Brother P.A.L. took the young Christian Rosenkreutz with him on his pilgrimage, but died en route in Cyprus, leaving his apprentice to go on without him. Christian Rosenkreutz arrived in Damascus at the age of sixteen, where he learned Arabic and translated an enigmatic text known only as "the Book M." into "good Latin." From Damascus he went to Egypt and then on to Fez, in Morocco, where he was initiated into the arts of magic and Kabbalah. As the *Fama* puts it, "Of these of Fez he often did confess that their Magia was not altogether pure, and also that their Cabala was defiled with their religion; but notwithstanding he knew how to make good use of the same, and found still more better grounds [*sic*] for his faith, altogether agreeable with the harmony of the world."[1]

After two years, C.R. (the Rosicrucian manifestoes often refer to him by his initials) left Fez for Spain, where he attempted to show the learned men something of his knowledge. "But it was to them a laughing matter; and being a new thing unto them, they feared that their great name should be lessened, if they should now again begin to learn and acknowledge their many years errors [*sic*]." Since "the same song was sung unto him by other nations," C.R. made his way back to his native Germany, where he assembled a collection of eight adepts, "all bachelors and of vowed virginity," and formed the Fraternity of the Rose Cross.

> Their agreement was this: First, That none of them should profess any other thing than to cure the sick, and that *gratis*. 2. None of the posterity should be constrained to wear one certain type of habit, but therein to follow the custom of the country. 3. That every year upon the day C. they should meet together in the house *S. Spiritus* [i.e., of the Holy Spirit] or write the cause of his absence. 4. Every brother should look about for a worthy person, who, after his decease, might succeed him. 5. The word C.R. would be their seal, mark, and character. 6. The Fraternity should remain secret one hundred years.[2]

The brothers dispersed to pursue their work in other countries. One brother, known only as A., died in "Gallia Narbonensis," that is, Languedoc. At this point, the *Fama* says, there was a gap in the transmission: "We must confess that after the death of the said A. none of us had in any manner known anything of brother R.C." except for some minor details. Even the year of his death and the location of his tomb had been forgotten. But while refurbishing their building (presumably the building *S. Spiritus*), the brothers opened a wall and discovered a hidden crypt adorned with mystical diagrams and mottoes and containing the remains of C.R. — "a fair and worthy body, whole and unconsumed." As we learn from the *Confessio*, Christian Rosenkreutz, born in 1378, had lived to the age of 106, which would mean that he died in 1484. His tomb was rediscovered 120 years after his death, which brings us to 1604 — close to the time these tracts were written.

The brothers take this discovery as a sign of a "general reformation both of divine and human things." The Rosicrucian treatises are firmly Protestant in their convictions. The *Confessio* states: "We do condemn the East and the West (meaning the Pope and Mahomet) blasphemers against our Lord Jesus Christ, and offer and present with a good will to the head of the Roman Empire our prayers, secrets, and great treasures of gold."[3] The "Roman Empire" is the Holy Roman Empire, the loosely strung confederation of states in Germany and Austria that lay claim to the mantle of the ancient Roman *imperium*. The *Fama* is a bit more equivocal about this entity: "In *Politia* we acknowledge the Roman Empire . . . for our Christian head; albeit we know what alterations be at hand."[4]

The "head of the Roman Empire" must have meant Emperor Rudolf II, who espoused religious tolerance and whose court was a mecca for occultists, Kabbalists, and alchemists. Rudolf died in 1612, between the writing of these treatises (around 1610) and their publication (in 1614). The brothers echo a widespread expectation at the time that the situation would change after Rudolf's death — which turned out to be true. In 1619, after a seven-year reign by Rudolf's ineffectual brother Matthias, Ferdinand II became Holy Roman Emperor. Ferdinand proved to be a vehement defender of Catholicism. Indeed, his zeal helped start the Thirty Years' War, which ravaged Europe between 1620 and 1648.

Rosicrucian Politics

One of the great themes of Western history has been the struggle between sacred and secular power. Since the fall of the Western Roman Empire in the fifth century A.D., Western civilization has taken the separation — indeed the adversity — between church and state as a given, something inevitable and possibly desirable. In the Middle Ages this opposition played itself out in the struggle between the popes, who claimed temporal as well as spiritual authority, and the Holy Roman Emperors, who sought to limit the church's ability to dictate to secular monarchs. One might think that Dante, the greatest of all Catholic poets, might have sided with the papacy in this matter, but he did not. He was a member of the Ghibelline — that is, the imperial — party, and even wrote a treatise, *De monarchia* (On Monarchy), which argued for the sacred nature of imperial authority.

Four hundred years later, we see the Rosicrucian manifestoes also siding with the secular powers and condemning the pope. It would be hard to draw a direct line between Dante and the Ghibellines on the one hand and the Rosicrucians on the other, but the thrust of their ideas is very much the same. Since the Middle Ages, strong voices in the esoteric currents of the West have urged that the church cannot be trusted with secular (and perhaps even spiritual) authority and that its power must be severely circumscribed. If there is a "secret history" of the West, this issue lies close to the heart of it. Eventually this would lead to the notion of the separation of church and state as embodied in the U.S. Constitution.

In the time of the Rosicrucian manifestoes, the struggle played itself out in the political arena — dramatically and disastrously. The Rosicrucian movement was closely connected with Frederick V, the Elector Palatine (1596–1632).[5] The Palatinate was a state in western Germany that was part of the Holy Roman Empire; the title "elector" meant that he was one of several princes entitled to vote in the election of the Holy Roman Emperor (which was not a hereditary office). Like the Rosicrucians of the manifestoes, Frederick was staunchly Protestant and devoted to the occult science of the age. His capital at Heidelberg was adorned with strange but beautiful Hermetic treasures: intricate mechanical figures, gardens designed around allegorical themes, water organs, singing fountains. Married in 1613 to Princess Elizabeth, the daughter of King James I of England, Frederick was also head of the Protestant Union of Princes.

The years 1610 to 1620 were a time of increasing tension in Europe. Catholicism, which had been in retreat from Protestantism for much of the sixteenth century, was in the midst of launching its counteroffensive, known as the Counter-Reformation. And the political mainstay of the Counter-Reformation was the Hapsburg dynasty, which ruled Spain, Austria, and many domains in between, including parts of present-day Italy, France, and the Low Countries. Ferdinand II was a Hapsburg (as were all the Holy Roman Emperors of that period, which helps explain the rather ambiguous acknowledgment of the Holy Roman Empire in the Rosicrucian manifestoes).

In 1617 the Catholic Ferdinand was crowned king of Bohemia (roughly equivalent to the modern-day Czech Republic). He rapidly moved to suppress the Protestant Bohemian Church, which had continued the legacy of the fifteenth-century reformer Jan Hus. Discomfited, the Bohemian nobles offered the crown to the Elector Palatine. He accepted in September 1619, writing in a letter to his uncle, "It is a divine calling which I must not disobey . . . my only end is to serve God and His Church."[6]

Frederick obviously knew that this move would set him against the Hapsburgs. Yet a number of considerations motivated him to make it. One was the urging of many Protestant leaders throughout Europe. Another was the fact that he was counting on his alliances with the Dutch, with German and French Protestants, and with his father-in-law, the king of Great Britain, to support him against the Hapsburgs.

Frederick and Elizabeth went to Prague that autumn and reigned briefly in an ethereal atmosphere reminiscent of the days of Rudolf II. But Frederick's hold on the Bohemian throne was not to last. The Hapsburgs marshaled their forces against him; the Protestant powers, including Britain, balked at coming to his aid. Frederick's army met Ferdinand's at the Battle of the White Mountain on November 8, 1620, and was utterly defeated. This event marks the beginning of the murderous Thirty Years' War, from which Germany would take a century to recover. The Hapsburgs occupied the Palatinate and devastated it, also destroying the Hermetic treasures of Heidelberg. Frederick and Elizabeth fled and spent the rest of their lives as exiles at The Hague.

What, apart from a similarity of interests, links the Rosicrucian movement with Frederick? Frances Yates, in *The Rosicrucian Enlightenment*, lists a number of things. In the first place, the *Fama* and the *Confessio* were published in the state of Hesse-Cassel, which was near the Palatinate and shared its Protestant and Hermetic allegiances. Other Rosicrucian treatises, some of them written in response to the *Fama* and the *Confessio*, were published in Oppenheim, in the Palatinate, as were a number of other Hermetic and alchemical works. The manifestoes also make some oblique allusions to politics. The *Confessio*, for example, says, "There are yet some Eagles' Feathers in our way, the which do hinder our purpose."[7] The eagle is a reference to the Hapsburgs, whose symbol was a double eagle. Even more tellingly, treatises on Rosicrucian themes abruptly ceased to appear after 1620 — the year of the White Mountain debacle.

The victorious Ferdinand moved swiftly against his enemies. Widespread purges eradicated the Bohemian Church. The Hapsburgs also launched a carefully planned propaganda campaign to discredit both Frederick and the Rosicrucians. Lampoons and satires survive that show him fleeing in humiliation, and a Rosicrucian motto — *Sub umbra tuarum alarum, Jehovah*, "Under the shadow of thy wings, Jehovah" — was vitriolically parodied by broadsides showing the wings as those of the Hapsburg eagle. In Germany, the forces of the Counter-Reformation also launched vicious and intense witch hunts in an attempt to connect the Hermetic magic of the Rosicrucians with witchcraft, that perennial bogeyman of the early modern era.

The most curious of these propaganda campaigns took place in France. In 1623, placards appeared throughout Paris proclaiming the arrival of the "principal College of the Brothers of the Rose Cross," who were "making a visible and invisible stay in this city."[8] A pamphlet appearing in the same year bore the title "Horrible Pacts Made between the Devil and the Pretended Invisible Ones."

These announcements caused a sensation, although, as the reference to the "Invisible Ones" suggests, no member of the Rose Cross Order ever revealed himself in public, in France or anywhere else. Even before the fall of Frederick, no Rosicrucians had ever made their presence known, despite many earnest entreaties. Hence they came to be nicknamed "the Invisibles."

Reading the Book of Nature

If the Rosicrucian movement was merely trying to advance the fortunes of the Elector Palatine as a bulwark for the Protestant cause, the brothers' aspirations were futile. But a closer examination of the texts reveals a deeper purpose. Near the beginning of the *Fama* we read:

> The pride and covetousness of the learned is so great, it will not suf-
> fer them to agree together; but were they united they might out of all
> those things which in this our age God doth so richly bestow upon
> us, collect *Librum Naturae* [the book of Nature], or a perfect method
> of all arts: but such is their opposition, that they still keep, and are
> loth to leave the old course, esteeming Popery, Aristotle, and Galen,
> yea and that which hath but a mere show of learning, more than the
> clear and manifested light of truth.[9]

Whether this passage was written out of mystical illumination or in a flight of fancy, it remains astonishing. These few convoluted lines set out an intellectual program that Western civilization would follow for the next four centuries; indeed we still follow it today. They deride the stale scholasticism of their time — "Popery, Aristotle, and Galen" — and call for a "perfect method" that involves reading the "book of Nature" directly rather than through the clouded lens of antique texts. In essence, this is the foundation of modern science.

This passage becomes even more astounding when we consider that the two names most directly connected with the birth of the scientific method had links to the Rosicrucian movement. One was the English philosopher and statesman Francis Bacon (1561–1626). Bacon decried the metaphysics of his day, which he likened to spiders' webs — beautiful and intricate, but in the end based on nothing. He called for a more precise method of experimentation so that scientific theories could be based on actual experience rather than on speculation. He preached what he called "the great instauration," a systematic investigation of nature that would restore to man the connection with (and power over) nature that he had had before the Fall.[10] Bacon was intimately connected with Rosicrucian currents. As Frances Yates remarks, "It was out of the Hermetic tradition that Bacon emerged, out of the Magia and Cabala of the Renaissance as it had reached him via the natural magicians."[11]

Even more remarkable is the case of the French philosopher René Descartes (1596–1650). It is he, more than any other thinker except perhaps Bacon, who has been most closely associated with the emergence of the modern scientific worldview. His *Discourse on Method* could be seen as a book-length extension of the brothers' injunction to study the *Librum Naturae*. As Descartes puts it, "As soon as I reached an age which allowed me to emerge from the tutelage of my teachers, I abandoned the study of letters altogether, . . . resolving to study no other science than that which I could find within myself or the great book of the world."[12] His *Discourse* sets out a program like Bacon's, calling for a method that would unify all the sciences by basing them on mathematical principles, particularly the Cartesian coordinate system, which he devised and which still bears his name.

Descartes' connections with the Rosicrucians are as fascinating as they are mystifying. A young man at the time the manifestoes were published, he went to Germany in 1619 to pursue his goal of learning through "travelling, seeing courts and armies, in mixing with people of different humours and ranks, in gathering a varied experience,"[13] but also in search of the Rosicrucian Brotherhood (which, of course, he never found). He thought about joining the

Catholic forces ranged against the Elector Palatine, but decided against it and sequestered himself away in a house on the Danube. "Finding no company to distract me, and having, fortunately, no cares or passions to disturb me, I spent the whole day shut up in a room heated by an enclosed stove, where I had complete leisure to meditate on my own thoughts."[14] These thoughts led him to the revolutionary conclusion that mathematics furnished the key to understanding nature.

By an odd coincidence, Descartes returned to Paris in 1623, when the Rosicrucian scare was at its height. Even more bizarrely, he found that his German sojourn had given him the reputation of being a Rosicrucian himself. His way of squelching this rumor was rather unusual. As Adrien Baillet, his seventeenth-century biographer, writes, "He made himself visible to all the world, and particularly to his friends who needed no other argument to convince them that he was not one of the Brotherhood of the Rosicrucians or Invisibles: and he used the same argument of their invisibility to explain to the curious why he had not been able to find any of them in Germany."[15]

The Reality of the Brotherhood

All this leads to an overwhelming question: did the Rose Cross Brotherhood exist? Even more than most, this is an area in which we cannot admit negative proof. The lack of hard evidence cannot prove the *nonexistence* of an order pledged to secrecy. And while the brothers proclaimed in the manifestoes that they would soon bring their order to public awareness, if they existed, given the hostile atmosphere of the times it's not surprising that they never fulfilled their promise.

On the question of the order's reality, opinion falls between two extremes. Academic scholars — of whom the late Frances Yates was the most distinguished — tend to discount their existence in any literal sense. They acknowledge that there were Rosicrucian currents — ideas and ideals that were linked to esotericism, including Kabbalah, Hermeticism, and alchemy, but they generally discount the existence of any literal Fraternity of the Rose Cross. On the other hand, modern organizations that call themselves Rosicrucian, laying claim to the brothers' legacy, tend to treat the story in the *Fama* and the *Confessio* as mostly factual. For those in between, it is not easy to tease out the truth. But several points can lead us to some tentative conclusions.

In the first place, nothing in the basic story of Christian Rosenkreutz's life is inherently implausible. Throughout the Renaissance, there was a rich and thriving trade between Europe and the Levant, and we do not have to stretch our imaginations far to believe that an itinerant seeker could have made his way to Syria and Morocco. In broad outline, Christian Rosenkreutz resembles many of the peripatetic scholar-mages we've already encountered in this narrative. Nor do we have to be insanely credulous to believe that such a man might make his way back to Germany and collect a small group of disciples around him.

That much said, much of the Christian Rosenkreutz mythos seems fictitious. In 1616, a short work called *The Chemical Wedding of Christian Rosenkreutz* was published. An elaborate alchemical tale, it is explicitly allegorical. In this case we *do* know who its author was: Johann Valentin Andreae, a German cleric and esotericist. *The Chemical Wedding* is quite close to the manifestoes in spirit, so Andreae would very likely have been connected to the circle that produced the *Fama* and *Confessio*. In later years, he would refer to the Rosicrucian myth as a *ludibrium* — a word often translated as "joke" or "farce," although it could also mean "entertainment," quite possibly with a serious purpose. In any case, this suggests that the Rosicrucian manifestoes contain an element of fiction, perhaps a large one.

So there is probably some mixture of fact and imagination in the tale of Christian Rosenkreutz. Certain things, such as the description of the discovery of his tomb, are almost certainly allegorical. Even the name "Christian Rosenkreutz" has the flavor of allegory about it, both esoteric (the rose has long served as a mystical symbol) and programmatic: Luther's personal coat of arms incorporated a rose and a cross. But the main story may have a core of truth. There *were* such seekers and adepts in those days, and the manifestoes could well conceal the story of one (or even a composite) of them. The same could be said of the society he founded.

All this aside, there is a deeper dimension to the rumor of the Brotherhood. In his biography of Descartes, Adrien Baillet makes a mysterious remark. Speaking of the Rosicrucians allegedly in France, he writes, "They could not communicate with people, or be communicated with, except by thought joined to the will, that is to say in a manner imperceptible to the senses."[16] The method of joining thought to the will bears a striking resemblance to Descartes' description of his "meditation." (What, after all, is meditation of any kind but a joining of thought to will?) Baillet's statement is one of the earliest known instances of a theme that from this time on becomes increasingly prominent in the Gnostic legacy: the idea of hidden masters who make their presence felt through clairvoyant means.

For some who have investigated these areas, the Rosicrucian manifestoes do not depict a society that exists on the physical level, but figuratively point to a group of individuals who operate at a higher level of consciousness. The twentieth-century esotericist Paul Foster Case observes:

> This fraternity is not an organized society like the Freemasons. One may not join it by making application for membership, paying entrance fees and dues, and passing through ceremonies. The Rosicrucian Order is like the old definition of the city of Boston: it is a state of mind. One *becomes* a Rosicrucian: one does not *join* the Rosicrucians. . . .
>
> The Order is designated as being invisible by the manifestoes themselves. It does not come in corporate form before the world, because by its very nature it cannot. True Rosicrucians know one another, nevertheless. Their means of recognition cannot be counterfeited nor betrayed, for these tokens are more subtle than the signs and passwords of ordinary secret societies.
>
> Let none suppose that because the Rosicrucian Order is invisible it is composed of discarnate human intelligences. Neither are its members supermen inhabiting a region vaguely designated by the term "higher planes." The Order is invisible because it has no external organization. It is not composed of invisible beings. Its members are men and women incarnate on earth in physical bodies. They are invisible to ordinary eyes because the minds behind those eyes cannot recognize the marks of a true Rosicrucian.[17]

This train of thought admittedly leads to unusual conclusions. Could Descartes, whose name has become synonymous with a linear, rationalistic approach to reality, have been inspired by hidden intelligences whose existence rationality could never prove? And could the scientific enterprise have been seeded by levels of consciousness that science itself tends to deny? It would be peculiar if it were so, but history offers many ironies that are just as droll. While skeptics may dismiss these ideas as nonsense, they are worth examining — if only to see how those who pursue esoteric teachings understand themselves.

The Divine Cobbler

As fascinating as it was, the Rosicrucian furor was only a part of the era's intense preoccupation with Hermeticism, alchemy, and Kabbalah, as well as theology of more conventional forms. One of the most powerful visionaries of the time had nothing to do with the Rosicrucian tracts, which, in fact, he thought were mad.[18]

Jacob Boehme (or Böhme) was born in 1575 in Görlitz, a town in what is now southeastern Germany.[19] Of humble origins, he lacked the physical strength to take up the backbreaking work of agriculture, so he became a cobbler. He led an unremarkable life until one day in 1600, when he found himself gazing on a glint of light reflected from a pewter dish. "In one quarter of an hour I saw and knew more than if I had been many years together at a university," he would later recount.

It took Boehme twelve years before he was able to formulate some of these insights in writing. His first book, the *Aurora*, was finished in 1612. He did not intend to publish it, but unfortunately a copy of the manuscript fell into the hands of Gregor Richter, the Lutheran pastor of Görlitz. Denouncing Boehme as a heretic, Richter managed to have a decree enacted that forbade him from writing for five years. Boehme even served time in prison. But in 1618, he started writing again and in the next five years composed the rest of his works, including *The Three Principles of the Divine Essence*, *The Threefold Life of Man*, and *The Way to Christ*. He died in 1624, surviving his nemesis, Richter, by a little more than six months. His followers, many of whom never met him, vested him with such extravagant epithets as "the Divine Cobbler" and *Philosophus Teutonicus*, "the Teutonic Philosopher."

What was it that so angered Richter? As Arthur Versluis, a scholar of esoteric movements, suggests, it may have been Boehme's contempt for mere book learning as a replacement for the living experience of the spirit. Boehme contended, "Man can undertake nothing from the beginning of his youth nor in the whole course of his time in this world that is more profitable than to know himself." Taking this stance put Boehme against the external authorities like Richter, for whom doctrines and the letter of scripture were the final authority.

For Boehme, this mandate, which echoes the ancient admonition of the Delphic oracle to "know thyself," extends beyond mere knowledge of the inner landscape. God has, in Boehme's words, enabled man to "penetrate into the heart of everything, and discern what essence, virtue, and property it has, in creatures, earth, stones, trees, herbs, in all moveable and immoveable things."[20] Although Boehme was not a part of the circle that produced the Rosicrucian tracts, his sentiments often echo theirs.

The most common response to Boehme's works is that they are extremely difficult. This is partly because even today many of them are available in English only in the seventeenth-century versions of Boehme's follower John Sparrow. And yet ultimately their difficulty seems to be due to the immensity of the task of compressing Boehme's mystical insights into the tiny yet cumbrous vehicle of human language.

Thanks to the indisputable power of his vision, Boehme managed to win friends among the learned and influential (one of whom had to pull strings to have Boehme given a Christian burial after his death). A number of them were versed in the esoteric traditions of the day, and Boehme seems to have picked up at least some of the concepts and terms of Kabbalah and alchemy from them. (One disciple, Balthasar Walter, had traveled to the East in search of "Kabbalah, magic, and alchemy," rather like Christian Rosenkreutz.)[21] But Boehme's vision remains uniquely his own. It led him to produce a *theosophy* — an esoteric exploration of how God makes himself known. Unlike conventional theology, which tends to restrict itself to interpretation and reinterpretation of dogmas and doctrines, theosophy is much more audacious. It attempts nothing less than to draw a mystical anatomy of the body of God.[22]

Boehme's spiritual vision begins with the wish of the divine to know itself. "Boehme does not hesitate to say that the Absolute does not know itself," writes the French scholar Pierre Deghaye. "Thus it is to himself that God is revealed as much as to the faithful. The hidden God is the unknown divinity which does not know itself. This divinity aspires to be known not only by the creature but also to itself."[23]

The divine wishes to know itself — but if the divine is all-encompassing, what is there for it to know, and what is there for it to be known *with*? So God must compress himself into something that *knows* and something that *is known* — or, viewed from another angle, something that *desires* and something that *is desired*. As Boehme puts it in his dark language, "The first property is a desirousness, like the magnet, viz., the compression of the will; the will desireth to be something, and yet it hath nothing of which it may make something to itself; and therefore it bringeth itself into a receivingness of itself, and compresseth itself into a something, and that something is nothing but a magnetical hunger, a harshness."[24]

Students of the Kabbalah will recognize echoes of its teaching here, for what Boehme is saying very much resembles the Kabbalistic concept of *tzimtzum*, the "withdrawal" of God from a part of reality so that the universe may arise, creating a mirror in which God can behold God. What is unique to Boehme is the force of his language. What the Kabbalists describe with serene abstraction here takes on an intense violence of expression. For the processes of divine manifestation, Boehme uses such terms as "hardness," "harshness," "sourness," "astringency," the "sting." The overall impression is one of vast cosmic forces, struggling and striving, each producing its opposite and, in the unendurable tension of their desire, giving birth to a world — nature, both earthly and celestial, as the mirror in which God beholds God. Underlying this all is the primordial tension between light and darkness — the darkness out of which all arises, and the light by which it comes to be known.

Boehme's thought thus echoes the ideas of the Manichaeans. But Boehme was not a Manichaean, and his doctrine differs from theirs in at least one profound sense: he does not regard the darkness as inherently evil or the light as inherently good. The darkness is merely unknowing, and the light is what makes it known. And yet Boehme's teaching does at times stray toward the edges of dualism; it's not surprising that one of his disciples, Johann Georg Gichtel (1638–1710), went so far as to defend Manichaeism.[25] Another disciple, Abraham von Franckenburg, compared Boehme's system to ancient Gnosticism, as did some of Boehme's eighteenth-century English disciples.[26]

These facts may lead someone to ask how close all these different teachings and movements really were to the Gnostic legacy. From a historical point of view, the connection is indirect, through the intermediaries of such traditions as Kabbalah and Hermeticism. Sometimes, too, it is a matter of independent visionaries attaining the same insights. As Arthur Versluis notes:

> There is little reason to posit some kind of historical continuity between [Boehme's] theosophy and early Christian gnosis; while there are certainly numerous historical enigmas involved here (the resemblance between some forms of Jewish Kabbalah, Mazdaean, Manichaean, and Gnostic Christian religions has been noted before), it seems unnecessary and conspiratorial to posit a grand historical

"initiatory transmission" when it should be obvious that in question
is not historical transmission, but the rediscovery of essentially the
same religion of light in different cultural contexts.[27]

Even so, the name of the Gnostics is invoked more than once, in connection not only with Boehme but with the Rosicrucians as well. The Restoration satirist Samuel Butler makes the following remark in a footnote to his
Hudibras: "The Fraternity of the Rosy-Crucians is very like the Sect of the
ancient Gnostici who called themselves so, from the excellent learning they
pretended to, although they were really the most ridiculous Sots of all
Mankind."[28]

Viewing the matter in a more positive light, Paul Foster Case observes:

> Rosicrucian religion . . . is Christian Gnosticism. It is opposed to or-
> ganized religious authority because that authority imposes creeds,
> plays on the fears and hopes of believers, and in Christendom founds
> itself on the essential ignobility and worthlessness of man. Rosicru-
> cian religion begins by proclaiming man's nobleness and worth and
> proceeds to declare its knowledge of the Christos. It describes that
> knowledge as being progressive and as leading eventually to con-
> scious immortality.[29]

The Rise of Masonry

As we've seen, the Rosicrucian brotherhood, if it existed, probably did not
exist in any form that would be recognizable from the manifestoes. And yet it
did in a sense prove to be a self-fulfilling prophecy. The *Fama* and the *Confessio* created a fascination with occult brotherhoods that has gripped the Western world up to the present time. And the most powerful and far-reaching of
these brotherhoods is Freemasonry (also known as Masonry, or sometimes
the Craft).

The Rosicrucian furor did not create Freemasonry: Masonic texts go back
to the fourteenth century. But something happened in the time of the Rosicrucian manifestoes that would galvanize Masonry and bring it to the center
of public attention. To understand how this happened, it would be helpful to
begin by exploring the extremely vexed question of where and when Freemasonry began.

Like the Kabbalists and Hermeticists, the earliest Freemasons had a rich if mythical account of their own genesis, summarized in the oldest surviving Masonic texts, called the "Old Charges." And the oldest surviving versions of these are preserved in two English manuscripts: the Cooke and the Regius manuscripts, dating to about 1400.[30] They contain a mythical history that traces Masonry back to antediluvian times, to "a mann that was clepyd lameth [*sic*]." "Lameth," presumably Cain's descendant Lamech (Gen. 4:18–19), produces two sons, "Iaballe [or Jabal] and the other hight juballe," the elder of whom "was the first mann that ever found gemetry and masonry and he mad howsis & [is] named in the bybulle."[31] When Jabal's descendants realize that God is about to punish the wickedness of humanity with fire or flood, they inscribe their learning on two different kinds of stone, one of which would not burn and the other "that wolle not sinke in water."

After Noah's flood, the pillars are found by two individuals, Pythagoras and "Hermes the philisophre." Later, Abraham, during his sojourn in Egypt, teaches the Egyptians the science of geometry; his principal disciple is Euclid. The Israelites learn Masonry in Europe, and Solomon uses it to build the temple in Jerusalem. Later still, Masonry in England is organized by St. Albans and established by King Athelstan.

As charming as this account is, it obviously has little if any historical truth. In true medieval fashion, figures from the Bible and classical antiquity are jumbled together without any comprehension of actual chronology. Pythagoras, who lived in the sixth century B.C., comes before Abraham, whose life is traditionally dated to around 1900 B.C. Even so, two things are striking about the story in the Old Charges. In the first place, it resembles the legendary histories of the Kabbalah and Hermeticism, which are also traced back to antediluvian times and evoke the heritage of Egypt. In the second place, it foreshadows later Masonic themes: for example, the names of the sons of "Lameth," Jabal and Jubal, anticipate the names of the three "ruffians," Jubelo, Jubela, and Jubelum, who, in the rite of the Master Mason degree, slay the Master Mason Hiram Abiff.[32] Thus at least some of the later Masonic teachings may be traced back to this period.

All in all, though, the story in the Old Charges is a legend. More recent and more historical accounts can generally be ranged into two categories. The first connects Masonry with the Knights Templar. The Templars, a military order of knights established in 1118 to protect pilgrims to the Holy Land, rapidly became one of the most successful organizations in history. Within a century of their founding, they commanded an empire of fortifications and estates that spanned from Palestine to the British Isles. But with the recapture of the Holy Land by the Muslims in the late thirteenth century, the Templars seemed to have lost their raison d'être. They were brutally suppressed in 1307 by King Philip the Fair of France (who coveted their tremendous wealth) with the connivance of Pope Clement V. All Templars found were imprisoned, and a strange series of confessions was extracted from them. They were accused, for example, of spitting on the crucifix in their secret rites and worshipping an idol named Baphomet.

All of this is well-documented historical fact (although it's hard to say how much of the Templars' confessions is to be believed, since they were for the most part extracted under torture). From here, proponents of alternate history take the matter in quite a different direction. By this account, some of the Templars managed to flee to Scotland, which had been placed under excommunication in 1312 and which was struggling to fight off an English invasion. Indeed a Templar contingent is said to have turned the tide at the crucial Battle of Bannockburn in 1314, in which the Scots under Robert the Bruce decisively drove out the English.

In Scotland, according to this theory, Templar tradition went underground. The chief evidence for its continuation is in stone. It is a curious building called Rosslyn Chapel, several miles outside of Edinburgh. For proponents of alterative history, the carvings at Rosslyn represent a kind of missing link between the Templars and the Freemasons. By this view, the Templars were architects first and fighters second. It was their arcane sacred geometry that was preserved in Scotland and resuscitated in the late sixteenth century to create the Freemasonry that is known from history.

Such is the first theory. It has gained currency over recent decades, being expounded in such popular books as John J. Robinson's *Born in Blood* and Michael Baigent and Richard Leigh's *The Temple and the Lodge*. Rosslyn Chapel provides the backdrop for the climax of *The Da Vinci Code*. Moreover, the Templar-Mason connection has been embraced by many Masons, who have given Templar names to some of their higher-grade degrees. A youth organization sponsored by Masons is known as the Order of DeMolay in honor of Jacques de Molay, the last Templar Grand Master, who was burned at the stake in Paris in 1314.[33]

But there are some key problems with the Templar-Freemason connection. To begin with, there is the plain fact that the Templars were primarily a military order. Whatever esoteric knowledge they had probably had little to do with geometry or sacred architecture. Furthermore, there is the evidence of such texts as the Old Charges themselves, which draw a very clear and strong connection between the ancient builders and the stonemasons of their own time. There is no suggestion, overt or veiled, that the Templars had anything to do with Masonry.

The most plausible version of the origins of Masonry is the standard one — or at least a version of it. It's well known that in the Middle Ages guilds were predominant in many trades, serving as a combination of union, technical school, benevolent society, and guarantor of professional standards. Because the medieval world was focused on the sacred, the guilds had a spiritual element as well; they resembled lay religious fraternities. Some of them, including the trade guilds of France, known as the *compagnonnages*, even transmitted a kind of initiatic wisdom.

The Masons were among these guilds. They differed from most guilds in two ways. On the one hand, the nature of their work ensured that masons would spend more time traveling from job to job than would men of most trades. This made it necessary to create certain signs and words by which a mason could make himself known in a strange city. In the second place, as we can see from the Old Charges, the Masons had a much richer tradition about their past than most guilds. Both of these characteristics would help transform Masonry from a trade organization into one of the most influential movements in Western history.

The transformation began in Scotland, and its key figure was a man who is hardly remembered today. His name was William Schaw (c. 1550–1602), and he was master of works to King James VI of Scotland. This position gave him authority over the nation's lodges of masons, and he soon regularized their organization and incorporated new elements into their practice. In 1598 and 1599, he issued two sets of statutes that were to radically alter the face of Masonry. One of the most curious provisions enjoined the lodge warden to test every applicant for membership in "the art of memorie and science thairof."[34] As I've noted in regard to Giordano Bruno, the Renaissance art of memory involved intense powers of visualization, including the construction of a "memory palace." We do not know whether Schaw introduced the art of memory to the Masonic lodges of Scotland or whether it had been practiced before his time. Nor is it certain that this "art of memorie" was akin to Bruno's; it may have been something simpler designed to facilitate rote learning of rituals. At any rate, this provision suggests that Masonic training at the end of the sixteenth century included some esoteric knowledge.

This knowledge began to exercise an increasing attraction for men who were not working (or "operative") masons. Soon after the Schaw Statutes, we see Masonic lodges beginning to admit gentlemen, who in most circumstances would have been loath to admit any connection to ordinary trades. The fact that they were drawn to Masonry suggests that they believed some hidden knowledge was to be gained there.

Such was the situation when the Rosicrucian furor burst upon the public. No one would seriously argue that the Rosicrucian manifestoes were talking about the Masonic lodges. On the other hand, the similarity between the invisible brothers of the Rosy Cross and the highly visible brothers of the Masonic fraternity was evident to many. By 1638, an obscure Scottish poet named Henry Adamson could write these lines:

> For what we presage is not in grosse,
> For we be brethren of the *Rosie Crosse*;
> We have the *Mason Word* and second sight,
> Things for to come we can foretell aright.[35]

The "Mason Word" was a kind of secret password that would enable Masons to recognize each other. Rituals of identification — passwords, grips, and scripted questions with responses — became more and more elaborate as Masonry continued to evolve in the seventeenth century. Some of these cast light on the esoteric nature of Masonic teachings.

The Mason Word, for example, has been known to the public since the late seventeenth century. The password for the Entered Apprentice (the first and lowest of Masonic degrees) is *Boaz*; that for the Fellow Craft (the second degree) is *Jachin*. These allude to Solomon's Temple in the Bible: "And he set up the pillars in the porch of the temple: and he set up the right pillar, and called the name thereof Jachin; and he set up the left pillar, and he called the name thereof Boaz" (1 Kings 7:21; cf. 2 Chron. 3:17). Around the beginning of the eighteenth century, a third degree, that of the Master Mason, was introduced; its word was *Mahabyn*. The meaning of this word is obscure, and many highly ingenious and highly implausible explanations have been offered for its origins.

The pillars have another meaning that will be obvious to any student of the Kabbalah.[36] Kabbalistic teaching speaks of two "pillars": the Pillar of Mercy and the Pillar of Severity, or, to phrase it differently, Force and Form, respectively. Force, or Mercy, is generally pictured on the right; Form, or Severity, on the left. (Kabbalists would also say that this is the inner meaning of the two pillars in front of the Temple in Jerusalem.) Because Kabbalistic ideas had such a wide currency in this period, this association must have been evident to many who took these degrees. It also harks back to the two pillars of stone in the Old Charges on which the antediluvians sought to preserve their knowledge from cataclysm.

Another detail resonates still more powerfully with the Rosicrucian manifestoes. Here is a question-and-answer sequence from a late seventeenth-century Masonic catechism:

Q. Where shall I find the key of your lodge?
A. Three foot and a half from the lodge door under a perpend esler and a green divot. But under the lap of my liver where all the secrets of my heart lie.
Q. What is the key of your lodge?
A. A weel [sic] hung tongue.
Q. Where lies the key?
A. In the bone box.[37]

This passage makes it clear that the true lodge was not a physical building, but was contained in the human heart and head — the latter being the "bone box" that holds the tongue. Historian David Stevenson contends, "There is a strong case for regarding the mental lodge described in the catechisms as a memory temple, crude and confused perhaps by the process of being handed down over the generations." What this means is that the true lodge is a temple not built by human hands; it is an invisible temple that exists in the realm of thought. This in turn would explain why Schaw insisted that Masons be versed in the art of memory, since this art hones the skills of imagination and visualization to a high degree.[38] Note also how this invisible temple resembles the invisible "house of the Holy Spirit" in which the Rosicrucian brothers were said to meet.

None of this means that the Rosicrucian manifestoes were talking about the Masonic brotherhoods of their day. But it does suggest that the Masonic ritual and symbolism that evolved from Schaw's time on drew consciously and deliberately upon esoteric sources, including Rosicrucianism and Kabbalah. This in turn would mean that men seeking esoteric knowledge would naturally gravitate toward the Masonic lodge.

Masonry in the Public Domain

But the thirst for occult knowledge does not in itself explain the extraordinary expansion of Freemasonry in the eighteenth century. A more compelling reason is suggested by an entry in the journal of an Englishman named Elias Ashmole. Ashmole (1617–92) was an alchemist, astrologer, and most of all an indefatigable amasser of antiquities: his collection forms the nucleus of the Ashmolean Museum at Oxford. On October 16, 1646, Ashmole says in his diary, he was admitted to a Masonic lodge in Warrington, Lancashire. What is notable about this — apart from the fact that it is one of the first documented Masonic initiations in England — is the company. Also present was his cousin Henry Mainwaring, who was a member of the Parliamentary faction in the English Civil War that was then raging. Ashmole himself was a Royalist, fighting on the other side. Other Masons present included Catholics. (Catholics had not yet been forbidden to become Masons.) So this early Masonic lodge was able to join Anglicans, Puritans, and Catholics together in fraternal fellowship at a time when religious strife in England was at a peak.

This detail goes far to explain the success of Masonry. Masonic membership in those days was offered to all Christians; in the eighteenth century it would be extended to all who believed in a Supreme Being. Masonry, which came of age at the end of over a century and a half of bitter religious warfare that had ravaged much of Europe, offered a haven from the endless strife over faith that inflamed so much of public opinion in those days. To this day it is forbidden to discuss religion or politics in the lodge.

Nevertheless, man is a political animal, and politics soon began to seep into the Masonic world. One example was the Gold- und Rosenkreutz (or "Golden and Rosy Cross") of eighteenth-century Germany.[39] The Gold- und Rosenkreutz was not a shadowy entity like the Brotherhood of the manifestoes. It actually existed, and we know a considerable amount about its membership and its practices; for example, it had ten grades of initiation, based on the ten *sefirot* of the Kabbalah. Moreover, it was only open to men who had already passed through regular Masonic initiation.

By the 1770s the Gold- und Rosenkreutz had lodges all over Central Europe. It reached the height of its power in Prussia in the years after 1786, when one of its members, a nephew of Frederick the Great, came to the throne as Frederick William II. For much of Frederick William's reign, his court was dominated by a small Rosicrucian clique that gained a reputation for right-wing reaction, attempting — ironically, considering the original nature of the Rosicrucian impulse — to tighten religious orthodoxy. Such abuses, as well as internal conflicts, caused the dissolution of the Gold- und Rosenkreutz after Frederick William's death in 1797.

Another, much more notorious quasi-Masonic lodge was the Bavarian Illuminati, started by a young Bavarian university professor named Adam Weishaupt in 1776.[40] The Illuminati were the opposite of the Gold- und Rosenkreutz: they were radicals attempting to combat Catholicism and particularly the Jesuits, then the leading religious influence in Bavaria. Weishaupt's aim was to foster the egalitarian program of the Enlightenment, but his arrogant and capricious behavior nearly destroyed his own organization, which he only managed to preserve by hitting on the ingenious device of infiltrating regular Masonic lodges in Germany and Austria. In the 1780s, however, this scheme came to light, and in 1785 the Elector of Bavaria issued an edict condemning both Freemasonry and the Illuminati.

In all likelihood this was when the Illuminati fell apart as an organized entity, though various right-wing forces (including the Gold- und Rosenkreutz) circulated the idea that the Illuminati were still operating and endangering the safety of well-ordered states, an idea that has continued to surface ever since. To this day rumors about this fascinating but short-lived body survive, sometimes seriously (in the works of conspiracy theorists), sometimes as a kind of *ludibrium,* or half-serious joke (as in the works of the contemporary writer Robert Anton Wilson, coauthor of the *Illuminatus!* trilogy).

Even apart from the Illuminati, Masonry in the eighteenth century came to be associated with social change — the overturning of the *ancien régime,* dominated by monarchs and the church, in favor of the then-revolutionary concept of representative government. A number of the Founding Fathers of the United States were Masons, including George Washington and Benjamin Franklin. One estimate says that of the fifty-five men who signed the Declaration of Independence, nine are known to have been Freemasons.[41] The Masonic lodges were similarly influential in the French Revolution, though, as historian J. R. Roberts suggests, chiefly in the sense that "both the lodge organisation and the familiarity which it created meant that freemasonry was in principle helpful to collective action."[42]

Catholics versus Masons

Currents such as these help explain the increasing discomfort of the Catholic Church about Masonry. In 1738 Pope Clement XII promulgated the bull *In eminenti*, excommunicating all Masons. The stated grounds were that Masonry fostered the association of persons of different religious faiths, which the pope evidently regarded as undesirable. Further reasons included the misuse of the oath of secrecy as well as "other just and reasonable motives known to us." (These are not specified.) Other documents from the period indicate that the church regarded Masonry as an enemy of Christendom, although it remains unclear why.[43]

At any rate, Clement's bull was reissued by his successor, Pope Benedict XIV, in 1751; further condemnations followed in 1786, 1789, and later. Although the church did not strictly enforce its ban on Freemasonry during those years, the opposition between the two would harden in the nineteenth century, when it would cost the church dearly. As in the American and French revolutions, Masons played a key role in the unification of Italy in the period between 1850 and 1871. Giuseppe Garibaldi, for example, one of its greatest leaders, was Grand Master of the Grand Orient Lodge of Italy. And it was the unification of Italy that finally took temporal power away from the church. In 1871, when the city of Rome voted to join the unified Italian nation, the papacy finally lost its hold on the region of central Italy that since medieval times it had ruled as the Papal States. All in all, then, the church may have been right to suspect the Freemasons.

We need not demonize Catholicism in order to appreciate the ideals that the Rosicrucians and their descendants have contributed to our civilization. The beginning of the *Fama* says that one goal of the coming age would be "that man might . . . understand his own nobleness and worth"[44] — an ideal that harks back to Pico della Mirandola, one of whose most famous works is *The Oration on the Dignity of Man*. Today all this may sound unremarkable, but in those days it was revolutionary. The Christianity of the Middle Ages was far more likely to emphasize the baseness of human nature than its "nobleness and worth" and to view church and king as better safeguards of

conscience than the individual himself. With the inevitable abuses and excep-
tions, the Rosicrucian legacy has helped realize this aim. Whoever they were,
whatever they knew or did not know, the Rosy Cross Brothers seemed to fore-
see a time when all human beings might live in dignity, self-respect, and, perhaps, self-government. We are, of course, not yet in such an age. But we may
be closer than we were four hundred years ago.

Adventurers and Visionaries

Although it has been called the Age of Reason, the eighteenth century was fascinated with occultism. Interest in the subject was so high in France just before the Revolution that the king's police found more useful informants in
astrologers and fortune-tellers than in the more conventional sources of
priests or doctors. The feverish Paris of the 1780s was much taken with an
Austrian doctor named Franz Anton Mesmer, who practiced "animal magnet-
ism," later known as "mesmerism." In Mesmer's view, illness was caused by
disruptions in the invisible life force, or "magnetic fluid"; by setting this right,
Mesmer believed he could cure practically any ailment. His success rate was
good but not flawless, eventually leading the fickle Parisian public to tire of
him. Even so, his legacy persists: a follower of his, the Marquis de Puységur,
would develop hypnotism as it is known today.[45]

The eighteenth century was also replete with exotic occult characters
whose names still carry resonance — Cagliostro, the Comte de St.-Germain.
About these men, who spun an aura of mystery about themselves, we know
very little, and we know even less that is reliable; often even their real names
are in question. They were magician-adventurers, descendants of the Renaissance magi living in a more tolerant — or more disenchanted — age,
when evidence of occult power could earn one a welcome among blasé aris-
tocrats.

The Comte de St.-Germain may have been a Sephardic Jew born in Portu-
gal in 1710; he may also have been a Transylvanian nobleman named Francis
Ragoczy. Wild rumors about him circulated — that he was centuries old, that
he lived on nothing but an elixir that he made himself, that he had invented
Freemasonry. He died in Germany in 1782 — but then was seen in Paris during the Revolution several years later.[46] To this day, as an "ascended master," he
remains a vivid presence for devotees of the New Age, a number of whom
claim to have had communications from him.

Count Cagliostro, who styled himself "the Grand Copt," was probably an Italian adventurer named Giuseppe Balsamo.[47] "About me," he declared, "many lies and nonsensical stories have been written, but the truth is known to no one at all." Certainly he made little effort to set the record straight. Most scholars believe he was born in Sicily in 1743, the son of a jeweler. Cagliostro claimed to have knowledge of the Elixir of Life, and made most of his living by selling remedies derived from it. He also devised an Egyptian Rite of Freemasonry that he promoted heavily in the 1770s and 1780s. (Some versions of his story say he was initiated into this rite by the Comte de St.-Germain.) Like Giordano Bruno, Cagliostro saw a return to the religion of ancient Egypt as the remedy for the sects and schisms of his era, which by this time had begun to afflict Freemasonry as well. Implicated (though not convicted) in the famous affair of the Queen's Necklace in 1785, in which a couple of adventurers swindled a French prelate over a fabulously expensive necklace supposedly intended for Marie Antoinette, Cagliostro never recovered either his reputation or his aplomb. In 1789, he visited Rome in a quixotic attempt to convert Pope Pius VI to his version of Freemasonry. Instead he soon found himself in a prison run by the Inquisition. He died there in 1795 — one of the Inquisition's last victims.

Another powerful figure, less pretentious but ultimately no less mystifying, was Emanuel Swedenborg (1688–1772), a Swedish philosopher and engineer who began to have elaborate visions of the unseen worlds when he was in his mid-fifties.[48] Swedenborg's visions, described in lengthy, often ponderous volumes ("In dry Latin he went on listing / The unaccountable last things," as Jorge Luis Borges would write of him), spoke of elaborate resemblances — or "correspondences" — between the celestial and the earthly realms.

Swedenborg's ideas fed the imaginations of artistic geniuses from William Blake to Honoré de Balzac to Charles Baudelaire. Blake spoke of using Swedenborgian themes in his poetry and art, contending that "the works of this visionary are well worthy [sic] the attention of Painters and Poets; they are foundations for grand things."[49] (Blake would later turn away from his master, as we'll see in chapter 9.) Baudelaire's celebrated sonnet "Correspondences," which speaks of resonances between invisible worlds and our own, was inspired by Swedenborg's thought; the poem would in turn inspire the entire Symbolist movement in art. In 1835 Balzac published an extremely curious "Swedenborgian" novel (as he described it) entitled *Seraphita*, which is set in the remotenesses of the Norwegian fjords and centers on a strange hermaphroditic being, a "Christian Buddha" known as Seraphitus/Seraphita. Swedenborg's writings helped convince Balzac of the reality of the spiritual dimension. Speaking of *Seraphita* in his 1842 introduction to *La comédie humaine*, Balzac invokes "the mystics, the disciples of St. John, and . . . those great thinkers who have established the spiritual world — the sphere in which are revealed the relations of God and man."[50] Swedenborg's ideas permeated Masonry as well, leading to the creation of Swedenborgian degrees in certain lodges.

It may seem odd that the Enlightenment and its aftermath, which textbooks portray as the high point of rationalism and skepticism, should have felt such an intense thirst for the esoteric. On a closer look, however, it is not so strange. The Enlightenment was an age when intellectual horizons were widening at an unprecedented pace. When such expansion is in the air, it is not easy — or, perhaps, desirable — to make fine distinctions between the "rational" and "irrational," the mystical and the practical. We can see an analogy in the California of the last fifty years. California is often the butt of jokes for its zany mysticism and its enthusiasm for the outlandish, but during exactly the same period it has also been the center of technological innovation in the United States and possibly the world. This is probably not mere coincidence. Rather it is that in certain times and places, the sense of what is possible begins to spontaneously expand. And precisely because it is expanding, the spirit of the time is uninterested in drawing arbitrary distinctions; the creative mind discovers unforeseen connections in many realms, which feed and inform each other. So it may have been in the Enlightenment. If nothing else, it might serve as a reminder that the dimensions of thought dismissed as dreamy and impractical have their own uses, and that practical applications might not be possible without them.

CHAPTER 8

The Gnostic Revival

In 1772, a doctor named A. Askew made a curious purchase in a London bookshop. A collector of old manuscripts, he bought a codex of unknown provenance, written in Coptic, the lineal descendant of ancient Egyptian. He asked a scholar named C. G. Woide to examine it. Woide gave it the name of *Pistis Sophia*, which is Greek for "Faith-Wisdom," and made a copy of it for himself. After Askew's death, his estate sold it to the British Museum for £10 (then a substantial sum), where it resides today.

The *Pistis Sophia*, a previously unknown Gnostic writing probably dating to the third century A.D., contains a lengthy description of how Pistis Sophia, "Faith-Wisdom," fell from her high position in the heavens and had to be redeemed through repentance. Apparently the text itself was believed to have magical power. As a result, no one in antiquity dared edit it. The scribes who transcribed it copied down everything they had before them, repeating whole passages verbatim. Even apart from this, the text is often tedious and repetitive.

Given all this, it's easy to see why the *Pistis Sophia* made no great impression when it first came to scholarly attention. Woide did not publish his copy, and the text did not see print until 1851, when it appeared accompanied by a translation into Latin done by a German scholar named M. G. Schwartze. Only in 1896 did it begin to receive widespread notice when the British scholar G. R. S. Mead brought out a translation in English.[1]

Nevertheless, Askew's purchase marks a turning point in the history of Gnosticism. Up to now, our story has focused on its descendants, sometimes direct, sometimes oblique, as they have made themselves felt in the currents of Western civilization. But in the nineteenth century, the climate changed radically. There would be more interest in directly examining the Gnostic texts that were coming to light and in trying to see what the Gnostics had said about themselves.

This transition stems from the birth of the critical approach toward scripture, which arose during the Enlightenment of the eighteenth century. The educated public, disgusted with the religious strife that had torn Europe apart for the previous two hundred years, began to lose faith in Christianity and to examine its origins more skeptically. Scholars came to suspect that the Gospels themselves might not be entirely composed of "Gospel truth" and started to try to tease out mythical or legendary elements from these books. Once this approach was under way, an obvious step was to look more closely at other texts that might cast light on the origins of Christianity.

This process continues to this day, and it still exerts an intense fascination. The fact that the question of Christian origins can neither be forgotten nor laid to rest suggests that no really satisfactory answer has been found. Any documents that could have cast some definitive light on them have probably long since been lost or destroyed. Even so, a great deal of material has come to our attention that suggests the history of Christianity was not what it was believed to be. The *Pistis Sophia* is an early example. *The Nag Hammadi Library*, which I discussed in chapter 1, is another, far more influential one.

The development of the critical method and of what Albert Schweitzer famously styled "the quest of the historical Jesus" is beyond the scope of this book. Nor is it the whole story. Just as crucially, during this period the Gnostics were invoked more and more as forgotten heroes rather than as heretics. This fact can be explained partly in terms of academic trends. In the nineteenth and twentieth centuries, the field of Christian origins came to be dominated by liberal scholars who found their investigations useful in undermining the claims of their conservative counterparts.[2] The German scholar Kurt Rudolph summarizes the views of the liberals when he writes, "The development of orthodoxy [in early Christianity] was a lengthy process, which did indeed build upon certain basic statements but grew out of a very manifold variety of early Christian thought and action. This entirely valid multiplicity, to which the Christian gnostic movement also belongs, was only declared to be heretical and unorthodox in the course of the discussion, and this was a disqualification which rested purely upon theological judgements."[3] Rudolph's words encapsulate the views of many if not most current scholars who are not fundamentalists.

But the Gnostic revival cannot be explained exclusively in terms of academic discoveries. If it had merely been a matter of scholarship, these insights would very likely have reached the public much later and in a much more muted form than they did. What brought the Gnostic heritage to widespread attention was the work of a number of esoteric practitioners who invoked the Gnostics as ancestors.

To mention this fact is to introduce some awkwardness into the discussion. Academic scholars tend to give the esotericists of the last two centuries only the most equivocal and grudging acknowledgment as part of the intellectual currents of our time. Wouter Hanegraaff, a Dutch scholar of esotericism, explains why. As he observes, modern scholars did not see investigation of Gnosticism as a threat to them; on the contrary, it was useful ammunition against the conservatives. But Hanegraaff goes on to say:

> With respect to modern esoteric traditions, the situation was differ-
> ent. Not only were these less distant [than classical Gnosticism] in a
> strictly chronological sense, they were also much closer in spirit. Hav-
> ing flowered in the same period which saw the emergence of modern
> science and rationality (and, as we now know, crucially involved in
> that emergence), they evidently touched upon the very roots of
> modernity itself. If gnosticism had traditionally been perceived as the
> enemy of Christendom . . . modern esotericism held a comparable
> position in relation to the newly-established modernist worldview. To
> the intellectual heirs of the Enlightenment, it appeared very much as
> gnosticism had appeared to the early Church Fathers: as a collection
> of superseded but potentially dangerous superstitions.[4]

Although Hanegraaff phrases this passage in the past tense, it would create hardly any distortion to recast these words in the present. Thus one runs the risk of straying past the bounds of intellectual respectability by portraying modern esoteric spirituality as a crucial factor in the Gnostic revival. But we have to run this risk if we are to be true to the facts.

Isis Unveiled

Chief among these esotericists was Helena Petrovna Blavatsky (1831–91). Mainstream intellectuals often deride Blavatsky as a generator of half-baked mystical claptrap and cheesy occult parlor tricks. But her role in the modern era is far more significant than that. As Christopher Bamford, a contemporary scholar, observes:

Although Madame Blavatsky is not yet counted with Marx, Freud, and Nietzsche among the "creators" of the twentieth century, that surely is her place — despite her wild eccentricity and almost willful freedom of spirit. Certainly there is no "alternative thinker" of our time, in no matter what field, whose accomplishment does not at some level rest on her strenuous effort. Behind the "New Age" — whether we think of Rudolf Steiner, Gurdjieff/Ouspensky, Peter Deunov, Schwaller de Lubicz, Krishnamurti or a host of other and apparently unrelated "spiritual" streams, from the "perennialism" of René Guénon to the magic traditions, the renewal of Pythagore-anism, Hermetism, and the Kabbalah, or the search for a synthesis between science and mysticism exemplified by such as Fritjof Capra, Rupert Sheldrake, Lyall Watson and others — behind all this lies Madame Blavatsky.[5]

Admittedly, Blavatsky's story is a strange one, and even sympathetic ob-servers have cast some doubt on many of its details. Helena Petrovna Hahn was born in Russia in 1831 to an aristocratic Russian family. As a child she im-mersed herself in occult literature in the library of her great-grandfather, Prince Paul Dolgoruki, a Freemason. Headstrong from her youth, she defied her family's wishes and married an elderly general, Nikifor Blavatsky, at the age of seventeen. They soon separated, although her husband continued to provide her with financial support for many years afterward.

The decisive moment in Blavatsky's life came on August 12, 1851 (her twen-tieth birthday), when she was in London in her father's company. According to her confidant, Countess Wachtmeister, "she was one day out walking when, to her astonishment, she saw a tall Hindu in the street with some Indian princes." She immediately recognized him as her teacher. The next day she saw the "tall Hindu" again in Hyde Park. He told her of a mission that he would give her, including the formation of what would become the Theosophical Society. In preparation, she would have to spend three years in Tibet. After some consultation with her father, she accepted the task and departed straightaway for India.[6]

The next twenty years of Blavatsky's life furnish a rich but confusing tale of travels and adventures in places from India to Egypt to the Americas. She even claimed to have fought alongside Garibaldi's army against papal forces in the Battle of Mentana of 1867, in which she was apparently wounded. But the mis-sion given her by the tall Hindu did not begin to materialize until 1873, when she met an American lawyer named Henry Steel Olcott. In New York in 1875, she and Olcott established the Theosophical Society, an organization that is still thriving worldwide today.

In 1877 Blavatsky (known as HPB to her associates) published her first major book, a massive exposition of occult thought called *Isis Unveiled*. The first edition sold out in nine days. It is a long, diffuse work, and its main theme is the main theme of Blavatsky's life and teaching — the "Secret Doctrine" that, she believed, went far back into prehistory and could still be found in the esoteric traditions of Asia and the West.

Blavatsky was the quintessential iconoclast. She could hardly resist making a jibe at conventional authority when the occasion arose, and there was much in the thought of her day that provided such opportunities. She lived at the zenith of Western triumphalism. In the late nineteenth century, a handful of European nations ruled most of the world, and these nations took it as self-evident truth that the "primitive" and "savage" peoples would come to accept the superiority of Western civilization, including its religion. Blavatsky stood this idea on its ear. "The only characteristic difference between modern Christianity and the old heathen faiths is the belief of the former in a personal devil and in hell," she contended.[7] For Blavatsky to insist, as she gleefully did, that conventional Christianity was a cumbersome heap of half-understood doctrines that were little better than superstition was shocking to much of the reading public — and thrilling to much of the rest.

For Blavatsky, what was true in the Christian faith was not the creeds and dogmas of the church, but the esoteric doctrine that had been taught in the beginning by the Gnostics and by their Jewish kin, the Kabbalists:

> If the Gnostics were destroyed, the Gnosis, based on the secret
> science of sciences, still lives. It is the earth which helps the woman
> and which is destined to open her mouth to swallow up medieval
> Christianity [cf. Rev. 12:1–16], the usurper and assassin of the great
> master's doctrine. The ancient Kabbala, the Gnosis or traditional
> secret knowledge, was never without its representatives in any age
> or country.[8]

For Blavatsky, in the West these representatives included not only the Gnostics and Kabbalists, but the Essenes, the Platonists and Neoplatonists, the Hermeticists, and the Templars. Much of what she was saying was not new. Previous authorities — including Ficino with his *aurea catena* — had asserted the continuity of this tradition. Others, such as Giordano Bruno, had contended that there was nothing special in the Christian revelation: it was in many ways an inferior and literalized version of truths that had been known for millennia. But it was Blavatsky who was the first to impress these ideas upon the general public.

Blavatsky is a crucial, though often overlooked, figure in the rehabilitation of Gnosticism. In her magnum opus *The Secret Doctrine*, published in 1888, she asserted that "each of the Gnostic sects was founded by an Initiate, while their tenets were based on the correct knowledge of the symbolism of every nation."[9] She had several reasons for emphasizing this claim. One, which we have glimpsed above, was to invoke the memory of the Gnostics in opposition to the dogmatic Christianity of the Catholic and Protestant churches of her day. Another, closely related, reason has to do with a subtler issue, about which Blavatsky writes:

> It requires *a lower order of creative angels* to "create" inhabited globes — especially ours — or to deal with matter on this earthly plane. The philosophical Gnostics were the first to think so, in the historical period, and to invent various systems upon this theory. Therefore in their schemes of Creation, one always finds their *Creators* occupying a place at the very foot of the ladder of spiritual Being. With them, those who created our earth and its mortals were placed on the very limit of *mayavi* [illusory] matter, and their followers were taught to think — to the great disgust of the Church Fathers — that for the creation of those wretched races, in a spiritual and moral sense, no high divinity could be made responsible, but only angels of a *low hierarchy*, to which class they relegated the Jewish God, Jehovah.[10]

She argues that the Gnostics held this figure of Jehovah in contempt because "he was a proud, ambitious, and impure spirit, who had abused his power by usurping the place of the *highest God*, though he was no better, and in some respects far worse than *his brethren Elohim*."[11] (By the term *Elohim*, which means "gods" in Hebrew, Blavatsky means the "angels of a low hierarchy.")

We have already glimpsed this controversy in discussing Origen in chapter 2. The Gnostics were saying that the God of the Old Testament was an inferior deity who was claiming to be the one true God. But he could not *be* the one true God, because, in Blavatsky's view, this "highest God" is beyond all conception or thought. Thus Jehovah, whom both she and many of the ancient Gnostics identified with the demiurge, was a usurper.

The controversy here is intricate and difficult to disentangle, but it's worth the effort. Blavatsky is invoking the Gnostic legacy to claim that the "secret doctrine," the essential esoteric teachings that underlie all religions, is universal. The claim of the Jews that they alone worshipped the one true God — a claim that the Christians took up afterward — was thus condemned as a piece of sectarian arrogance. (Blavatsky was always careful to distinguish exoteric Judaism from the esoteric Judaism of the Kabbalah, much as she distinguished the esoteric Christianity of the Gnostics from the conventional religion.) Exoteric Jews and Christians did not worship the one, true God, but merely another deity in the celestial hierarchy — and moreover one who had the arrogance to claim that he alone was God. Thus she tried to strip the Judeo-Christian tradition of its pretensions to a monopoly on spiritual truth.

With this method of attack, Blavatsky was doing nothing more than employing a time-honored tactic. If you are trying to discredit another religion, there are basically two options open to you: you can claim the others' gods are illusory or you can claim they are evil. Blavatsky used the second approach, suggesting the Judeo-Christian God was a usurper from the lower ranks of the cosmic hierarchy who was essentially identical to the Gnostic demiurge. Proto-orthodox Christianity had used the same approach in its long combat with Greco-Roman paganism: the gods of the old pantheon existed, the ancient Christians said, but they were really demons. As Paul wrote, "The things which the Gentiles sacrifice, they sacrifice to devils, and not to God" (1 Cor. 10:20).

Blavatsky invoked the Gnostics for other purposes as well. Her "secret doctrine," expressed in the teaching she called Theosophy, holds that there are seven levels to the human structure, of which the physical is merely the bottom story. (These seven levels are the *atman,* or Self; *buddhi,* or higher intellect; *manas,* or mind; *kama,* or desire; *linga sharira,* or etheric double; *prana,* or life force; and the physical body.)[12] To back up her views, Blavatsky cited the *Pistis Sophia.* "According to this extraordinary piece of religious literature — a true Gnostic fossil —" she wrote, "the human Entity is the septenary ray from the One, just as our school teaches." She then goes on to relate the teachings of the Gnostic text to seven levels as understood by Theosophy.[13]

In 1878–79, Blavatsky, together with Olcott, moved to India, which would mark a major shift in their orientation. *Isis Unveiled* is fundamentally a work about Western esotericism. After her stay in India, Theosophy was much more thoroughly suffused with Eastern wisdom — particularly the "esoteric Buddhism" that she said lay behind Buddhism and Hinduism in their familiar outward forms. *The Secret Doctrine* is her compendious statement of this wisdom. Consequently, most interpreters have seen Blavatsky's later period as an embrace of Eastern esoteric teachings as opposed to those of the West. In a strange but fascinating series of lectures delivered in 1893, the British esotericist C. G. Harrison even claimed that the American occult lodges, fearing Blavatsky's power and suspicious of her motives, had used magical operations to put her into a kind of "occult imprisonment," which Harrison described as "a kind of spiritual sleep characterized by fantastic visions." When she went to India, certain spiritual masters there helped her break out in return for pledges of her assistance in promoting the cause of the Eastern traditions. "To cut a long story short," Harrison sums up, "Madame Blavatsky emerged from 'prison' a Tibetan Buddhist and the prophetess of a new religion."[14]

Even if this account is true, the story is not so simple. If Blavatsky was a "Tibetan Buddhist," her version of this tradition bears little resemblance to any form of Tibetan Buddhism that has come to the West over the last generation. It is inaccurate to say that Blavatsky's Theosophy is "Eastern" in any simplistic sense. Scholars who have compared her teachings to those of Hinduism and Buddhism have seen as many, or more, influences from Western esotericism as from Eastern on her Theosophy; one scholar even asserts that her sevenfold breakdown of the human structure has no parallels in the East, despite her use of Sanskrit terms. In his exhaustive study of esoteric currents in the New Age, Wouter Hanegraaff concludes that "theosophy — although it has been instrumental in stimulating popular interest in Indian religions — is not only rooted in western esotericism, but has remained an essentially western movement."[15]

It is thus no coincidence that G. R. S. Mead (1863–1933), who first brought the Gnostics to the attention of the English-speaking public with his edition of the *Pistis Sophia* and his *Fragments of a Faith Forgotten*, was a close associate of Blavatsky's. He served as her personal secretary from 1889 to her death in 1891 and as editor of the theosophical journal *Lucifer*, which he renamed *The Theosophical Review*. Mead was not a scholar of the conventional sort: he did not maintain a hands-off approach to his topic, but produced his works on the Gnostics as a means of enabling readers to move toward gnosis for themselves. On the other hand, Mead's work was thorough, conscientious, and intelligent, and scholars today still refer to it with respect.

Mead was a seminal figure, and his works did a great deal to help revive interest in the Gnostics, not only directly, but through his influence on a figure who would become far better known than Mead himself: the Swiss psychiatrist C. G. Jung (1875–1961). Richard Noll, whose book *The Jung Cult* provides a highly critical yet often insightful examination of Jung's thought, writes: "Mead remains an enormous — but still unacknowledged — influence on Jung. Jung's personal library contains no fewer than eighteen different scholarly studies written by Mead, all published by the Theosophical Publishing Society. Many of these were volumes in the Theosophical Society's *Echoes from the Gnosis* series, and thus Mead was Jung's 'stepping-stone to higher things.'"[16] Eventually Jung made Mead's personal aquaintance and even traveled to London to visit him.

Jung and the *Seven Sermons*

C. G. Jung remains one of the most influential, and one of the most uncategorizable, thinkers in modern psychology. Unlike many of the people discussed in this book, Jung had an education that was thoroughly mainstream. He studied at some of the leading psychiatric institutions of his time, and early in his career he was adopted by Sigmund Freud as an heir apparent to the nascent psychoanalytic movement. Jung insisted that his work was scientific in nature — and to the extent that it was grounded in extensive clinical work with patients, this is true. And yet Jung was also a visionary, in some ways like Swedenborg or Boehme. Both as a clinician and as a visionary, Jung invoked the Gnostic heritage and was probably the single most powerful force in bringing it back to mass consciousness.

Jung's background and his relations with Freud have been so widely discussed that I don't need to go into them here, except to say that the two men parted company in 1912 partly over theoretical, partly over personal matters. The next few years proved a time of psychic upheaval for Jung. Protected from the ravages of World War I by his Swiss citizenship, he nonetheless came to a personal crisis that would define his life and work from that time forth. This crisis had powerful resonances with Gnosticism.

Jung's inner struggle reached its climax in 1916. "There was an ominous atmosphere all around me," he recollected in his memoirs. "I had the strange feeling that the air was filled with ghostly entities." One Sunday Jung heard his doorbell ring, although no one was there. "I was sitting near the doorbell, and not only heard but saw it moving. . . . The whole house was filled as if there were a crowd present, crammed full of spirits." They cried out in unison, "We have come back from Jerusalem where we found not what we sought."[17]

This experience inspired Jung's strangest work — a short testament called *Septem Sermones ad Mortuos*, or *Seven Sermons to the Dead*, "written by Basilides in Alexandria, the city where the East toucheth the West." We have already encountered Basilides as one of the greatest Gnostic teachers of the second century A.D. The name may have a double meaning, for, as Richard Noll suggests, "Jung is perhaps also hinting by this pseudonym that someone from Basel" — as Jung was — "has written this piece." Using the persona of this shadowy figure, "one of those great minds of the early Christian era which Christianity obliterated," as Jung put it, he sets down a myth very much like the Gnostic systems of antiquity.[18] He even uses some of Basilides' terms, speaking of the deity, for example, as Abraxas.

But the keynote appears in the book's first sentence, which echoes the utterance of the ghostly apparitions: "The dead came from Jerusalem, where they found not what they sought." Jerusalem — the holy city of the Abrahamic religions, the center of religious hope and aspiration for half the world. What did the dead fail to find there? Maybe it was spiritual experience. Mainstream Christianity has provided much doctrine and ethical guidance, but in offering genuine inner experience to the spiritually dead, it has fallen short. And so, in Jung's vision, the dead go to Basilides the Gnostic in Alexandria — the ancient center of mysticism and occultism — in search of something new. Jung seems to be saying that this was the situation in his day, as it may be in ours.

Looking back shortly before his death, Jung viewed this period as the pivotal point of his life. "All my works, all my creative activity has come from those initial fantasies and dreams which began in 1912."[19] From his own experiences and those of his patients, he came to regard dreams and fantasies as expressions of certain fundamental structures in the human mind, which Jung called "archetypes." These archetypes have their own reality, not necessarily in some external dimension, but as innate structures of our own minds.

Early in his career, Jung was struck by how much his patients' dreams resembled ancient myths. In one famous case, he tells of a schizophrenic patient who said "he could see an erect phallus on the sun. When he moved his head from side to side, he said, the sun's phallus moved with it, *and that was where the wind came from.*" Jung found a remarkably similar image in a liturgy of the Mithraic religion, a mystery cult of late antiquity (which he had in a translation by Mead). The Mithraic text reads, "And likewise the so-called tube, the origin of the ministering wind. For you will see hanging down from the disc of the sun something that looks like a tube." And yet, Jung noted, "the patient was a small business employee with no more than a secondary school education." Jung thus ruled out the possibility that the patient might have come across this image by actually reading this obscure text. Instead, the resemblance entailed "a mythological statement . . . coming alive again under circumstances which rule out any possibility of direct transmission." Jung went on to say:

> This observation was not an isolated case: it was manifestly not a question of inherited ideas, but of an inborn disposition to produce parallel thought-formations, or rather of identical psychic structures common to all men, which I later called the archetypes of the collective unconscious.[20]

Jung concluded that esoteric texts, such as those of the Gnostics and the alchemists, could cast light on these archetypes. He was particularly fascinated by the central Gnostic myth, which, in speaking of the journey from oblivion to knowledge, seemed to him to resemble the path a contemporary analytic patient had to take to reach the level of integrated self-knowledge that Jung called "individuation." "Between 1918 and 1926," he later recalled, "I . . . seriously studied the Gnostic writers, for they had been confronted with the primal world of the unconscious and had dealt with its contents," although, he adds, "it seems to me highly unlikely that they had a psychological conception of them."[21]

This last statement is important. Even many of Jung's most ardent followers forget how heavily he was influenced by Immanuel Kant. Kant taught that we as humans never experience reality directly, as it is in itself, but through innate structures in our minds that he called the "categories." For Kant, the categories included such basic modes of perceiving as time, space, quantity, and causation. Jung, for his part, saw them as the archetypes, which manifest in dream images, art, and religious symbols. In saying that the ancient Gnostics did not have a "psychological conception" of these images, Jung means that they probably took them as real entities rather than as images arising out of the structure of the psyche.

Jung did not want to take the final step of endowing these archetypes with an objective reality outside the psyche. "Revelation is an 'unveiling' of the depths of the human soul first and foremost, a 'laying bare'; hence it is an essentially psychological event, though this does not, of course, tell us what *else* it might be. That lies outside the province of science."[22] Jung believed that these images tell us much about the mind, but not necessarily about the world. Consequently, he tried to limit himself to giving psychological rather than religious or metaphysical interpretations to myths and dreams (although he did unavoidably stray into these areas as well).

To take a simple example, Jung connects the Gnostic demiurge with the "cosmogonic jester of primitive peoples."[23] A familiar example of the latter is Loki, the trickster god of the ancient Norse, whose pranks eventually bring about the end of the age in the Twilight of the Gods. In essence, Jung is saying, there is an archetype that puts things awry, that brings destruction and imperfection into the world. This principle exists in our own psyches; we live it through in our lives, in the mistakes we make, half-blindly, half-knowingly. The Norse personified it in Loki; the Gnostics perceived it as the demiurge — the deity who has created the misshapen world we inhabit, even though both the god and his world may exist only in the mechanism of our brains.

Jung drew much criticism from theologians such as Martin Buber, who accused him of being a Gnostic himself. Jung's reply is summed up in the postscript to a letter to Victor White, an English Dominican with whom Jung corresponded for many years. "I will send you an offprint of my answer to Buber, who has called me a Gnostic. He does not understand psychic reality."[24] By this statement Jung is saying that he is speaking solely of psychological truths, which were expressed in the myths of the Gnostics as they were in many other sources. As he writes elsewhere, "The archetypal motifs of the unconscious are the psychic source of Gnostic ideas, of delusional ideas (especially of the paranoid schizophrenic forms), of symbol-formation in dreams, and of active imagination in the course of an analytical treatment of neurosis."[25]

All this is to say that Jung refuses to commit himself to a belief in the figures of the Gnostic myths (or of any other myths). "The designation of my 'system' as 'Gnostic' is an invention of my theological critics," he contends. "I am not a philosopher, merely an empiricist."[26] This empiricism consisted of examining psychic images in religion and myth as well as in the dreams of his patients. He did not claim that his discoveries about the psyche necessarily led to any theological or metaphysical truths.

Such, at any rate, was Jung's official position. It fit in well with his Kantian orientation, which suggested to him that we can never know how the world is in itself; we can only know how it *appears* to us. On the other hand, Jung did stray into theological turf, most famously in an interview he gave at the very end of his life. When asked if he believed in God, he replied, "I don't need to believe. I know."[27] The echo of the dominant theme of the Gnostic legacy is very clear.

Jung was a profound and insightful thinker; nonetheless his perspective presents some difficulties. Beyond a certain point, we are unlikely to be satisfied with psychological explanations alone. We want answers that reveal how things actually are rather than merely saying how the mind works. Even if (as Kant and Jung seem to say) this is not possible, we still long for it.

To go farther along these lines would take us into an intricate and probably irresolvable philosophical discussion. Nonetheless, Jung made a tremendous contribution. In seeing esoteric texts and myths as having a *psychological* truth, he made it possible to read them afresh. One no longer had to accept them at a literal or even theological level to see that they had something powerful to say to the contemporary mind. Jung and his followers, such as the celebrated author and teacher Joseph Campbell, thus opened up the world of myth in a way that it had not been for centuries.

Existential Gnosticism

Jung's training may have been conventional and his influence has penetrated much further into the intellectual mainstream than Blavatsky's, but in many ways he, too, remains a marginal figure. As popular and influential as it is, Jungian psychology hovers on the margins of academic respectability; Jungian analysts receive accreditation not from universities but from the C. G. Jung Institute in Zurich or its affiliates. We're therefore left asking if and how the rediscovery of Gnosticism in a strictly academic context has fostered the Gnostic revival.

A key figure in this regard was Hans Jonas, a German scholar who published a seminal study entitled *Gnosis und spätantiker Geist* (Gnosis and the Spirit of Late Antiquity) in 1934. A later version, published in English as *The Gnostic Religion*, remains a standard introduction to the subject. Like Jung,

Jonas made it possible for twentieth-century readers to approach the Gnostics with fresh eyes, but Jonas did so from an existentialist perspective.

The word *existentialism* on the printed page is likely to make one's eyes glaze over. In brief, existentialism is an attempt to deal with an abstruse philosophical question: what is the difference between a thing as it is in itself (its *essence*, to use philosophical jargon) and a thing as it manifests in the world (its *existence*)? Existential philosophers, such as Jean-Paul Sartre, generally hold that things — including human beings — have no fixed, determinate nature. Existence precedes essence: we make ourselves up as we go along. (Older philosophers, such as Aristotle and Aquinas, had believed the opposite.)[28]

As abstract as it is, this idea has radical implications. In the first place, if it is true, it means that human beings are free: having nothing that we are at the core, we are free to make anything of ourselves. In the second place, if (as many of the existentialists assumed) there is no God who has created our essences, then we are ultimately alone in a universe that is absurd. And this leads to the common picture of existentialism, a term that for most people will probably evoke a mood rather than a concept — images of European intellectuals drinking endless cups of espresso in a room thick with smoke, morosely contemplating the isolation of man in an alien world.

The Gnostics agreed that the world we see is meaningless. As Jonas expresses their views, "Whoever has created the world, man does not owe him allegiance, nor respect to his work. . . . The world . . . is the product, and even the embodiment, of the negative of *knowledge*."[29] Jonas also noted that the Gnostics used images that evoke Martin Heidegger, the existentialist philosopher who most influenced him. Heidegger spoke of *Geworfenheit*, or "thrownness," the fact that we find ourselves in a world we did not create, not knowing how we got here. Jonas quotes Gnostic texts that have a similar flavor, for example, "Save us out of the darkness of this world into which we have been thrown."[30]

But Jonas also saw a radical cleft between the ancient Gnostics and the modern existentialists. He quotes a famous formula of Valentinus: "What makes us free is the knowledge of who we were, what we have become; where we were, where we have been thrown; whereto we speed, wherefrom we are redeemed; what is birth and what is rebirth." Superficially there is a resemblance here too, for both Gnostics and existentialists speak of freedom. But the Gnostics say that "though thrown into temporality, we had an origin in eternity, and so also have an aim in eternity. This places the innercosmic nihilism of the Gnosis against a metaphysical background which is entirely absent from its modern counterpart."[31] In other words, for the Gnostics, there is a world beyond this one, to which we belong and by which we are redeemed. Existentialism offers no such hope.

Jonas ends *The Gnostic Religion* by arguing that existentialism leads to nihilism, a step that he himself does not want to take. He does not want to agree that there is an indissoluble gulf between the universe and the human being, which condemns the latter to an "isolated selfhood"; nor, however, does he want to take the opposite step — concluding that humanity and the universe (or nature) are one, which, he says, "would abolish the idea of man as man." He concludes his book with the nebulous hope that some middle ground might be found between these two extremes. And yet, being an intellectual of the early twentieth century, he cannot bring himself to accept the Gnostics' attempt at a middle ground: the idea that there might be a higher dimension of reality that gives meaning to existence.

Whatever we conclude about Jonas's philosophical conclusions, he did make it possible for thinkers in his own time to explore their affinities with the Gnostics. Like Jung, although coming from a totally different orientation, he took a major step in rehabilitating the Gnostic legacy. He enabled the intellectuals of the midcentury, infatuated with existentialism, to see the Gnostics as kindred and possibly as forebears.

Gnosis as a Mass Phenomenon

All the sources I have discussed above prepared the ground for widespread fascination with Gnosticism. But it did not come to mass awareness until the late 1970s, with the publication of two quite different books.

The first was a one-volume edition of the Nag Hammadi scriptures in English that appeared in 1977. Edited and translated by the most eminent experts in the field, *The Nag Hammadi Library in English* immediately commanded attention as the century's most important publication of early Christian texts. Today, nearly thirty years later, scholars are still grappling with the insights it provides into the foundations of the faith.

Not all of these texts, of course, attracted a widespread readership. Even those who profess devotion to Gnosticism have probably not read, say, the *Allogenes* or the *Trimorphic Protennoia*. In fact, of all the Nag Hammadi texts, there is one, above all others, that has captured the attention of a large public:

the *Gospel of Thomas*. Since *Thomas* first appeared in English in a complete form (the Nag Hammadi texts provided the first intact version, although fragments had been known previously), it has been published in innumerable editions, each having its own slant on this enigmatic Gospel. One recent example, *The Gnostic Gospel of St. Thomas*, consists of brief homilies on each verse. The author begins his work by stating:

> There is a need for a new gospel, a Gospel of the Cosmic Christ —
> one that restores the mystical and magical elements to Christianity,
> and yet more, one that teaches a path of conscious evolution toward
> the enlightenment that Yeshua Messiah (Jesus Christ) himself em-
> bodied — the state of Christ-consciousness. . . .
>   At the heart of this inner tradition is a spiritual art of conscious
> living and conscious dying, and the development of consciousness
> beyond the body, through which the initiated is able to consciously
> enter into higher planes of existence, both in this life and the afterlife.
> The result is a conscious continuity of self-awareness throughout all
> states of existence, including what we call "death," so that, in effect,
> there is no more death and no more need for physical incarnation.
> When we speak of enlightenment and liberation, self-realization or
> Christ-consciousness, this is ultimately what is meant.[32]

The author of this work, "Tau Malachi," says he was introduced to these teachings by an elderly gentleman named Tau Elijah, who was heir to "a lineage of mystical or Gnostic Christians." ("Tau," the last letter of the Hebrew alphabet, apparently denotes a master.) "Through personal or individual conversations, group discourse, instruction on methods of mystical prayer, prophetic meditation, rituals of initiation, and such, he imparted the teachings of the tradition," writes Tau Malachi, who traces this tradition to the Rosicrucian Enlightenment of the seventeenth century and, farther back, to the Kabbalah and the *merkavah* mysticism of the first century. For him, Christian Gnosticism is "a weave of Gnosticism, Kabbalah, and Rosicrucian philosophy."[33]

Whether or not Tau Malachi's tradition really has such ancient roots, it is interesting to see the *Gospel of Thomas* tied to many of the esoteric traditions we have explored here. The passage above gives the flavor of many teachings that invoke the Gnostic heritage today and suggests how New Age teachers have traced a full circle back to some of the earliest Christian texts. By emphasizing "Christ-consciousness" as opposed to faith in the historical Jesus, they attempt to ground spiritual experience in an individual's own being rather than in a deity who is envisaged as radically "other."

The second extremely influential work on the rediscovery of Gnosticism was published in 1979 by Elaine Pagels, then a professor at Barnard College. (Today she is at Princeton.) Entitled *The Gnostic Gospels*, it was greeted with resounding acclaim. More than any other book, possibly even *The Nag Hammadi Library* itself, it has brought the ancient Gnostics to the general reading public.

Pagels was not the first scholar to write a general introduction to Gnosticism; Hans Jonas did, as we've just seen. What distinguished her book was not only its unusually deft handling of the material, but also the revolutionary conclusions she drew from it. She characterized the struggle between the Gnostics and the proto-orthodox church as a dispute not only over doctrine but over the nature of authority itself. The nascent orthodox church stressed the literal fact of the Resurrection. Why did it do this, when the New Testament accounts (as vague as they are) leave room for many interpretations? Pagels replies:

> I suggest that we cannot answer this question adequately as long as we consider the doctrine only in terms of its religious content. But when we examine its practical effect on the Christian movement, we can see, paradoxically, that the doctrine of bodily resurrection also serves an essential *political* function: it legitimizes the authority of certain men who claim to exercise leadership over the churches as the successors of the apostle Peter.[34]

Pagels argues that the Gnostic approach — whereby spiritual authority rests on direct inner experience — was too destabilizing for the early orthodox church, which sought to rest its power on the rock of apostolic succession. Moreover, Pagels notes, many early Christian groups recognized the spiritual authority of women. This was in part because of the influence of Mary Magdalene, who, according to the most ancient traditions, was the first one to see the risen Christ. But as the male bishops began to appropriate spiritual authority more and more for themselves, Mary Magdalene became an increasingly obscure figure. As we saw in chapter 1, she was eventually equated with the woman taken in adultery. Some sources tried to present Peter, the embodiment of apostolic authority, as the first witness to the Resurrection.

The Gnostic Gospels is in many ways a brilliant book, but many brilliant books capture the public imagination belatedly or not at all. Pagels's work was so successful largely because its conclusions fit in extraordinarily well with the needs of the time. In the late 1970s, the New Age was becoming a mass phenomenon, and one of the central themes of the New Age as a whole is the need for personal spiritual experience (as the Gnostics believed) rather than trusting in dogma or authority.[35] Moreover, in saying that many of the earliest Christians did not believe in a literal, physical Resurrection, Pagels spoke to many modern readers who have difficulty with the more miraculous aspects of Jesus's story. In addition, her claim that women possessed spiritual authority in early Christianity struck a resonant chord at a time when feminism was coming to the fore in American society. Finally, in seeing political rather than spiritual motives for many developments in the early church, her approach was extremely modern — or rather, postmodern. Until recently, scholars of Christian origins saw the struggles between proto-orthodoxy and various "heresies" purely as matters of religious truth. It is part of the legacy of the contemporary "hermeneutics of suspicion" that we find it more plausible today to view such disputes in terms of political and organizational power. For all these reasons, Pagels' book galvanized public attention, as have her later works, *Adam, Eve, and the Serpent* and *Beyond Belief*.

The Gnostic Church

This discussion of the popularity of Gnosticism should not create a false impression. Interest may be wide, but it's often shallow. Innumerable people may be drawn to Gnosticism in a vague way, but there are extraordinarily few who pursue it beyond the point of reading one or two books. A few more may explore Gnosticism in study groups in the more liberal churches, where participants may read *The Gospel of Thomas* or one of Pagels's works.[36] But the number of people who have explored these subjects in any depth is, in relation to the general population, infinitesimal. I don't know of any attempt to reckon the number of people in the United States who may identify with Gnosticism in some fashion or another: it's hard to imagine that they exceed 100,000, and they may well number much less.

Nevertheless, there are some organizations that call themselves Gnostic. One is La Asociación Gnóstica, founded by a Colombia-born teacher named Victor Rodriguez, also known as Samael Aun Weor (1917–77). The association espouses a "Gnosis of the Cosmic Christ" that "synthesizes the practise of all Yogas, Lodges, orders, religions, schools, systems, and so on."[37] It has a far-flung following in Latin America.

There are also some Gnostic churches, which usually trace their lineage back to the "wandering bishops" of the nineteenth century.[38] These bishops owe their status to a peculiarity in Roman Catholic doctrine, first espoused by Augustine and held by the church to this day: a bishop's ordination remains valid even if he leaves the church or differs with it on doctrinal matters. In 1724, one wandering bishop founded the Dutch Old Catholics as the result of one such split. Another lineage is the succession of the Church of South India, which traces itself back to the apostle Thomas, who, legend has it, traveled there after Christ's death and whose bones are said to be interred at Madras.

In nineteenth-century France, these two lineages converged to create the Église Gnostique, a Gnostic organization centered in France.[39] The founder was a man named Jules-Benoit Doinel du Val Michel, who in 1890 had a mystical experience that impelled him to reestablish the Gnostic church. He collected a number of prominent French esotericists together in this venture, notably Gérard Encausse, better known by his pen name "Papus," who had founded an esoteric society called the Martinist Order. (Martinism, a Christian esoteric tradition that is better known in the French world than in the English-speaking countries, takes its name from the eighteenth-century occultists Martinez de Pasqually and Louis-Claude de St.-Martin, to whom Papus traced its origins.)

The intricate spiritual genealogy of the various Gnostic churches is of interest chiefly to devotees and specialists. In the United States today, the most prominent spokesman for a renascent Gnosticism is Stephan A. Hoeller, a Hungarian esotericist who heads the Ecclesia Gnostica in Hollywood, California. Hoeller's works connect Gnosticism with both Blavatsky's Theosophy and Jung's thought.[40]

Hoeller has consecrated other bishops, including Rosamonde Miller, who leads the Ecclesia Gnostica Mysteriorum in Palo Alto, California. In addition to her lineage as a Gnostic bishop, Miller claims to be part of a society that was passed down from the earliest days of Christianity called the Order of Mary Magdalene. For most of its history, this society, centered in the south of France, was kept secret and restricted to women, but in more recent times it has made itself public (in a limited fashion) and now accepts men as well.

One member of Miller's congregation, Jay Kinney, a cartoonist, writer, and former editor of *Co-Evolution Quarterly* (later *Whole Earth Review)*, was inspired by his experiences with the Ecclesia and his long-standing interest in esotericism to start *Gnosis*, a quarterly journal of the Western inner traditions. The first issue of *Gnosis* was published in 1985. I began to write for it in 1986 and became editor in 1990, a position I held until the magazine stopped publication in 1999, chiefly because of long-standing financial pressures. Although *Gnosis* was never meant to serve as a house organ for a renascent Gnostic movement — its intent was to provide a respectful and wide-ranging forum for the Western esoteric traditions as a whole — many writers connected with this movement wrote for the publication at some point. Stephan Hoeller, for example, was a frequent contributor and had a column in the magazine for several years.

These groups and individuals all represent the most direct and obvious continuation of the Gnostic legacy in the present day. It would be possible to trace it much farther in any number of directions, since traditions ranging from Kabbalah to alchemy to Eastern Orthodox mysticism owe their roots to this heritage. But it would hardly be possible to do justice to these subjects in a book of this length; moreover, I've covered much of this ground in my previous books, *Hidden Wisdom* and *Inner Christianity*. It remains now to talk about the Gnostic influence in a form that has been less direct but more pervasive — in its echoes in modern literature and philosophy.

CHAPTER 9

Gnosis and Modernity

Tracing the tendrils of the Gnostic legacy is a delicate task. In one respect, it seems to surface everywhere — in the "great heresy" of the Manichaeans and Cathars, in the occult philosophy of the Renaissance and the modern era, in Hermetic currents and Neoplatonic speculations. Jung, for example, believed that alchemy was a direct continuation of Gnosticism, an assertion that he based on the similarities of their symbolism but which most scholars would hesitate to confirm.

Sorting out actual Gnostic influences becomes more difficult the closer we come to the present. This is partly because Gnosticism has been alleged to influence a dizzyingly wide panoply of writers and philosophers. A partial list would include Hegel, Blake, Goethe, Schelling, Schleiermacher, Emerson, Melville, Byron, Shelley, Yeats, Hesse, Albert Schweitzer, Toynbee, Tillich, Heidegger, Conrad, Simone Weil, Wallace Stevens, Doris Lessing, Isaac Bashevis Singer, Walker Percy, Jack Kerouac, and Thomas Pynchon. Unfortunately, even those who advocate such connections often end up admitting that these figures never read the Gnostics or were influenced by them in any meaningful way. One critic who labels the novelist Doris Lessing as Gnostic concedes, "I know of no evidence that Lessing is directly familiar with Gnosticism."[1]

Nonetheless, there are leading figures whose names can be meaningfully invoked in terms of a Gnostic legacy. Some of them seem to have drawn inspiration from the Gnostic heritage. Others have seen it from a more orthodox perspective — as an arch-heresy that is responsible for all the evils of our time.

In both cases, one theme that constantly recurs is revolt. While revolt against established authority — whether viewed in political or cosmic terms — has been a given in human life for millennia, revolt as a conscious, reasoned

stance arose only in the eighteenth century, as an outgrowth of the Enlightenment and the Romantic movement. Revolt was often characterized in political
terms — against the remnants of feudalism and theocracy that bourgeois Europe was sweeping away — but in metaphysical terms as well. The nineteenth-century French poet Charles Baudelaire evokes this spirit in his poem
"Abel et Caïn," which ends, "Race of Cain, to heaven climb / And onto earth
throw down God!"[2] It's easy to see in this an echo of the Gnostic theme of revolt against the demiurge and the powers of "spiritual wickedness in high
places." It would be much harder to claim that Baudelaire was thinking of the
Gnostics when he wrote these words. Nevertheless, such resonances suggest
why many critics and thinkers have seen Gnostic themes in the art and philosophy of modernity, whether or not they are really present.

In this chapter, I will look at some of the figures in the last two centuries
who can reasonably be connected to the ideas of the classical Gnostic systems
of the early centuries A.D., either because they have invoked them or because
they clearly bear the traces of this influence. I'll also examine some twentieth-
century thinkers who have invoked the Gnostic legacy in the context of
revolt — viewing it in both positive and negative ways.

Blake and the Demiurge of Cognition

One of the first figures in modern times to bear the Gnostic stamp was the
English artist and poet William Blake (1757–1827). He is often connected with
the Romantic revolt against political oppression — the subtitle of his best-
known biography styles him "Prophet against Empire" — but the metaphysical aspect of his work is at least as important, and possibly more so.[3]

Blake, who was apprenticed at age fourteen to an engraver, was largely self-
taught in regard to book learning. Not having gone through the usual mills of
schools and universities, like many self-educated men he shaped his learning
to his own character. His primary influences included Swedenborg (the only
church he is known ever to have attended was a newly formed Swedenborgian
congregation in London), Plato (which he read in the highly influential translations of Thomas Taylor), Hermeticism, and the Gnostics. None of the Gnostic texts had been published in Blake's day; the Askew Codex, for example, still
lay in the British Museum untranslated. But Blake did have access to ecclesiastical histories, which, although prejudiced against the Gnostics, would have
given him a reasonably clear idea of their basic beliefs.

The first man to connect Blake with Gnosticism was his contemporary Henry Crabb Robinson, who recounts a conversation with him:

> The eloquent descriptions of Nature in Wordsworth's poems were conclusive proof of atheism, for whoever believes in nature, said B[lake], disbelieves in God. For Nature is the work of the Devil. On my obtaining from him the declaration that the Bible was the word of God, I referred to the commencement of *Genesis* — "In the beginning God created the Heaven & the Earth." But I gained nothing by this, for I was triumphantly told that this God was not Jehovah, but the Elohim, & the doctrine of the Gnostics repeated with sufficient consistency to silence one so unlearned as myself.[4]

Here Blake seems to be alluding to an ancient esoteric teaching: the idea that these two names of God, *YHWH*, or "Jehovah," and *Elohim*, refer to two different aspects of the deity, or even to two different deities. Jehovah would be presumably be the true, high God; Elohim would be the Gnostic demiurge.

The British poet and Blake scholar Kathleen Raine suggests that the idea of the demiurge may lie behind Blake's most famous poem, "The Tyger."

> Tyger Tyger, burning bright,
> In the forests of the night;
> What immortal hand or eye
> Could frame thy fearful symmetry? . . .
> Did he who made the Lamb make thee?[5]

The poem is asking whether the same God who made the innocent lamb could also have fashioned the fierce tiger. If they were made by different Gods, then one is the God of eternity, the other, the demiurge of temporality. But as Raine goes on to say, in the end "Blake . . . left his question unanswered not because he did not know the answer or was in doubt, but because the answer is itself a no and yes of such depth and complexity."[6]

The figure in Blake's personal pantheon that most resembles the demiurge is Urizen, who may well have been partly inspired by the Gnostic figure. The name *Urizen* appears to be a multivalent pun, evoking the Greek verb *ourizein*, meaning "to limit"; also the English "horizon"; "your reason"; and "your eyes." And Urizen is connected both to perception and to limitation.

Blake tells the story of Urizen's birth in *The Book of Urizen*, published by Blake himself in 1794 and illustrated with his own designs. The work is vivid in the violence and tension of its language:

> Lo, a shadow of horror is risen
> In eternity! Unknown, unprolific!
> Self-clos'd, all-repelling: what Demon
> Hath form'd this abominable void
> This soul-shudd'ring vacuum? — Some said
> "It is Urizen."[7]

The visual imagery is equally violent and tortured. Many of the images depict an ancient, white-haired figure — which is particularly striking since the beginning of this book describes the *birth* of Urizen; indeed it takes its structure from the stages of fetal development as they were understood in Blake's day.[8] In essence, *The Book of Urizen* is a book about the gestation and birth of an old man.

Who is Urizen? He seems to embody perception bound by the senses, hence images of freezing and confinement characterize his development: "Bones of solidness froze / Over all his nerves of joy." Blake seems to be saying that the development of sensation as we know it — sensation divorced from what elsewhere he calls "Imagination" — incarcerates the individual in an aged and frozen tomb. It is the ancient motif of *Soma sema*, "The body is a tomb," recast in Blake's inimitable words and images.

All of this would be of merely literary interest except for one thing. Blake is making a connection that was only implicit in the Gnostic myths. The demiurge is not a figure of theology; he is not a god hovering in some stratosphere above our heads; he personifies the structure of our own consciousness and experience. Possibly the ancient Gnostics understood as much, but if so, it is difficult to tell. Their insights are embedded in the cryptic myths of their scriptures; the mask of allegory never drops. Blake, by contrast, lets down the mask enough to make his fundamental point clear. Or perhaps it is rather that we are close enough to him in time and culture to hear his message more clearly.

In any case, Blake's insight brings the message of the Gnostics far closer to home. We are unlikely to take much interest in half-forgotten myths of remote and improbable gods. But when we realize that these gods sit within our own brains, serving as nets and filters over our encounter with reality, we may be more inclined to pay attention.

Blake's solution to this imprisonment lies in what he calls "Imagination." This is far from idle fantasy. "Forms must be apprehended by Sense or the Eye of Imagination. Man is All Imagination," he writes.[9] As his use of the term *Forms* suggests, in speaking of Imagination, Blake is pointing toward the higher states of cognition as described by Plato and his followers, which can perceive the eternal Ideas or Forms directly, without the mediation of the senses. For Blake, Imagination in this sense is as much as a matter of perception — perception, that is, of a higher reality — as it is of creation.

Blake's embrace of revolt is perhaps most apparent in *The Marriage of Heaven and Hell*. One section of this work is entitled "The Voice of the Devil," who sets out a list of "errors" caused by "all Bibles, or sacred codes." The devil contends that Milton wrote so well about Satan in his *Paradise Lost* "because he was a true Poet and of the Devils party without knowing it."[10] Blake also reviles his old master Swedenborg, whose writings, he contends, are a "recapitulation of all superficial opinions," because "he conversed with Angels who are all religious, & conversed not with Devils who hate all religion, for he was incapable thro' his conceited notions."[11]

Blake's contentions raise a question that may already have occurred to the reader at some point in this narrative: if the god who created the world we see is evil, does that mean the devil is good? For their part, the ancient Gnostics did not conceive of a personal devil apart from the demiurge and his minions; their hierarchies of evil were already well stocked. But for certain Gnostic sects, such as the Naasenes and the Ophites, the serpent of Genesis — which conventional Christianity equates with the devil — was a sacred symbol. (This attitude is echoed in the names of the sects: *nahash* means "serpent" in Hebrew, as *ophis* does in Greek.) The serpent was an emissary of the true God, sent to awaken Adam and Eve to the knowledge of their actual identity as gods, a knowledge that had been hidden by the craft of the demiurge.

How, then, did the Gnostics regard good and evil? Many of the ancient Gnostics tried to invert conventional moral values. One sect, known as the Carpocratians, allegedly held that the only way to escape the false world of the demiurge was to discharge one's debt to him by experiencing everything in this world, both evil and good. This would of course involve exhausting all the possibilities of wicked acts as well as beneficent ones.[12] Such a stance helps suggest why so many modern thinkers equate Gnosticism with revolt.

Blake's answer to this age-old issue appears in the title of *The Marriage of Heaven and Hell*. He is not advocating an embrace of evil but a reconciliation of opposites. "Opposition is true Friendship," he writes. Toward the end of the book he relates a "Memorable Fancy" (the title is a jab at Swedenborg, who inserted "Memorable Relations" of his encounters with spirits into his theological writings) in which an angel embraces a devil who appears as a flame of fire, "& he was consumed and arose as Elijah," the greatest of the prophets.[13]

Voegelin's Modern Heresies

Like the other modern thinkers we have examined, Blake thus regards the Gnostic legacy as a metaphysical and psychological issue — but not exclusively, for Blake's work has a strongly political element as well. In *America: A Prophecy*, published in 1793, he even portrays Urizen as the embodiment of political tyranny, "weeping in dismal howling" at his defeat by the rebellious Americans.[14] For Blake, the liberation of consciousness is intimately connected with freedom from oppression by kings and nobles and clergymen.

Blake is not the only figure to associate the Gnostic legacy with revolt in a political sense. One of the most ambitious attempts to connect gnosis with revolt was made by Eric Voegelin (1901–85) — although Voegelin's stance is the opposite of Blake's. A German-born political philosopher educated in Vienna, Voegelin emigrated to the United States in 1938 and became a doyen of the conservative movement among American intellectuals of the late twentieth century. At the time of his death he was a senior fellow of the Hoover Institution at Stanford University.

Voegelin saw himself as a traditionalist, a champion of the core values of Christianity and Western civilization against various usurpers and underminers. Prime among these, he believed, were the Gnostics. Voegelin's criticism of the ancient Gnostics is a common one: that their religion was world-denying and solipsistic, seeking an escape from reality in a transcendent realm. Certainly there is some truth to this claim as far as it goes. Viewing the world as radically flawed, the Gnostics saw the remedy not in fixing the world but in liberating the mind from it.

And yet Voegelin took his critique to a peculiar extreme. In the end he went so far as to characterize virtually all of the forces that threatened Western civilization as "Gnostic." In his 1952 book *The New Science of Politics*, he contends:

> Modern gnosticism has not spent its drive. On the contrary, in the
> variant of Marxism it is expanding its area of influence prodigiously
> in Asia, while other variants of gnosticism, such as progressivism,

positivism, and scientism, are penetrating into other areas under the title of "Westernization" and development of backward countries.[15]

The reader who has followed the argument of this book so far is apt to be amazed by Voegelin's claim. What on earth could Gnosticism and its descendants have to do with "progressivism, positivism, and scientism"? And both Marxists and Gnostics would indignantly deny any connection with one another.

Voegelin admits that the ancient Gnostics bore little resemblance to these movements; his objection to the original Gnostics (a familiar one) lies in their embrace of transcendent knowledge rather than faith. The turning point, he contends, came in the High Middle Ages, with the twelfth-century visionary Joachim of Fiore, who proclaimed the imminent coming of the Age of the Holy Spirit. (It is not clear what makes Joachim a Gnostic, since he was a Catholic monk.) The advent of this age would be marked by the coming of a leader, a *Dux ex Babylone*, a "leader out of Babylon," who would arrive no later than 1260. With Joachim and his heirs (who, for Voegelin, include practically all the movements of modernity), the Christian eschaton, that is, the Last Judgment, was taken out of God's hands and placed into those of man.

This "fallacious immanentization of the Christian eschaton" — to use Voegelin's barbarous phraseology — has spawned all the evils of the modern world. The idea that there is meaning and progress in history has begotten progressivism; the idea that humans can better themselves through technical knowledge begets scientism. The Joachimite *Dux ex Babylone* eventually becomes the Nazi führer. Joachim also taught "the brotherhood of autonomous persons": "This third age of Joachim, by virtue of its new descent of the spirit, will transform men into members of the new realm without sacramental mediation or grace."[16] In Voegelin's view, this monstrous doctrine would later mutate into Puritanism and still later into Marxism. Voegelin goes so far as to say that "totalitarianism, defined as the existential rule of Gnostic activists, is the end form of progressive civilization."[17]

Such arguments, however strange, are certainly ingenious. It requires some intellectual adroitness to blame Gnosticism for its world-denial and then to turn around and blame it for movements such as Marxism and scientism, which deny the existence of anything *apart from* this world. For Voegelin, Gnosticism becomes a catchall term that embraces everything in Western civilization that he hates and fears.

Despite these absurdities, one must be fair to Voegelin. He does hit upon one of the main causes of the tragedies of the twentieth century: the tendency to sacrifice the present to some imagined future, whether it is the dictatorship of the proletariat or the Thousand-Year Reich. In this respect, Voegelin is right: over the last hundred years the future has become a Moloch demanding constant human immolation. But he is wrong in foisting the blame on the Gnostics, who did not see enormous hope for this world either in the present or in any foreseeable future. For the Gnostic, history does not offer salvation; the Gnostic could say, with Joyce's Stephen Dedalus, "History is a nightmare from which I am trying to awake."[18]

We would only have to make a slight adjustment in Voegelin's terminology to bring it far more in line with actuality. This tendency to drug oneself with the future is the legacy not of Gnosticism but of apocalyptic. Apocalyptic is the genre of religious writing that predicts an imminent end to the world, with God rewarding the virtuous and visiting wrath on the wicked. Its earliest instances can be found in the Old Testament, notably the Book of Daniel, written in the second century B.C.; in the New Testament, the most prominent example is Revelation. Joachim of Fiore stands firmly in this tradition.

In essence, apocalyptic writing tries to deal with two contradictory ideas: the presumed justice of God and the continued injustice of the world, usually envisaged as the suffering of God's people (for example, the children of Israel or the Church of Christ). Since it's impossible to reconcile these two ideas under ordinary circumstances, it becomes necessary to invoke supernatural ones: God will soon come to set it right. The fact that no such divine intervention has appeared in the 2,300 years of the apocalyptic genre — even though this redemptive act is always supposed to be just around the corner — has not kept people from continuing to believe in it. Throughout much of history, the hope of such an apocalypse has been held out to the masses in order to get them to put up with the inequities of the present. Updating Marx, one could say that apocalypse is the opium of the people.

Taking Voegelin's view further, we can see that modern secular society has transmuted the apocalyptic eschaton into a bright, shiny future as envisaged by scientism and progressivism, as well as by communism and fascism. And the crimes enacted in the names of these ideologies are justified by the hope of the wonders they would soon bring. Voegelin is right to see these delusions as causes of many of the woes of recent history. But again, he is wrong in connecting them with the Gnostics, who put little emphasis on apocalypticism of any kind. On the contrary: apocalyptic thought has been a standby of mainstream Christianity ever since Paul composed 1 Thessalonians — the first book in the New Testament to have been written — to explain to his disciples what would happen to Christians who died before Jesus came back.

I have dwelled on Voegelin's ideas at such length for several reasons. In the first place, as we'll soon see, his capricious use of the word *Gnosticism* opened the field for other misleading applications of the term, leading some to question whether it still has any meaning. In the second place, his thought has shaped contemporary conservative thought to an extraordinary degree. It is hard to imagine an issue of *National Review* that does not bear some marks of Voegelin's influence. This in turn has had a great impact on contemporary politics. Voegelin's followers seem to conclude that any attempt at social justice is "immanentizing the eschaton" or holding out some false hope of the perfectibility of man; trying to better the human condition is at best mistaken and at worst sacrilegious. Such quietism is convenient for the powers that be, which helps explain the munificent funding that has been lavished on conservative institutes and think tanks over the last generation.

It's curious to think that Voegelin's disciples imagine they are fighting Gnosticism. If they do, perhaps the fight will be more than ideological. In 1952, Voegelin wrote:

> A democratic government is not supposed to become an accomplice
> in its own overthrow by letting Gnostic movements grow prodi-
> giously in the shelter of a muddy interpretation of civil rights; and if
> through inadvertence such a movement has grown to the danger
> point of capturing existential representation by the famous "legal-
> ity" of popular elections, a democratic government is not supposed
> to bow to the "will of the people" but to put down the danger by
> force, and, if necessary, to break the letter of the constitution to save
> its spirit.[19]

No doubt he conceived these words in light of the struggles of his own day. Nonetheless, they evoke some reflections about the present political scene. While civilizations notoriously pitch back and forth in their progress, it would be peculiar if the West were to return to the spirit of the Middle Ages in putting down the "danger" of imagined Gnosticism by force.

Bloom's Gnostic Misreading

Another influential intellectual who appears to misunderstand the Gnostic legacy is the literary critic Harold Bloom. Unlike Voegelin, who paints Gnosticism as an arch-heresy that is behind all our civilization's ills, Bloom is sympathetic to the tradition. He even describes himself as a Gnostic:

> I return to personal history to explain how I understand Gnosis and Gnosticism. You don't have to be Jewish to be oppressed by the enormity of the German slaughter of European Jewry, but if you have lost your four grandparents and most of your uncles, aunts, and cousins in the Holocaust, then you will be a touch more sensitive to the normative Judaic, Christian, and Muslim teachings that God is both all-powerful and benign. That gives one a God who tolerated the Holocaust, and such a God is simply intolerable, since he must be either crazy or irresponsible if his benign omnipotence was compatible with the death camps.[20]

Bloom's own Gnosticism seems to arise out of a world-weariness, a pessimism about the world we see. This is certainly compatible with the classical Gnostic systems. But Bloom takes his view of Gnosticism in a strange direction. Curiously, he says it lies at the core of "the American Religion":

> Mormons and Southern Baptists call themselves Christians, but like most Americans they are closer to ancient Gnostics than to early Christians. . . . [M]ost American Methodists, Roman Catholics, and even Jews and Muslims are more Gnostic than normative in their deepest and unwariest beliefs. The American Religion is pervasive and overwhelming, however it is masked, and even our secularists, indeed even our professed atheists, are more Gnostic than humanist in their ultimate presuppositions.[21]

What could this mean? What could classical Gnosticism — often gloomy and exclusivist — possibly have to do with the relentless egalitarianism and manufactured cheer of American culture, much less with evangelical Christianity, which shuns the Gnostic legacy with abhorrence? Bloom might have stressed the blind dualism of fundamentalist and secularist thought, like Frederic Spiegelberg, who saw the black-and-white thinking of the mass mind as a degenerate form of Manichaeism. But Bloom doesn't go in that direction.

Instead he finds the answer in the "transcendent self" that, he says, lies at the core of all American religious belief and expression:

> The American finds God in herself or himself, but only after finding
> the freedom to know God by experiencing a total inward solitude.
> Freedom, in a very special sense, is the preparation without which
> God will not allow himself to be revealed in the self. And this free-
> dom is itself double; the spark or spirit must know itself to be free
> both of other selves and of the created world.[22]

Stating Bloom's views more plainly, we could say that for him, the American search for self-realization and self-fulfillment is identical to the Gnostic desire for liberation of the "true I." And the American quest for freedom parallels the Gnostic urge to rise above the shackles of the world. At the same time, there must be something wrong with this equation if it enables Bloom to style Mormons, Methodists, and Southern Baptists as Gnostics. Like Voegelin's definition, it renders the term all but meaningless.

Bloom's perspective comes into clearer focus if we see it in the light of his literary theory. He is best known for his theory of *misreading* — the idea that each great poet carves out his own imaginative universe by misreading (that is to say, misunderstanding) his predecessors. It was only by misreading Milton, for example, that Blake could conclude that he was "of the Devil's party." Using such a theory, Bloom might conclude that the "American Religion" is a misreading of Gnosticism.

This makes sense up to a point, but then we are thrown back on the fact that the Gnostics were hardly invoked at all by any of the major religious or philosophical thinkers of America. Blake could misread Milton, but in order to do so he had to have read him. There is little evidence that any of the formative figures of American thought cared at all about the Gnostics. As Bloom notes, there *are* Gnostic echoes in American literature — most famously Melville's Captain Ahab, who sees Moby-Dick as a "mask" for "an outrageous strength . . . an inscrutable malice" in the universe, against which man must strike.[23] But to find echoes is not quite the same as showing that Gnosticism lies at the core of the American Religion.

As for Bloom's equation of the transcendent self of the "American Religion" with the "true I" of the Gnostics, this too is fascinating but implausible. The Gnostics saw their quest in light of the liberation of the consciousness from materiality itself; freedom for self-realization in this world had little to do with their aspirations. The American transcendent self resembles more the self as imagined by the existentialists — radically free to make what it wants of itself in a vast but meaningless universe. Bloom would have been closer to the truth if he had said that at its core the American Religion was existentialism.

All this said, Bloom is a subtle thinker, and it may be oversimplistic to say he is missing the point of Gnosticism or American religion or both. A clue to his intention may appear in a statement he makes about a passage from Ronald Knox's *Enthusiasm*, a heresiology from the mid-twentieth century: "I think that this is quite wrong, and needs to be very strongly misread if it is to be of use."[24] This remark suggests that for Bloom, misreading may be intentional. Could he be engaging in a deliberate misreading of the American religious sensibility? It's possible. If so, his misreadings are in some ways more profound than the insights of lesser minds; they are a hall of mirrors, forcing us to see familiar things from many unfamiliar angles all at once. Even so, it's unlikely that Bloom will convince many people that Methodists or Southern Baptists are really Gnostics at heart.

The Black Iron Prison

Bloom and Voegelin, both men of monumental erudition, misread the Gnostic legacy, one inadvertently, the other perhaps deliberately. It's strange, then, that the man who understood Gnosticism most profoundly in recent times was a science-fiction writer with comparatively little education (he was a dropout from the University of California at Berkeley). And yet there are few individuals of any era who felt the Gnostic worldview so viscerally and expressed it so well.

On February 3, 1974, Philip K. Dick found himself in terrible pain from a root canal procedure. He phoned his pharmacy to have a prescription delivered for a painkiller his surgeon had prescribed. When it arrived, it triggered an experience that would overturn his view of reality.

At the door with the prescription was a girl wearing a gold pendant with a fish. As Dick recounted:

> For some reason I was hypnotized by the gleaming golden fish: I forgot my pain, forgot the medication, forgot why the girl was there. I just kept staring at the fish sign.
> "What does that mean?" I asked her.
> The girl touched the glimmering golden fish with her hand and

said, "This is a sign worn by the early Christians." She then gave me
the package of medication.[25]

In that instant, what Dick described as a "beam of pink light" flashed at
him directly from the necklace. "I remembered who I was and where I was. In
an instant, in the twinkling of an eye, it all came back to me. And not only
could I remember it but I could see it. The girl was a secret Christian and so
was I. We lived in fear of detection by the Romans. We had to communicate in
cryptic signs. She had just told me all this, and it was true."

Like most such moments of revelation, this one would change Dick's life.
After that, he believed he was in touch with what he called VALIS — an
acronym for "Vast Active Living Intelligence System." The experience inspired
him to start a journal filled with mystical and theological speculation that he
called the *Exegesis*. By the time of his death in 1982, the *Exegesis* would amount
to two million words and would fill two file drawers. Of it he later said, "I suppose that all the secrets of the universe lay in it somewhere amid the rubble."
He would also expand upon his insights in his three last novels: *VALIS, The
Divine Invasion*, and *The Transmigration of Timothy Archer*.

Dick, who is best known as author of the novels that inspired the films
Blade Runner and *Minority Report*, frequently wrote about tears and rends in
the space-time continuum. In 1977 he wrote an essay entitled "If You Find
This World Bad, You Should See Some of the Others," and one of his most admired books, *The Man in the High Tower*, tells of an alternate reality in which
the Axis won the Second World War. His VALIS-inspired vision led him to see
world history in the same terms. The period from 70 A.D. (when the Romans
sacked the temple in Jerusalem) to 1974 was a mass hallucination: a strange,
false blip in time fabricated by spiritual powers of wickedness. The flash of the
pink beam (and the fall of Richard Nixon in the same year) served as a signal
to Dick that this fake era of history had come to an end and that real time had
begun to tick again.

Dick's *Exegesis* includes a capsule summary of Gnosticism, written in a
hasty, disjointed style:

WE ARE IN THE BLACK IRON PRISON

1. Ignorance (Occlusion) keeps us unaware of this & hence
   unresisting prisoners.

2. But the Savior (Valis) is here, discorporate; he restores our memory & gives us knowledge of our true situation (1) and nature (4).

3. Our real nature — forgotten but not lost — is that of being fallen or captured bits of the Godhead, whom the Savior restores to the Godhead. His nature — the Savior's — and ours is identical; we are him and he is us.

4. He breaks the power which this world of determinism & suffering has over us.

5. The Creator of this world is irrational & wars against the Savior who camouflages himself & his presence here. He is an invader.

6. Thus it is a secret that he is here, nor do we recognize the irrationality of this world & its frauds: that it lies to us.

7. We must balk against this world (more specifically against its irrationality) in order to align ourselves with the Savior.

8. It is us & the Savior vs. this irrational world.

9. To a degree, this world is irreal, counterfeit, esp. time.

Here, in Dick's jagged notes, is a capsule summary of the worldview of the Gnostics thousands of years ago. The world is a trap, constructed by the irrational "Creator of this world" to imprison us, the "fallen bits" of the true Godhead. The Savior — Christ, VALIS — has launched a divine invasion of this defective, "irreal" cosmos to help us break out.

Dick describes his views of the universe most clearly and concisely in a 1978 essay entitled "Cosmogony and Cosmology."[26] Citing Jacob Boehme, who used a similar term, he refers to the ultimate source of everything as the *Urgrund*, or "primordial ground." This Urgrund has "'created' (actually only projected) our reality as a sort of mirror or image of its maker, so that the maker can obtain thereby an objective standpoint to comprehend its own self." Dick calls this "image" the "artifact" and identifies it with the Gnostic demiurge. But "the artifact is unaware that it is an artifact; it is oblivious to the existence of the Urgrund . . . , and imagines itself to be God, the only real God."

Acting on its own, the artifact creates a version of reality, which reflects the Urgrund, although defectively. The history of the universe is nothing more than a process by which the artifact becomes more and more like its creator "until finally that reality is a correct analog, truly, of the Urgrund itself." At that point the Urgrund will absorb the reality the artifact has made, and "the artifact or demiurge will be destroyed."

The artifact thus is not exactly evil, since through its processes it is leading us humans to the Urgrund; on the other hand, it *is* ruthless and mechanical. Moreover, "the servant has become the master and is, perhaps, very strong." Dick's 1974 vision led him to believe that the Urgrund was trying to bring the drama to an end by launching a "divine invasion," which is "a subtle invasion, taking place in stealth," because if the artifact knew of this interference, it "would step up its cruelty to a maximum degree."[27]

The coming of Christ was part of this invasion by stealth. Knowledge of these truths was preserved by "the true, hidden, persecuted Christian Church, working through the centuries underground, with direct ties to the esoteric oral traditions, gnosis, and techniques dating back to Christ."[28] Dick believed that he, like the girl with the golden fish, had been part of this early persecuted church; his experience with the pink beam had awakened his memory to this truth.

What was the source of Dick's strange experiences? The readiest answer is schizophrenia or some other mental disorder. Dick himself wondered about this possibility:

> I saw Valis outside me modulating reality. Ah; but that was a projection (cf. Jung). Projection explains it. . . . It was my own mind that I was seeing external to me. I traveled down to the phylogenic (collective) unconscious. God had nothing to do with it. Right?
>
> Then what about the messenger who comes in time and bilks the retribution machine by withholding from it the bill of particulars against you? Is the messenger an archetype of the collective unconscious? And the AI voice [Artificial Intelligence voice — Dick's name for the hypnagogic voice he heard frequently in 1974–75 and intermittently thereafter until his death]; that is my anima?[29]

In the end, madness is not an entirely plausible explanation for Dick's visions. Mental disorder usually causes dysfunction: the sufferer is less able to deal with ordinary reality. Dick's experience was the opposite. The intelligence behind the pink light "immediately set about setting my affairs in order. It fired my agent and my publisher. It remargined my typewriter. . . . My wife was impressed by the fact that, because of the tremendous pressure this mind put on people in my business, I made quite a lot of money very rapidly. We began to get checks for thousands of dollars that was owed me, which the mind was conscious existed in New York but which had never been coughed up."[30]

If we want to account for Dick's experiences in conventional terms, the direction lies probably not in madness but in psychedelics, which he had used periodically over the years. The pink beam revelation certainly resembles an LSD trip; soon afterward Dick had an eight-hour vision of thousands of colored graphics resembling "the nonobjective paintings of Kandinsky and Klee."[31] It would be too easy to write off Dick's vision as a glorified LSD flashback, but his experiences with the drug may have primed his consciousness for this experience in some indeterminable way.

On a larger scale, widespread psychedelic experimentation in the 1960s and 1970s no doubt helped prepare the ground for a revival of the Gnostic vision. In their book, *The Psychedelic Experience*, Timothy Leary, Ralph Metzner, and Richard Alpert (Ram Dass) point out that certain types of LSD visions make the tripper aware that "he is involved in a cosmic television show which has no more substantiality than the images on his TV picture tube."[32] The conclusions one draws from this insight will vary depending on one's experience. If it is positive, the tripper may decide that the universe is *lila*, the cosmic dance envisaged by Hindu sages. If the experience looks threatening, one may decide that the cosmos is an evil charade enacted by a demiurge. Even apart from all this, anyone who has experimented with LSD has probably had to face the stupefying realization that an infinitesimal amount of chemical change in the brain (LSD is taken in micrograms, not milligrams) can alter one's sense of reality so deeply.

This, perhaps, leads us to the heart of the matter. Such reflections dovetail with other currents in psychology and philosophy that point in the same direction. Most of these see the cosmic deception in cognitive and psychological rather than theological terms: the demiurge resides in our brains.

The father of these insights was Immanuel Kant, who, as I've already noted, contended that we don't experience the world directly, as it is, but through the filters of certain modes of experience that he called the "categories," which include time, space, and causality. Not every philosopher has accepted Kant's theory, but every philosopher since his time has had to deal with the disconcerting possibility that the world is not exactly as we imagine it, that even the most fundamental elements of reality may be the constructs of our own minds. Advances in cognitive psychology have fed this suspicion by showing us how much our perceptions are conditioned by our sensory apparatus.

More recently, the virtual-reality craze in the 1990s fed hopes (and fears) that we would soon be able to immerse ourselves in totally convincing if totally fictitious realities. In the late 1990s, these ideas penetrated into mass culture through films like *ExistenZ, The Truman Show,* and *The Matrix.*

Free Your Mind

Of these films, *The Matrix,* produced by the Wachowski brothers and released in 1999, has undoubtedly left the greatest impact. The film's plot is well known by now. Neo (played by Keanu Reeves) is a young man working in a respectable software company by day; by night he is a computer hacker. He is about to be apprehended by government agents when he is rescued by a group of "terrorists" led by the mysterious Morpheus (played by Laurence Fishburne). Morpheus provides him with a surprising revelation: that the world Neo knows, the world of apparent solidity, is nothing more than the construction of the Matrix, a grid of virtual reality that keeps humans in a state of somnolence while their enemies, a sophisticated race of androids, use their bodies as a source of renewable energy. The action of the film (and its sequels, *The Matrix Reloaded* and *The Matrix Revolutions*) pits Neo, Morpheus, and their comrades against the androids and their "agents" — especially Neo's archenemy, Agent Smith — both in the virtual world of the Matrix and in the real world, a burnt-out dystopian earth situated some centuries in the future.

The Matrix has evoked a wide range of interpretations. Philosophy professors lecturing at the time of the movie's release found their students raising their hands and saying that Plato's cave or similar philosophical concepts were "just like *The Matrix*."[33] As usual, people see what they want to see. Marxists view the film as an allegory of humans trying to escape a mindless and exploitative capitalism. For existentialists, it is a drama in which individuals free themselves from "inauthenticity" into the bleak but radically free "authenticity" of the human condition. For Buddhists, it speaks of liberation from *samsara,* or illusion; conventional Christians see Neo as a type of Christ.

It's not surprising, then, that some observers find a Gnostic thread in *The Matrix,* although when asked in an interview, "Have you ever been told *The Matrix* has Gnostic overtones?" the Wachowski brothers equivocally replied, "Do you consider that a good thing?"[34] At any rate, the parallels are easy to see. Neo is "saved" not through faith but through a secret knowledge that liberates his consciousness and also reveals the ultimate nature of the reality he has believed in up to now. Before Neo makes the choice that frees him from bondage to the Matrix, Morpheus exhorts him, "Free your mind." Even his name in the Matrix — Thomas Anderson — has Gnostic connotations for some, who take "Anderson" as being derived from the Greek *andros*, "of man," so that Neo is the "Son of Man." And his first name, Thomas, is that of the apostle who is most closely connected with gnosis.

On the other hand, there are differences as well. Illumination gives the Gnostic entry into a world beyond pain and suffering, whereas the reality into which Neo is liberated is even more dismal than the late twentieth-century America replicated in the delusory realm of the Matrix. Moreover, as one commentator points out:

> The only character who expresses anything close to true Gnosticism is, ironically, Agent Smith — the truly disembodied mind who is forced to take on physical form and interact in the simulated physical world within the Matrix. As he says to Morpheus: "I can taste your stink and every time I do, I fear that I've somehow been infected by it." He is desperate to return to a pure state of disembodied existence, just as any true Gnostic would. Yet he is the embodiment of the enemy.[35]

All in all, then, it is probably most sensible to take *The Matrix* as a combination of themes — Gnostic, Buddhist, conventional Christian, existentialist, Marxist, and others — that have been recast into a unique whole. But the film does raise one issue that has surfaced both in Gnosticism and elsewhere: why should the demiurge and the archons bother to keep humanity in bondage?

In *The Matrix*, the answer is clear: as a source of renewable energy. At one point in the film, Morpheus says, "What is the Matrix? Control. The Matrix is a computer-generated dream-world built to keep us under control in order to change a human being into *this*" — and he holds up a Duracell coppertop battery. Previously another character had even addressed Neo as "Coppertop."[36]

Strikingly, this idea echoes the teachings of some ancient Gnostics. The ancient heresiologist Epiphanius reports: "They [the Gnostics] say that the soul is the food of the Archons and Powers without which they cannot live, because she is of the dew from above and gives them strength."[37]

This idea appears in other contexts as well. Michael Harner, an expert on shamanism, describes an experience he underwent while using the South American psychedelic ayahuasca. In his vision he sees "large, shiny, black creatures with stubby pterodactyl-like wings and huge whale-like bodies" who explain to him "how they created life on the planet" in order to hide from extraterrestrial enemies. "I learned that the dragon-like creatures were thus inside of all forms of life, including man." Harner adds, "In retrospect one could say they were almost like DNA, although at the time, 1961, I knew nothing of DNA." Amusingly, he describes his experience to a missionary couple, who find in it an astonishing parallel to the "serpent" of Revelation 12. Later he tells a shaman the same story. The shaman laughs and says of the reptilian beings, "Oh, they're always saying that. But they are only the Masters of Outer Darkness."[38]

The spiritual teacher G. I. Gurdjieff (1866?–1949) expressed a similar idea when he said that "everything living on the earth, people, animals, plants, is food for the moon." In Gurdjieff's view (which he said represented an ancient and previously unrevealed esoteric teaching), the moon is not a dead planet, but a planet that is "growing and developing" and which "will, possibly, attain the same level as the earth." Organic life, including humanity, exists so that its vibrations can feed the moon. Spiritual liberation consists in freeing oneself from the influences of the moon.[39]

It would be easy to dismiss Harner's and Gurdjieff's views — or those of Epiphanius's Gnostics — with the ease with which we step back from a viewing of *The Matrix*. And yet for all their outlandishness they seem to represent an intuition of a profound truth: that human beings are the product of vast cosmic forces whose nature and purpose we do not entirely understand. We may regard them as benign, malevolent, or indifferent, or, with modern science, we may regard them as utterly unconscious and random. But behind it all is the awareness that they are not necessarily, or primarily, our servants. We may be theirs.

The worldview of the modern West is often said to have begun with Descartes, that erstwhile Rosicrucian; indeed it is often called the Cartesian worldview in his honor. It's interesting to go back and see where Descartes begins his philosophical speculations. In his *Meditations*, he starts by supposing that there is "not a true God, who is the sovereign source of truth, but some evil demon, no less cunning and deceiving than powerful, who has used all his artifice to deceive me. I will suppose that the heavens, the air, the earth, colours, shapes, sounds and all external things that we see, are only illusions and deceptions which he uses to take me in."[40] Descartes was probably not thinking of the Gnostic demiurge here, but his "evil demon" sounds remarkably similar.

In the end, Descartes rejected this supposition. Yet the great scientific enterprise that he launched has pushed us closer toward it. Like Blake, we are more and more aware that our experience is conditioned and constrained by the limits of our nervous systems. Like Michael Harner, we may sense that the "serpent" of Genesis may be akin to our own DNA. While few would agree that we are misled by some conscious malevolence, it is scarcely more reassuring to consider that the cunning and deceiving demon may be embedded in the structure of our bodies and minds.

The Ego and the Demiurge

Who or what, then, is the demiurge? To say it is embedded in our nervous systems, even in our DNA, is to say anything and nothing. And yet we seem haunted by the idea that the fundamental problem with the world lies within *us*. Otherwise we would not invest so much time and energy in trying to fix ourselves.

Of recent attempts to address this conundrum, among the most powerful is *A Course in Miracles*. It was begun in 1965, when a New York psychologist named Helen Schucman heard an inner voice telling her it would dictate "a course in miracles" and that she should take notes. She complied (with some reluctance), and over the next several years took down material that would amount to some 1,200 printed pages, including a text, a workbook containing 365 daily lessons, and a manual for teachers.

The *Course* was first published in 1975 and since then has sold more than a million and a half copies. Despite this grassroots success, the *Course* has been given short shrift by conventional theologians and spiritual leaders. But then the circumstances of its transmission make it unlikely that the *Course* would be accepted in conventional circles, since the voice that dictated the material to Helen Schucman claimed to be that of Jesus Christ correcting two thousand years of misrepresentation of his teaching.

Even if we grant that transmission of this kind (usually known as "channeling") is possible, there's no way of proving this assertion true or false: to use the language of the philosopher Karl Popper, it is not "falsifiable." It can't be checked against the conventional or even the apocryphal Gospels, since most modern scholars agree that these contain much material that probably does not go back to Jesus himself. There are no other sources for the life and teachings of Christ that are any more reliable.

In the end, the *Course* has to be taken at face value, on the strength of its ideas alone. It restates many themes of the Gnostic legacy. Indeed one of the barriers to its acceptance arises from its echoes of the ancient Gnosis. We see these most clearly in its attitude toward the visible world, which, the *Course* asserts, is not real and was not created by God: "There is no world! This is the central thought the course attempts to teach."[41]

According to the *Course*, the world we see, the physical world of suffering and loss and change, is the result of a primordial separation from God — or rather, a *belief* that separation from God is possible. "Into eternity, where all is one, there crept a tiny, mad idea, at which the Son of God remembered not to laugh. In his forgetting did the thought become a serious idea, and possible of both accomplishment and real effects."[42]

This "tiny, mad idea" is what the *Course* calls the ego — the stance the fallen Son of God (which is each of us) takes in his deluded belief that he can exist apart from the Father. The apparently "real effects" include the physical world and the body itself, the "hero of the dream."

So far the ideas seem to echo those of classical Gnosticism as well as the great dualist heresy. But the *Course* takes these premises to a very different conclusion. If God did not create the meaningless world we see, if there is no ultimate reality to the body, then the only appropriate response is to look past these illusions. It's no coincidence that the *Course* speaks of laughing at the "tiny, mad idea" of separation. The *Course* also teaches that the only sane response to any form of madness in the world is to forgive it.

A Course in Miracles thus takes one of the central precepts of the Gospels — forgiveness — and elevates it to a status that it does not have and cannot have in mainstream Christianity. If, as the latter teaches, the world does have a genuine ontological reality, then the evil in it is also real. Forgiveness then becomes a kind of favor bestowed upon the unworthy, an attitude that the *Course* material calls "forgiveness-to-destroy." By contrast, the *Course* teaches the undoing of the illusory phenomenal world by literally overlooking it, by seeing past its appearances to what the *Course* calls the "real world" underneath. This "real world" does not exist in some millennial future; it is present now, in the "holy instant."

The *Course*'s approach to the ego (its name for the illusory sense of a separated self) also reformulates the Gnostic heritage in a radical way. Originally the Gnostics seem to have seen the demiurge as a real entity who generated the world. Later echoes of this heritage, notably Blake's, have focused on the cognitive aspect of this myth: the demiurge, Urizen, is a mythic portrayal of the limits our own brains and sense organs have imposed upon experience. The *Course* combines these two approaches. The demiurge — what the *Course* calls the ego — is not a god apart from ourselves; it does not exist in some spiritual stratosphere; it is the embodiment of our own desire to exist apart from God.

> This fragment of your mind is such a tiny part of [the universe] that, could you but appreciate the whole, you would see instantly that it is like the smallest sunbeam to the sun, or like the faintest ripple on the surface of the ocean. In its amazing arrogance, this tiny sunbeam has decided it is the sun; this almost imperceptible ripple hails itself as the ocean. Think how alone and frightened is this little thought, this infinitesimal illusion, holding itself apart against the universe. The sun becomes the sunbeam's "enemy" that would devour it, and the ocean terrifies the little ripple and wants to swallow it.
>
> Yet neither sun nor ocean is even aware of all this strange and meaningless activity. They merely continue, unaware that they are feared and hated by a tiny segment of themselves. Even that segment is not lost to them, for it could not survive apart from them. And what it thinks it is in no way changes its total dependence on them for being. Its whole existence still remains in them. Without the sun the sunbeam would be gone; the ripple without the ocean would be inconceivable.[43]

This passage echoes a section of the Gnostic *Apocryphon of John* that describes the demiurge Ialdabaoth: "And he is impious in his madness which is in him. For he said, 'I am God and there is no other God beside me,' for he is ignorant of his strength, the place from which he had come."[44] Possibly the author of the *Apocryphon* had a meaning in mind similar to that in the *Course*, which, using the language and thought of his time, he expressed in mythic terms. Because this ancient text speaks only symbolically, we will probably never know. In any case, the *Course*, whether it was written by Jesus Christ, Helen Schucman, or some other being, restates some of the profoundest themes of the Gnostic legacy in a fresh and remarkably self-consistent way. That may be one of the chief sources of its appeal.

Secrets of *The Da Vinci Code*

Of all the books that touch on the Gnostic legacy, by far the most successful has been Dan Brown's thriller, *The Da Vinci Code*, which has sold 25 million copies worldwide since it first appeared in April 2003. At this writing, it is being made into a feature film starring Tom Hanks.[45]

As even the sketchiest outline of its plot suggests, *The Da Vinci Code* is a thriller. It begins with a curator at the Louvre who is imperfectly murdered by an albino monk and realizes he has fifteen minutes to live. In the time remaining to him, the dying curator scrawls a series of enigmatic clues to his fate on his body and on artworks in the museum. These clues draw the curator's granddaughter Sophie, along with a Harvard cryptographer named Robert Langdon, into an elaborate adventure to solve the crime and, incidentally, to unveil the best-kept secret of the past two thousand years.

The Da Vinci Code overflows with last-minute escapes, high-tech surveillance, ruthless thugs, and sinister conspiracies at the highest circles of power. None of these devices — which by now have gone past cliché and at this point simply form part of the vocabulary of the genre — accounts for the astounding success of *The Da Vinci Code*. Even unsophisticated readers complain of its cardboard characters and its improbable plot. The book's popularity can only be explained by its subject matter. The crime and its solution have nothing to do with drug rings, underworld lords, or political chicaneries. Instead they involve the Catholic Church, a reactionary Catholic organization called Opus Dei, a mysterious secret society called the Priory of Sion, and the quest for the Holy Grail — not to mention Mary Magdalene and Jesus Christ himself.

During the frantic chases and close escapes of *The Da Vinci Code*, the hero and heroine unearth an astonishing revelation: Jesus Christ was not celibate. In fact, following standard practice for Jewish men then and now, he was married. His wife was Mary Magdalene, and their offspring survived to form the bloodline of the Merovingian dynasty, which ruled France from the fifth through the eighth centuries. The Catholic Church, with its horror of anything that might connect the feminine with the divine, did its best to repress this fact, but it was always preserved underground. During the Crusades, the secret was entrusted to the Knights Templar, who used it to blackmail the Catholic Church into granting the Templars virtually limitless power. The church bided its time, however, and managed to suppress the Templars in the fourteenth century. At this point the secret was passed on to the Priory of

Sion, an order that numbered among its leaders Isaac Newton, Victor Hugo, and of course Leonardo da Vinci. The Priory guards it up to the present (or at least up to the time of the novel), intending, perhaps, to reveal the truth to the world in the current era.

These themes make the novel's success much easier to understand. The Templars, the Priory of Sion, the Catholic Church, and Mary Magdalene are all proven sales draws. So, of course, is Jesus himself. Newsmagazines such as *Time* and *U.S. News & World Report*, finding that issues featuring Jesus outsell practically all others, constantly put the Carpenter of Nazareth on their covers, usually to announce amazing new "facts" about his life that turn out not to be news at all. So it was a brilliant stroke on Dan Brown's part to take these themes and offer them in the easy-to-swallow form of a suspense novel.

The Da Vinci Code is a work of fiction, and Brown would be within his rights to have made up every last detail in it, but much of the material in his book is based on alleged fact. The story about the sacred bloodline of Jesus and Mary Magdalene — as well as its preservation in the Merovingian dynasty — is taken from the bestseller *Holy Blood, Holy Grail* by Richard Leigh, Henry Lincoln, and Michael Baigent. The Priory of Sion exists, or has existed, as does Opus Dei (which has publicly protested its portrayal in the novel).[46] So it would be interesting to see how much factuality there is in *The Da Vinci Code*. As usual, the truth is both more interesting and more complicated than a novel can make it appear.

A careful reading of the book suggests that Brown has, as he claims, done a considerable amount of research. Unfortunately, his research is often wrong. He seems, for example, to endorse a claim by one of his characters that "the Bible, as we know it today, was collated by the pagan Roman emperor Constantine the Great."[47]

There is no truth to this assertion. The Old Testament canon was established by Jewish sages in a process that culminated in the two councils of Jamnia in 90 and 118 A.D., two centuries before Constantine. And while the final canon of the New Testament was not set until the fourth century, when Constantine lived, there is no evidence that the emperor set it. It *is* true that the first list of the twenty-seven books of the New Testament now recognized as canonical appears in a letter of the fourth-century Church Father Athanasius the Great. Moreover, Athanasius's views on the Trinity had prevailed at the Council of Nicaea in 325, which Constantine had convened. But this is far from saying that the emperor "collated" the Bible as we know it today.

Brown also says that Mary Magdalene was a descendant of the "House of Benjamin," and that Jesus's marriage to her created a dynastic link between the House of Benjamin and the House of David.[48] It is certainly correct to say that Jesus belonged, or was believed to belong, to the House of David; the Gospels frequently allude to this lineage. But there was no House of Benjamin. Benjamin was a small tribe that had been incorporated into the biblical kingdom of Judah, and though Saul, Israel's first king, was of the tribe of Benjamin (1 Sam. 9:1–2), there is nothing to suggest that this line survived to Christ's time or that Mary Magdalene was part of it.

Nor is there any evidence that Jesus was married to Mary Magdalene, much less that they had descendants who have survived to our own time. This leads to the question of the alleged divine bloodline of Jesus, a legend that Brown did not invent but took wholesale from *Holy Blood, Holy Grail*. Who would want to propound such an idea? The most convincing view I have seen comes from Robert Richardson, who argues in detail that the Priory of Sion, allegedly a secret society entrusted for centuries with protecting the Grail and the secret of the divine bloodline, does in fact exist.[49] It is not, however, an ancient esoteric order, but the creation of ultra-right-wing French monarchists of the twentieth century.

In fact, there was once an authentic Catholic order called the Priory of Sion. Originally centered in Palestine, it later transferred its headquarters to Sicily. But it ceased to exist in 1617; at that time it was absorbed into the Jesuit order. The modern "Priory of Sion" was the creation of a Frenchman named Pierre Plantard. Born in 1920, Plantard became influential in his late teens as a leader of Catholic youth groups. Around the outbreak of World War II he became titular head of an alleged esoteric order named Alpha Galates. During the German occupation of France in the early 1940s, Plantard and Alpha Galates published a newspaper called *Vaincre* (Conquer). *Vaincre* was pro-German and anti-Semitic, combining its political messages with discussions of chivalry and Celtic esoterica. It published only six issues.

After the war, Plantard promoted himself as the heir to the Merovingian dynasty. To this end, in 1956 he founded an organization called the "Priory of Sion," which had no connection with the extinct Catholic order. In the 1950s and 1960s, Plantard and his organization promoted a mélange of anti-Semitic, anti-Masonic views while espousing a rightist view of French nationalism.

All of this may seem mystifying to the English-speaking reader, for whom this blend of intrigue and extremist politics may seem better suited to a

thriller than to reality. But there are some major differences between the esoteric climate of the English-speaking world and that of the European continent. In Britain and the United States, esoteric groups have long followed the
lead of the Freemasons, who promoted liberal ideals in the eighteenth and
nineteenth centuries, including republican government. In these nations, the
Masons have long since been integrated into the power structure. Members of
the British royal family have served as titular heads of the Masonic United
Grand Lodge of England, and a number of U.S. presidents have been high-
degree Masons.

In continental Europe the situation has been quite different. The power of
the Catholic Church — and its loathing for secret societies of any type —
spawned Masonic groups that were revolutionary and anticlerical. In response or reaction, occult orders arose to guard the privileges of church
and nobility against the inroads of bourgeois republicans. (The Gold- und
Rosenkreutz in the eighteenth century is one example of these orders.) In the
nineteenth and twentieth centuries, these groups were drawn toward nation-
alistic, monarchistic, and fascistic ideals. Among such groups is, apparently,
the Priory of Sion. As Richardson observes:

> The first objective of the "Priory" is to position itself in the mind of
> an unknowing public as the supreme Western esoteric organization.
> It dreams of utilizing that constituency in a synarchy-like fashion to
> promote its hybrid agenda of right-wing politics and turn-of-the-
> [twentieth-]century esoteric teachings. It does not represent the real
> teachings of any positive esoteric order. It is materialistic, obsessed
> with attaining influence, and has fabricated documents without re-
> gard for any ethical considerations. Its program is to manipulate
> people through lies in order to promote itself.[50]

In the early years of the twenty-first century, when the dishonesties of political leaders have become ever more glaring, the threat posed by a Priory of
Sion can hardly seem terrifying. Regardless, the claims of this order have
made their way to a wide audience, first in *Holy Blood, Holy Grail,* and now in
The Da Vinci Code. These books inform us that the surnames of the descendants of the Merovingians — and hence of Jesus too — were Plantard and
Saint-Clair. Thus we see Plantard's dubious claim to divine lineage vindicated
in the pages of a popular novel.

Most crucially, however, *The Da Vinci Code* portrays the Catholic Church as an enemy of the Divine Feminine. In the end, the secret of the Grail has less to do with the sacred bloodline than with the holiness of the feminine, which, Brown tells us, the church has constantly denied and denigrated.

Taken at face value, this idea is absurd. The Virgin Mary is a central figure in Catholic devotion — for many believers, far more vivid and immediate than God the Father or Christ himself. As the British newsmagazine *The Economist* has pointed out, a visitor entering a church at Christmastime with no prior knowledge of Christianity "might well conclude that the main person being celebrated and adored was not a newborn boy, but his mother."[51] And as one reader on the Amazon.com Web site grumbled about *The Da Vinci Code*, "The anti-Catholic bias of this nonsense reaches ridiculous proportions. I mean, come on: for the last five centuries we have been taught that the Catholic Church was evil precisely because it had PERPETUATED goddess worship in the form of the cult of Mary and the saints. Now we are supposed to believe that the Catholic Church is evil for exactly the opposite reason, that it SUPPRESSED goddess worship?"

But the point in the novel goes beyond the issue of mere goddess worship. It is true that the Catholic Church deems Mary worthy of a veneration only slightly less than is due to God himself. Historical evidence suggests that the proclamation of Mary as Theotokos, or "Mother of God," in the fifth century A.D. was partly intended to fill the vacuum left by the suppression of the worship of Isis, the all-compassionate Egyptian mother goddess popular in the Greco-Roman world.[52] But Mary is a *virgin* goddess. And here lies the crux of the issue. Brown puts these words into the mouth of his hero:

> For the early Church, . . . mankind's use of sex to commune directly with God posed a serious threat to the Catholic power base. It left the Church out of the loop, undermining their self-proclaimed status as the *sole* conduit to God. For obvious reasons, they worked hard to demonize sex and recast it as a disgusting and sinful act. . . . Is it surprising we feel conflicted about sex? . . . Our ancient heritage and our very physiologies tell us sex is natural — a cherished route to spiritual fulfillment — and yet modern religion decries it as shameful, teaching us to fear our sexual desire as the hand of the devil.[53]

Whatever one wishes to make of *The Da Vinci Code*, this part of its message is hard to refute. While no sensible person would deny that some control over sexual urges is desirable and necessary, mainstream Christianity went far be-yond this and vilified sexuality as a whole. Its attitude can be partly explained in the light of Christian origins — the religion arose in the late Roman Em-pire, when sexuality had become unusually brutalized and degraded — but even so, Brown's point is not to be dismissed. The demonization of sexuality has indeed proved a potent form of social manipulation. The Jewish Law for-bade sexual expression in certain circumstances, but Christianity came close to condemning it in virtually all instances, even in marriage. As the Church Father Jerome declared, "He that is insatiable of his wife commits adultery."[54] This blanket condemnation would inevitably produce tremendous amounts of guilt in believers — since no normal person is devoid of sexual feelings — thus enabling the church to set itself up as the sole provider of remission of these "sins." Indeed the church's assertion that it possesses exclusive rights to dispensing God's grace on earth — expressed in the aphorism *Extra ecclesiam nulla salus* (Outside the church there is no salvation) — has been one of its most audacious but most successful tactics.

At the end, *The Da Vinci Code* says the goal of the Priory is neither to pre-serve the secret of Jesus's marriage to Mary Magdalene nor to promote the in-terests of his bloodline. Rather, it is to foster awareness of the Divine Feminine, and, we are told, this purpose can be discerned in art, literature, even in the productions of Walt Disney. "Look around you," Sophie's grand-mother, a descendant of Christ and Mary Magdalene, tells Langdon. "Her story is being told in art, music, and books. The pendulum is swinging. We are starting to sense the dangers of our history . . . and of our destructive paths. We are beginning to sense the need to restore the sacred feminine."[55]

This states a theme that recurs in much contemporary spiritual writing: Humanity has been in bondage to masculine values of hierarchy, war, and domination for thousands of years, and now the tide is beginning to turn. The blossoming of interest in the feminine face of God — Mary Magdalene, Sophia, and the Virgin herself, not to mention the Great Goddess of paganism — attests to this fact. Masculine values are receding, and we are wit-nessing the dawn of a new era of peace, cooperation, and caring.

There is only one problem with this vision: the contemporary scene does not bear it out. Even if we simplistically equate masculinity with dominance and femininity with caring and compassion, we see less and less of the latter in society, supplanted by an ever more pervasive profit motive. In much of the developed world, the "nanny state" of the mid-twentieth century, which was intended (with whatever degree of success) to provide a level of support for all citizens, is being replaced by a laissez-faire system that assumes that market forces will somehow establish social justice.

Thus the resurgence of the Divine Feminine may represent, not a swinging of the pendulum in the other direction, but what psychologists call *compensation*. The more the virtues associated with femininity — caring, beauty, compassion — are trampled down in the culture at large, the more they make their presence felt at an unconscious level. In individuals this manifests in dreams and neuroses, while at a collective level it manifests in spontaneous and inexplicable occurrences (such as the numerous Marian apparitions), as well as in works like *The Da Vinci Code* that seize the popular imagination. Thus these evidences of the Divine Feminine may represent not the dawning of a brilliant new age but a coping mechanism for our contemporary discomfort.

And yet, I suspect *The Da Vinci Code*'s appeal runs still deeper than these concerns. It reflects a widespread sense — which I mentioned in the introduction — that something is missing in Christianity. *The Da Vinci Code* belongs to the genre of detective fiction, and like all such books, it is driven by the hero's need to find out facts: the culprit in the murder, and ultimately the alleged cover-up of the central truths of Christianity. But part of the book's magic is that it leads the hero (and implicitly the reader) to something beyond factual knowledge: it culminates in a quasi-mystical experience. "For a moment," we read at the end, "he [Langdon] thought he heard a woman's voice . . . the wisdom of the ages . . . whispering up from the chasms of the earth."[56]

Thus *The Da Vinci Code* culminates in a dimension of experience that goes beyond dates and times and personages. Its facts, as we have seen, are shaky. But in the end, what would it matter if Jesus was married to Mary Magdalene or not? What difference would it make if they had descendants who have survived to this day? At this point in history, it would be practically impossible ever to find out. But the need for awakening to a higher consciousness is not false or fictional. By suggesting that the way to this experience is still open, *The Da Vinci Code*, for all its faults, has made a great contribution to the discourse of our time.

The various currents of the Gnostic heritage that we've examined in this chapter seem — and indeed *are* — highly disparate. In some cases this legacy is antinomian; it takes a stance against the social conventions that imprison the individual. In others, the forces that enchain us are closer than our own jugular veins. But this very disparity suggests a thread that can lead to spiritual liberation.

Often an individual begins the spiritual path with a vague dissatisfaction with ordinary life. She may have brushed up against society's conventions and come to realize that they are foolish and arbitrary. The spiritual path then becomes a means of escaping this social incarceration. But if there is any authenticity to this path, one soon realizes that the forces that constrain us are not merely exterior but much closer to ourselves and to whom we think we are. Ultimately we discover that the enemy is the tendency in ourselves to set ourselves up against the universe and to say, with the Gnostic Ialdabaoth, "I am God and there is no other God beside me." Without this insight, it may be impossible to break free of the Black Iron Prison.

CHAPTER 10

The Future of Gnosis

Isaac Bashevis Singer, the great preserver of the lore and atmosphere of the old Jewish *shtetls* of Eastern Europe, was once asked if the Yiddish language had a future.

"Ask me first if it has a present," he replied.

This story comes to mind when I think about the future of gnosis. In this context it seems appropriate to take a look at a small and endangered community often described as the last Gnostics — the Mandaeans of Iran and southern Iraq.[1]

The Mandaeans are one of innumerable small groups throughout the Middle East — such as the Yezidis of Kurdistan and the Druzes of Lebanon — as well as the Parsis of Gujarat in western India, who have clung to an ancient religious heritage despite the hostility of much larger nations and faiths around them. Although the Mandaeans are characterized as Gnostics, they do not trace their origins back to any of the Gnostic schools of the second century A.D. They claim to be followers of John the Baptist. As befits their background, the Mandaeans attach great importance to ritual purification by water, which is necessary after a wide number of forms of defilement, ranging from menstruation to contact with Muslims. Moreover, the water must be "living water" — it must come directly from a stream or river. Water in bottles or artificial conduits is "dead," useless for bestowing life or purity.

As this detail alone might suggest, the Mandaeans have faced intense threats to their survival in recent times. Entire communities have moved when a water source is depleted, so modern pollution presents an entirely new threat to their existence. To make matters worse, the Mandaeans have long been centered in the marshy regions of southern Iraq. Here, in the last few decades, they have been subjected to the ravages of war as well as to virulent persecution by the Iraqi dictator Saddam Hussein. Suspecting the Mandaeans, or "Marsh Arabs," as possible sources of opposition, Saddam attempted to destroy their community by destroying their environment. During the 1990s, he drained the marshes, turning 95 percent of wetlands the size of Massachusetts into desert — an act that has been described as the environmental crime of the century.[2]

It is hard to say how well the Mandaeans have survived these onslaughts. One estimate says there were some twenty thousand practicing Mandaeans in Iran and Iraq before the wars of the past twenty-five years. This number must be much smaller now.

If the Mandaeans are followers of John the Baptist (they regard Jesus as a false Messiah), what makes them Gnostics? Chiefly their theological views.[3] Although Mandaean theology is flexible and embraces many systems (which are not always mutually compatible), in essence it speaks of a First Principle that is known as Life, Great Life, or First Life. The First Principle generates realms of light inhabited by celestial intermediaries that Mandaeans themselves have equated with the angels of Christianity. But there are sinister forces as well. One principle, known as Ruha ha-Qudsa, "The Spirit of Holiness," has an incestuous relationship with her brother, which generates a cosmic serpent named 'Ur that resembles the Ourobouros, the "tail-eating serpent" of Western esotericism. 'Ur in turn produces the manifest cosmos, governed by the planets and the signs of the zodiac. This is a place of darkness. To redeem this realm, a cosmic savior named Hibil Ziua descends, but he becomes entrapped. Like the hero of the Gnostic "Hymn of the Pearl," he is himself in need of liberation.

Even this skeletal description suggests how the Mandaeans' teaching resembles many Gnostic and similar esoteric systems. There is a process of emanation that generates the universe; there is a principle of darkness that limits and circumscribes it; and there are different levels of being, of which ours, the earthly, is the darkest and most defective. There is also a descent into this realm of darkness by what Philip K. Dick would call a "divine invasion," with ambiguous results. Eventually all will be redeemed, but only at the end of this age, which, the Mandaeans say, will be destroyed by the powers of the air.

A Dubious Category?

To look at Mandaean teachings may lead one to think that their cosmology is like the ecosystem that supports them — intricate, frail, and prone to collapse. It's hard to imagine, say, the typical student at an American divinity school taking any interest in their theology except as the source of a dissertation. Taking such ideas seriously consigns one to the theological fringes — to starting a church in California or writing novels along the lines of Philip K. Dick.

Not surprisingly, perhaps, Gnosticism as a concept is under attack in certain circles of academe. Recent years have seen the publication of two books by mainstream academics — *Rethinking "Gnosticism": Arguments for Rethinking a Dubious Category* by Michael Williams and *What Is Gnosticism?* by Karen King — arguing that the term itself is too problematic to be meaningful anymore. To recapitulate their arguments would be both complicated and tiresome, but in essence they are both saying the term "Gnosticism" is too simplistic and doesn't fit many of the texts and movements it claims to cover. Williams, for example, suggests that the standard view of the Gnostics as "world-haters" is incorrect, since they were actually less at odds with the powers that be of the Roman Empire than were the proto-orthodox Christians.[4] King says that "the variety of phenomena classified as 'Gnostic' simply will not support a single, monolithic definition, and in fact *none of the primary materials fits the standard typological definition*."[5]

Although they limit their discussions to studies of Christian origins and ancient religion, Williams and King perhaps also have in mind such bizarre uses of the term as we find in Voegelin, Harold Bloom, and other modern sources. One peculiar usage of the term Gnosticism appears in a 2003 report on the New Age by the Vatican's Pontifical Council for Culture.[6] It quotes Pope John Paul II as saying:

> Gnosticism never completely abandoned the realm of Christianity. Instead, it has always existed side by side with Christianity, sometimes taking the shape of a philosophical movement, but more often assuming the characteristics of a religion or a para-religion in distinct, if not declared, conflict with all that is essentially Christian.

The authors of the report add: "An example of this can be seen in the enneagram, the nine-type tool for character analysis, which when used as a means of spiritual growth introduces an ambiguity in the doctrine and the life of the Christian faith."

While it is understandable that the Vatican would want to define Christianity in contradistinction to Gnosticism, it is hard to see how the enneagram is "Gnostic" in any meaningful sense. The enneagram is indeed a "nine-type" system for determining certain psychological distortions and imbalances.[7] But it has nothing to do with Gnosticism or gnosis, nor is it a "religion or a para-religion." Ironically, the enneagram has attracted a substantial following among Jesuits and Benedictines, partly because the system (with some modification) adapts itself well to the Seven Deadly Sins of traditional Catholic teaching. Labeling the enneagram "Gnostic" seems to show some confusion about what Gnosticism is.

Partly as a result of such confusions, Williams's and King's critiques have left an impact on their colleagues. Even Elaine Pagels avoids the term *Gnosticism* in her latest book, the enormously popular *Beyond Belief*. But should the term be discarded completely? Certainly there is some merit in pointing out oversimplifications in what we call "Gnostic," and to this extent Williams and King are persuasive. And insofar as they warn us against viewing the Gnostics simplistically as "world-denying" or "body-hating," their suggestions are constructive.

And yet Williams's and King's views arouse a measure of suspicion. Some of their objections seem motivated by an exaggerated sense of political correctness. King, for example, says, "Many typological definitions of Gnosticism . . . are based on an unarticulated but implicit comparison with normative constructions of Christianity and Judaism or some more vague notion of 'true religion.'"[8] That is, Gnosticism was designated for so long as a heresy that the term itself usually implies a value-laden — and negative — approach to the subject. But this seems overconscientious. It's hard to see a term as pejorative when increasing numbers of people are embracing it.

Here lies another facet of the issue. Specialists tend to discard a term when it gains popular currency. We see this most vividly in psychology, where such words as *complex*, *neurosis*, and *hysteria* were once used clinically but were later jettisoned after they had come into common parlance. Are some scholars unhappy with the term *Gnosticism* precisely because more and more ordinary people are drawn to it? Williams suggests replacing *Gnosticism* with *biblical demiurgism*. Whatever the scholarly merits of this improbable usage, it is sure to be immune to public embrace. *Time* magazine is not going to be running stories about the rise of "biblical demiurgism" anytime soon.

Marvin Meyer, another scholar in the field, suggests a more balanced approach. In the introduction to his recent work, *The Gnostic Gospels of Jesus*, Meyer says:

> I remain confident that the terms *gnosis*, "gnostic," and "gnosticism" may still be used in a meaningful way to designate a series of religious movements that have existed since ancient times. After all, the word *gnosis* is commonly attested in gnostic and heresiological texts, and heresiological references to such references to such expressions as "falsely so-called knowledge (*gnosis*)" in Irenaeus of Lyons and elsewhere make it clear that a battle was being waged over whose knowledge was true knowledge.[9]

That is to say, *gnosis* and *Gnostic* were meaningful terms in antiquity, both to those who considered themselves to be Gnostics and to those who opposed them.

Personally, I have no great attachment to the term *Gnostic*. Having written this book, I'm quite aware of the disadvantages of this word, and I've sometimes had to take pains to distinguish classical Gnosticism from its descendants. But in the current debate, I suspect Meyer is closer to the truth than his opponents. Whatever the problems involved in calling something "Gnostic," both scholars and laypeople will probably continue to do so. Even if they don't, they will end up using another term that means more or less the same thing.

When I speak of the future of gnosis and Gnosticism, I am concerned with them not as designations but as a set of insights. Do they have any value today? If so, what's the best way to approach them?

To speak of the future of Gnosticism as such is like speaking about the future of the Latin language. The Latin language itself does not have much of a future. In each generation, fewer and fewer people are studying it, and even the Catholic Church has discarded it as a liturgical language. In this sense, Latin is a dead language. Yet from another perspective, Latin is not dead at all. It continues to survive in its descendants, the Romance languages, spoken by hundreds of millions of people in regions spanning from Romania to Patagonia.

Gnosticism is similar. The classical Gnostic systems disappeared. Despite current interest, they are not going to be revived on any large scale; they are too obscure and crabbed, and we know too little about how they worked in practice. But they, too, continue to live on in their descendants, the Western esoteric traditions in their many forms: Kabbalah, esoteric Christianity, Hermeticism,

Rosicrucianism, Freemasonry. Gnosticism did not die out; it simply changed its form in response to the needs of different times.

What, then, are the needs of our time, and how does the Gnostic legacy address them? To answer this question, we need to step back and look at the problems of mainstream Christianity as we find it today.

The Limits of Salvation

Christianity — that is, the Christianity of the churches, of Catholicism and Orthodoxy and Protestantism — holds out the hope of salvation. Essentially, salvation is the answer to the problem of sin. By sin, that is, by moral error, we have cut ourselves off from God. The redemptive act of Christ atoned for these failings and restored the bridge between God and man. By accepting Christ, we allow his redemptive act to cancel out our sins and clear our record with God.

The power of this idea is evident. Christianity would not be the religion of some two billion people — one-third of the world's population — if salvation did not speak to a deep-seated need. Humans are moral beings, and sooner or later we realize that we have moral failings. How can we redress them? Merely attempting to "make up for them" does not always do the trick. Recompense is not always total, and damage cannot always be undone. Even if it can, we may still be unable to rid ourselves of a lingering sense of guilt. By symbolically allowing Christ to take on our sins through repentance, the burden is lifted, and we can go on with our lives.

There is great truth — both spiritual and emotional — in this idea, and it provides a powerful answer to the universal problem of human guilt. But to say it has truth is not to say it is the whole truth.

As the apostle Paul showed, the Law in itself cannot redeem us. The Law — that is, whichever law we may find ourselves under — may be necessary for regulating human conduct, but in itself it cannot offer meaning and purpose to life. One could say the same about salvation. Salvation, if it is genuine, clears the boards, enabling one to go on to lead a meaningful and purposeful life. But salvation itself does not confer meaning or purpose; it is merely one step in that direction. To use the analogy of the Twelve-Step program, asking help of a Higher Power and making amends to those we have harmed are parts of the process; they are not the whole of it. To believe that sin and redemption constitute the whole of the spiritual path puts too much focus on sin. This is the trap into which conventional Christianity has fallen. The believer continues to lament and beat his breast because, as it were, he has nothing else to do.

At some point, we come to realize that the human condition has more than a moral dimension. It also reflects a lack of insight, a primordial ignorance or loss of awareness that certain Gnostic texts represent by the fall of Sophia. It's not simply that we do bad things, but that our minds have become distorted by fixating on a mistaken view of reality.

Seeing the fundamental problem of the human condition as cognitive rather than moral is often regarded as an "Eastern" teaching, but it also has ancient roots in the West — in Socrates' contention that all evil is due to ignorance, in Plato's famous metaphor of the cave, as well as in the teachings of the Gnostics. This idea has recently come to the fore not only thanks to various philosophical insights — such as Kant's theory of the categories — but through neurology. Science has shown us how much of our perception of reality is limited by the filters of our nervous systems (an idea that we can trace as far back as Blake's *Urizen*).

Physics has gone still further, contending that the filters over reality comprise more than the mere limitations of our own cognitive capacities. As is well known, quantum theory holds that the process of observation itself changes the thing observed. Werner Heisenberg, one of the founders of quantum physics, writes:

> We can no longer speak of the behavior of the particle independently
> of the process of observation. As a final consequence, the natural
> laws formulated mathematically in quantum theory no longer deal
> with the elementary particles themselves, but with our knowledge of
> them. Nor is it any longer possible to ask whether or not these parti-
> cles exist in space and time objectively.[10]

For science as it stands now, these limitations are total. There is no seeing past the "process of observation" itself. But the Gnostic tradition holds that these limitations are *not* total; if they were, we would have no hope of escape. We would not even be aware of a need to escape, because we would take the world totally at face value. But there is something within us that realizes that this is not the whole picture, that this is not how things were meant to be. To gain this insight is to begin the spiritual path proper. That which is conscious within us — the true Self, the "kingdom of heaven" — begins to turn away from the world and seeks a higher level of reality. At the core this is a process of detachment.

Much of Christianity holds up love as the supreme value, but Meister Eckhart does not agree. He writes, "I put detachment higher than love." For Eckhart, it is detachment from the world and its experiences that leads one toward God. "Experience must always be an experience of something, but detachment comes so close to zero that nothing but God is rarefied enough to get into it, to enter the detached heart."[11] This statement is practically a one-sentence summary of the path of gnosis, the liberation of the true "I" from its bondage to its own experience so that it can unite with God.

Liberation through gnosis can happen totally and spontaneously; many such cases appear in the religious literature of the world. But this rarely happens. For most people, the process of awakening is a gradual one, leading to different stages of experience. That is, experience changes its form many times before one passes beyond experience itself. While this process can vary from individual to individual, the general outlines are clear enough, and it's possible to talk meaningfully about them. Different images have been applied to these stages: the Gnostic's ascent through the invisible realms, Dante's journey through the spheres of heaven, the Kabbalistic way through the *sefirot*. This brings us to esotericism proper — the science of these inner stages of awakening. Esotericism is now, as it has always been, an integral part of the Western spiritual tradition, although churches have rarely provided a welcome haven for it.

This liberation of the true "I" from the world does not make moral behavior irrelevant; it makes it easier. Detachment from externalities makes it easier to love one's fellow humans, because one then is free from wanting things and nursing hidden agendas. Love becomes something more than a mere bargain or transaction. At the same time, the Gnostic is less preoccupied with moral rules and regulations, which are general guidelines only. This is what it means to be free of the Law.

The Imaginary Friend

Evangelical Christians reading these pages may complain that gnosis, thus described, is merely a vague and nebulous substitute for a personal relationship with Jesus Christ. But what exactly is a "personal relationship" with Jesus? Certainly it is possible to have a living experience of Christ, or of other great masters and teachers who are no longer living on the physical plane; such experiences are far too numerous and well documented to be casually dismissed. But while this experience is possible, it's not common. It is certainly not something that one gets automatically just by making a commitment, however sincere. Few people give any indication of having had it. This leads us to ask just what it is that people are experiencing when they are "born again."

Often, it seems, this is little more than a counterfeit of a personal relationship with Jesus. The believer creates a mental picture of Jesus from what he knows from reading the Bible or going to church, the mind then makes this picture come to life (which it can easily do), and then he has a relationship with this figment. For many people, Jesus amounts to little more than an imaginary friend. If by some chance the individual has a genuine experience of the divine, he only accepts it if it fits in with his preconceptions. Otherwise he hates and fears it as a snare of the devil.

As harsh as this characterization may sound, it is in many ways milder than the accusations flung by many evangelical Christians at the spiritual experiences of others, which (insofar as they are granted any reality at all) are frequently dismissed as delusions engendered by demons. This is not to deny that a person can have a genuine encounter with the presence of Christ, which in itself is a form of gnosis. But many people appear to have had "born-again" experiences largely because they were expected to. They soon discovered that these experiences were empty. Or, just as often, they found that the experience itself was powerful but their churches had hedged around it with so many unrealistic moral, doctrinal, and even political demands that they became disillusioned and embittered. Disbelieving in the church, they came to disbelieve in their own experience.

As I said in the introduction, there is an enormous need for teachers and counselors with enough experience in the spiritual realms that they can help seekers distinguish genuine experience from "gnosis falsely so called." This, too, points to a need for esoteric training, which concerns itself precisely with these matters. But esotericism is a pariah in mainstream Christianity. To the fundamentalists, it is the devil's work; to the liberals, it is an antique. Consequently, people who go to their priests and ministers with such experiences and receive the usual unsatisfying answers often cast off religion entirely, deciding it must be worthless if even the experts know nothing. Or they go to alternative religions or to teachers from the Eastern traditions, who, to their credit, have frequently provided better advice.

Faith, Reason, and Gnosis

What role, then, will — or should — the Gnostic legacy play in the civilization of the future? One of today's most prominent scholars of esotericism is
Wouter J. Hanegraaff, professor of the history of Hermetic philosophy at the
University of Amsterdam. At the end of his book *New Age Religion and Western Culture*, he makes some points that are worth repeating here.

For Hanegraaff, Western civilization is rooted in three major impulses:
reason, faith, and *gnosis.* Reason holds that "truth — if attainable at all — can
only be discovered by making use of the human rational faculties, whether or
not in combination with the senses." Faith, by contrast, says that reason in itself does not provide us with ultimate answers, which can only come from a
transcendental realm and are encapsulated in dogmas, creeds, and scriptures.
Gnosis teaches that "truth can only be found by personal, inner revelation. . . . This 'inner knowing' cannot be transmitted by discursive language
(that would reduce it to rational knowledge). Nor can it be the subject of
faith . . . because there is in the last resort no other authority than personal,
inner experience."[12]

For Hanegraaff, reason is epitomized in the scientific enterprise; faith, in
institutional Christianity. (He stresses, however, that these categories are not
radically exclusive: many forms of Christianity place a great deal of value on
reason, while faith in authority is far from unknown in science.) Western civilization, especially in recent eras, has been characterized by this polarity of
reason and faith.

Gnosis has been much less valued. Although Hanegraaff does not spell it
out, the reason is clear. By emphasizing direct spiritual experience, gnosis
often finds itself at variance with revealed religion: if God appears to you,
he — or, for that matter, *she* or *it* — may not look as he does on the Sistine
Ceiling. And since gnosis transcends reason, many have jumped to the conclusion that it is "irrational." Hence gnosis has been marginalized in most eras
of Western history (the Renaissance, as we have seen, is a major exception). As
Hanegraaff says, "The traditions based on gnosis can be seen as a sort of traditional western counter-culture."

Hanegraaff does not go further with these points, but it's logical to take
his premises to the next step: to suggest that gnosis, instead of being
marginalized — or even despised, as it often is — in Western society, needs
to be placed on a par with the dual authority of institutional science and

institutional religion. This need is growing all the more urgent today, as science and religion are becoming more polarized and hostile, as we see from current polemics about such issues as creationism and stem-cell research. Left to their own devices, faith and reason seem likely to continue to pull farther and farther apart. It does not require great creativity to imagine the disasters that could result.

Those who embody the third impulse — gnosis — could help bridge this chasm. In some ways, gnosis seems ideally suited for the task. Like science, it is rooted in experience; like religion, it acknowledges the existence of transcendental realities. It can never be reduced to mere faith or mere reason; otherwise it would simply be a subcategory of these. But, given a serious hearing, it could help produce a genuinely dynamic synthesis for what now look very much like opposing forces.

Admittedly, this seems unlikely to happen anytime in the near future. The established institutions of any description show little interest in gnosis. And in any case it is far from clear who the current representatives of this gnostic impulse would be. Even so, history teaches one lesson repeatedly: sudden reversals in trends are not only possible but probable. Gnosis may yet receive the place it deserves in our civilization.

No matter what the future of the Gnostic legacy may be, there is one thing whose future is certain, and that is gnosis itself — the direct spiritual awakening that comes, bidden or unbidden, to individuals great and small. It is not the property of any religion, though each religion tries to make it its property; it can be invited by meditation and spiritual practice, but just as often it is like the wind, "which bloweth where it listeth," arriving where it is least expected or even desired. Sought or unsought, honored or dishonored, gnosis will always be with us. It is both our birthright and the destiny to which each of us will sooner or later be called.

Selected Bibliography

Abdill, Edward. *The Secret Gateway: Modern Theosophy and the Ancient Wisdom Tradition.* Wheaton, Ill.: Quest, 2005.

Agrippa, Henry Cornelius. *Three Books of Occult Philosophy.* Translated by James Freake. Edited by Donald Tyson. St. Paul, Minn.: Llewellyn, 1993.

Alighieri, Dante. *La Vita Nuova.* Translated by Barbara Reynolds. Harmondsworth: Penguin, 1969.

The Anchor Bible: Galatians. Edited and translated by J. Louis Martin. New York: Doubleday, 1997.

Baigent, Michael, and Richard Leigh. *The Temple and the Lodge.* New York: Arcade, 1989.

Bailey, Alice. *The Consciousness of the Atom.* New York: Lucis, 1922.

Bamford, Christopher. *An Endless Trace: The Passionate Pursuit of Wisdom in the West.* New Paltz, N.Y.: Codhill, 2003.

BeDuhn, Jason David. *The Manichaean Body in Discipline and Ritual.* Baltimore, Md.: Johns Hopkins University Press, 2000.

Besant, Annie. *Esoteric Christianity, or the Lesser Mysteries.* Reprint. Kila, Mont.: Kessinger, n.d. (1918).

Blake, William. *The Book of Urizen.* Edited by Kay Parkhurst Easson and Roger R. Easson. Boulder, Colo.: Shambhala/Random House, 1978.

————. *The Complete Poetry and Prose of William Blake.* Edited by David V. Erdman. Revised edition. Berkeley: University of California Press, 1982.

Blakney, Raymond B. *Meister Eckhart.* New York: Harper & Row, 1941.

Blau, Joseph Leon. *The Christian Interpretation of the Cabala in the Renaissance.* Reprint. Port Washington, N.Y.: Kennikat Press, 1965.

Blavatsky, H. P. *Isis Unveiled: Secrets of the Ancient Wisdom Tradition.* Abridged edition. Edited by Michael Gomes. Wheaton, Ill.: Quest, 1997.

————. *The Secret Doctrine.* Third Point Loma edition. Point Loma, Calif.: Aryan Theosophical Press, 1926.

Bloom, Harold. *The American Religion.* New York: Simon & Schuster, 1992.

————. *Omens of Millennium.* New York: Riverhead, 1996.

Bradley, Ian. *Celtic Christianity: Making Myths and Chasing Dreams.* New York: St. Martin's Press, 1999.

Brown, Raymond E. *An Introduction to the New Testament.* New York: Doubleday, 1996.

Case, Paul Foster. *The True and Invisible Rosicrucian Order.* York Beach, Maine: Samuel Weiser, 1985.

Charles, R. H. *The Apocrypha and Pseudepigrapha of the Old Testament.* Volume 2: *Pseudepigrapha.* Oxford: Oxford at the Clarendon Press, 1913.

Churton, Tobias. *Gnostic Philosophy from Ancient Persia to Modern Times.* Rochester, Vt.: Inner Traditions, 2005.

———. *The Golden Builders: Alchemists, Rosicrucians, and the First Freemasons.* Boston: Weiser, 2005.

Clement of Alexandria. Edited and translated by G. W. Butterworth. Cambridge, Mass.: Harvard University Press (Loeb Classical Library), 1919.

Clement of Alexandria. *Stromateis.* In *The Ante-Nicene Fathers,* volume 2, edited by Alexander Roberts and James Donaldson. Reprint: Grand Rapids, Mich.: Eerdmans, 1994.

Copenhaver, Brian P., ed. and trans. *Hermetica: The Greek Corpus Hermeticum and the Latin Asclepius in a New English Translation with Notes and an Introduction.* Cambridge: Cambridge University Press, 1992.

A Course in Miracles. 3 vols. Tiburon, Calif.: Foundation for Inner Peace, 1975.

Dan, Joseph, ed. *The Christian Kabbalah: Jewish Mystical Books and Their Christian Interpreters.* Cambridge, Mass.: Harvard College Library, 1997.

Davis, Erik. *TechGnosis: Myth, Magic, and Mysticism in the Age of Information.* 2d ed. London: Serpents Tail, 2004.

De Rougemont, Denis. *Love in the Western World.* Translated by Montgomery Belgion. Rev. ed. Princeton, N.J.: Princeton University Press, 1983.

Descartes, René. *Discourses on Method and the Meditations.* Translated by E. F. Sutcliffe. Harmondsworth: Penguin, 1968.

Dick, Philip K. *The Shifting Realities of Philip K. Dick: Selected Literary and Philosophical Writings.* Edited by Lawrence Sutin. New York: Pantheon, 1995.

Dictionary of Gnosis and Western Esotericism. Edited by Wouter J. Hanegraaff et al. 2 vols. Leiden: Brill, 2005.

Durkheim, Émile. *The Elementary Forms of Religious Life.* Translated by Karen E. Fields. New York: Free Press, 1995.

Meister Eckhart. *German Sermons and Treatises.* Translated by M. O'C. Walshe. Vols. 1 and 2, London: Watkins, 1979–81; vol. 3, Shaftesbury: Element, 1987.

Eusebius. *The History of the Church.* Translated by G. A. Williamson. Edited by Andrew Louth. London: Penguin, 1989.

Evola, Julius, et al. *Introduction to Magic: Rituals and Practical Techniques for the Magus.* Translated by Guido Stucco. Rochester, Vt.: Inner Traditions, 2001.

Faivre, Antoine, and Jacob Needleman, eds. *Modern Esoteric Spirituality.* New York: Crossroad, 1995.

Feuerstein, Georg. *The Mystery of Light: The Life and Teaching of Omraam Mikhaël Aïvanhov.* Sandy, Utah: Passage Press, 1994.

Filoramo, Giovanni. *A History of Gnosticism.* Translated by Anthony Alcock. Oxford: Blackwell, 1990.

Foerster, Werner. *Gnosis: A Selection of Gnostic Texts.* Vol. 1. Edited by R. McL. Wilson. Oxford: Oxford at the Clarendon Press, 1972.

Freke, Timothy, and Peter Gandy. *The Jesus Mysteries.* New York: Three Rivers Press, 1999.

Gikatilla, Joseph. *Gates of Light: Sha'arei Orah.* Translated by Avi Weinstein. San Francisco: HarperSanFrancisco, 1994.

Gilbert, R. A. *The Golden Dawn: Twilight of the Magicians.* Wellingborough: Aquarian, 1983.

The Gnostic Bible. Edited by Willis Barnstone and Marvin Meyer. Boston: Shambhala, 2003.

Godwin, Joscelyn. *The Pagan Dream of the Renaissance.* Grand Rapids, Mich.: Phanes, 2002.

Goffman, Ken, and Dan Joy. *Counterculture through the Ages: From Abraham to Acid House.* New York: Villard, 2004.

Guénon, René. *Aperçus sur l'ésotérisme chrétien.* Paris: Éditions Traditionelles, n.d.

Halevi, Z'ev ben Shimon. *The Way of Kabbalah.* London: Rider, 1976.

Hallamish, Moshe. *An Introduction to the Kabbalah.* Translated by Ruth Bar-Han and Ora Wiskind-Elper. Albany: State University of New York Press, 1999.

Hanegraaff, Wouter J. *New Age Religion and Western Culture.* Albany: State University of New York Press, 1998.

Harnack, Adolf von. *History of Dogma.* Vol. 1. Translated by Neil Buchanan. New York: Russell & Russell, 1958.

———. *Marcion: The Gospel of the Alien God.* Translated by John E. Steely and Lyle D. Bierma. Durham, N.C.: Labyrinth, 1990.

Harner, Michael. *The Way of the Shaman.* New York: Bantam, 1982.

Harris, Lynda. *The Secret Heresy of Hieronymus Bosch.* Edinburgh: Floris, 1995.

Harrison, C. G. *The Transcendental Universe: Six Lectures on Occult Science, Theosophy, and the Catholic Faith.* Hudson, N.Y.: Lindisfarne, 1993.

Hawkins, David. *Power vs. Force: The Hidden Determinants of Human Behavior.* Sedona, Ariz.: Veritas, 1995.

Herodotus. Translated by A. D. Godley. 4 vols. London: Heinemann (Loeb Classical Library), 1931.

Hoeller, Stephan A. *Gnosticism: New Light on the Ancient Tradition of Inner Knowing.* Wheaton, Ill.: Quest, 2002.

Jenkins, Philip. *Hidden Gospels: How the Search for Jesus Lost Its Way.* Oxford: Oxford University Press, 2001.

Johnson, K. Paul. *The Masters Revealed: Mme. Blavatsky and the Myth of the Great White Lodge.* Albany: State University of New York Press, 1994.

Johnson, Paul. *A History of Christianity.* New York: Atheneum, 1987.

Jonas, Hans. *The Gnostic Religion.* 2d ed. Boston: Beacon, 1963.

Jung, C. G. *Memories, Dreams, Reflections.* Rev. ed. Translated by Richard and Clara Winston. New York: Vintage, 1989.

———. *Psychology and Religion. Collected Works,* vol. 11. 2d ed. Translated by R. F. C. Hull. Princeton, N.J.: Princeton University Press, 1969.

————. *Symbols of Transformation. Collected Works*, vol. 5. 2d ed. Translated by R. F. C. Hull. Princeton, N.J.: Princeton University Press, 1967.

Kaplan, Aryeh. *Meditation and Kabbalah*. York Beach, Maine: Samuel Weiser, 1982.

The Key of Solomon the King (Clavicula Salomonis). Translated by S. L. MacGregor Mathers. York Beach, Maine: Samuel Weiser, 2000.

King, Karen L. *What Is Gnosticism?* Cambridge, Mass.: Harvard University Press, 2003.

Kinney, Jay, ed. *The Inner West: An Introduction to the Hidden Wisdom of the West*. New York: Jeremy P. Tarcher/Penguin, 2004.

Klimkeit, Hans-Joachim. *Gnosis on the Silk Road: Gnostic Parables, Hymns, and Prayers from Central Asia*. San Francisco: HarperSanFranciso, 1993.

Knoop, Douglas, et al., eds. *The Two Earliest Masonic Mss*. Manchester: Manchester University Press, 1938.

Knox, R. A. *Enthusiasm: A Chapter in the History of Religion*. Oxford: Oxford at the Clarendon Press, 1950.

Lacarrière, Jacques. *The Gnostics*. Translated by Nina Rootes. New York: E. P. Dutton, 1977.

Lachman, Gary. *A Dark Muse: A History of the Occult*. New York: Thunder's Mouth, 2003.

Larson, Gerald J. *Classical Samkhya: An Interpretation of Its History and Meaning*. 2d ed. Delhi: Motilal Barnarsidass, 1979.

Layton, Bentley, ed. and trans. *The Gnostic Scriptures*. New York: Doubleday, 1987.

Lorimer, David. *Prophet for Our Times: The Life and Teachings of Peter Deunov*. Rockport, Mass.: Element Books, 1996.

Lossky, Vladimir. *The Mystical Theology of the Eastern Church*. Crestwood, N.Y.: St. Vladimir's Seminary Press, 1976.

Lupieri, Edmondo. *The Mandaeans: The Last Gnostics*. Translated by Charles Hindley. Grand Rapids, Mich.: Eerdmans, 2002.

MacDermot, Violet. *The Fall of Sophia: A Gnostic Text on the Redemption of Universal Consciousness*. Great Barrington, Mass.: Lindisfarne, 2001.

MacNulty, W. Kirk. *Freemasonry: A Journey through Ritual and Symbol*. London: Thames & Hudson, 1991.

Malachi, Tau. *The Gnostic Gospel of St. Thomas: Meditations on the Mystical Teachings*. St. Paul, Minn.: Llewellyn, 2004.

Markale, Jean. *The Church of Mary Magdalene: The Sacred Feminine and the Treasure of Rennes-le-Château*. Translated by Jon Graham. Rochester, Vt.: Inner Traditions, 2004.

————. *Courtly Love: The Path of Sexual Initiation*. Translated by Jon Graham. Rochester, Vt.: Inner Traditions, 2000.

Maxwell-Stuart, P. G., ed. and trans. *The Occult in Early Modern Europe: A Documentary History*. New York: St. Martin's Press, 1999.

Meyer, Marvin. *The Gnostic Gospels of Jesus*. San Francisco: HarperSanFrancisco, 2005.

Meyer, Marvin W., and Richard Smith. *Ancient Christian Magic: Coptic Texts of Ritual Power.* Princeton, N.J.: Princeton University Press, 1994.

Miller, D. Patrick. *The Complete Story of the Course.* Berkeley, Calif.: Fearless, 1997.

The Nag Hammadi Library in English. Edited by James M. Robinson. San Francisco: Harper & Row, 1977.

New Testament Apocrypha. Edited by Wilhelm Schneemelcher. Translated by R. McLachlan Wilson. 2 vols. Edinburgh: T & T Clark, 1991.

Noll, Richard. *The Jung Cult: Origins of a Charismatic Movement.* Princeton, N.J.: Princeton University Press, 1994.

Origen. *On First Principles.* Translated by G. W. Butterworth. Reprint. New York: Harper & Row, 1966.

Ouspensky, P. D. *In Search of the Miraculous: Fragments of a Forgotten Teaching.* New York: Harcourt, Brace, & Co.: 1949.

Pagels, Elaine. *Beyond Belief: The Secret Gospel of Thomas.* New York: Random House, 2003.

———. *The Gnostic Gospels.* Reprint. New York: Vintage, 1989.

———. *The Gnostic Paul: Gnostic Exegesis of the Pauline Letters.* Philadelphia: Trinity Press International, 1975.

Palamas, Gregory. *The Triads: Book One.* Translated by Robin Amis. South Brent, Devon, UK: Praxis, 2002.

Perkins, Pheme. *The Gnostic Dialogue: The Early Church and the Crisis of Gnosticism.* New York: Paulist, 1980.

The Philokalia: The Complete Text Compiled by St. Nikodimos of the Holy Mountain and St. Makarios of Corinth. Translated by G. E. H. Palmer, Philip Sherrard, and Kallistos Ware. 5 vols. London: Faber & Faber, 1979.

Pico della Mirandola, Giovanni. *De hominis dignitate.* Milan: Mondadori, 1994.

———. *Heptaplus, or Discourse on the Seven Days of Creation.* Translated by Jessie Brewer McGraw. New York: Philosophical Library, 1977.

———. *900 conclusions philosophiques, cabalistiques, théologiques.* Edited by Bertrand Schefer. Paris: Éditions Allia, 1999.

Plotinus. *The Enneads.* Translated by Stephen MacKenna. Burdett, N.Y.: Larson, 1992.

Raine, Kathleen. *Blake and Tradition.* 2 vols. Princeton, N.J.: Princeton University Press, 1968.

Ramakrishna, Sri. *The Gospel of Sri Ramakrishna.* Translated by Swami Nikhilananda. New York: Ramakrishna-Vivekananda Center, 1942.

Reuchlin, Johann. *On the Art of the Kabbalah (De arte cabalistica).* Translated by Martin and Sarah Goodman. Lincoln: University of Nebraska Press, 1993.

Roberts, J. M. *The Mythology of Secret Societies.* London: Secker & Warburg, 1972.

Robinson, Ira. *Moses Cordovero's Introduction to Kabbalah: An Annotated Translation of His Or Ne'erav.* New York: Yeshiva University Press, 1994.

Roché, Déodat. *Études manichéennes et cathares.* Arques, France: Éditions des Cahiers d'Étude Cathares, 1952.

Rudolph, Kurt. *Gnosis: The Nature and History of Gnosticism.* Edited and translated by Robert McLachlan Wilson. San Francisco: HarperSanFrancisco, 1987.

Runciman, Steven. *The Medieval Manichee: A Study of the Christian Dualist Heresy.* Cambridge: Cambridge University Press, 1947.

Sandoz, Ellis. *The Voegelinian Revolution: A Biographical Introduction.* 2d ed. New Brunswick, N.J.: Transaction, 2000.

Scholem, Gershom. *Kabbalah.* Reprint. New York: Dorset, 1987.

———. *Major Trends in Jewish Mysticism.* 3d ed. New York: Schocken, 1961.

Schweitzer, Albert. *The Quest of the Historical Jesus: A Critical Study of Its Progress from Reimarus to Wrede.* Translated by W. Montgomery. Reprint. New York: Macmillan, 1961.

Seesholtz, Anna Groh. *Friends of God: Practical Mystics of the Fourteenth Century.* Reprint. New York: A. M. S Press, 1970 (1934).

Segal, Robert A., ed. *The Gnostic Jung.* Princeton, N.J.: Princeton University Press, 1992.

Shumaker, Wayne R. *The Occult Sciences in the Renaissance: A Study in Intellectual Patterns.* Berkeley: University of California Press, 1972.

Smith, Morton. *The Secret Gospel.* New York: Harper & Row, 1973.

Smoley, Richard. *Inner Christianity: A Guide to the Esoteric Tradition.* Boston: Shambhala, 2002.

Smoley, Richard, and Jay Kinney. *Hidden Wisdom: A Guide to the Western Inner Traditions.* New York: Penguin Arkana, 1999.

Spiegelberg, Frederic. *Living Religions of the World.* Englewood Cliffs, N.J.: Prentice-Hall, 1956.

Steiner, Rudolf. *Spiritualism, Madame Blavatsky, and Theosophy.* Edited by Christopher Bamford. Great Barrington, Mass.: Anthroposophic Press, 2001.

Stevenson, David. *The Origins of Freemasonry: Scotland's Century, 1590–1710.* Cambridge: Cambridge University Press, 1988.

Stoyanov, Yuri. *The Other God: Dualist Religions from Antiquity to the Cathar Heresy.* New Haven, Conn.: Yale University Press, 2000.

[Tomberg, Valentin]. *Meditations on the Tarot: A Journey into Christian Hermeticism.* Translated by Robert A. Powell. Warwick, N.Y.: Amity House, 1985.

Trigg, Joseph W. *Origen.* London: Routledge, 1998.

Unseen Warfare, Being the Spiritual Combat and Path to Paradise of Lorenzo Scupoli, as Edited by Nicodemus of the Holy Mountain and Revised by Theophan the Recluse. Translated by E. Kadloubovsky and G. E. H. Palmer. London: Faber & Faber, 1952.

Van den Broeck, Roelof, and Wouter J. Hanegraaff, eds. *Gnosis and Hermeticism from Antiquity to Modern Times.* Albany: State University of New York Press, 1998.

Versluis, Arthur. *Wisdom's Children: A Christian Esoteric Tradition.* Albany: State University of New York Press, 1999.

Vivekananda, Swami. *Jnana Yoga.* New York: Ramakrishna-Vivekananda Center, 1955.

Voegelin, Eric. *The New Science of Politics.* Chicago: University of Chicago Press, 1952.

Wachtmeister, Countess Constance, et al. *Reminiscences of H. P. Blavatsky and the Secret Doctrine.* Wheaton, Ill.: Quest, 1976.

Wapnick, Kenneth. *Love Does Not Condemn: The World, the Flesh, and the Devil According to Platonism, Christianity, Gnosticism, and 'A Course in Miracles.'* Roscoe, N.Y.: Foundation for *A Course in Miracles,* 1989.

Waterfield, Robin. *Hidden Depths: The Story of Hypnosis.* New York: Brunner-Routledge, 2003.

Weldon, Jane L. *The Platonic Roots of Analytic Psychology: The Archetype of the Self and the Subtle Body of the Soul.* Ph.D. diss., Pacifica Graduate Institute, 2004.

White, Ralph, ed. *The Rosicrucian Enlightenment Revisited.* Hudson, N.Y.: Lindisfarne, 1999.

Williams, Michael Allen. *Rethinking "Gnosticism": An Argument for Dismantling a Dubious Category.* Princeton, N.J.: Princeton University Press, 1996.

Wirszubski, Chaim. *Pico della Mirandola's Encounter with Jewish Mysticism.* Cambridge, Mass.: Harvard University Press, 1989.

Yamauchi, Edwin M. *Pre-Christian Gnosticism.* Grand Rapids, Mich.: Eerdmans, 1973.

Yates, Frances A. *Giordano Bruno and the Hermetic Tradition.* Chicago: University of Chicago Press, 1964

———. *The Occult Philosophy in the Elizabethan Age.* London: Routledge & Kegan Paul, 1979.

———. *The Rosicrucian Enlightenment.* London: Ark, 1987.

Notes

INTRODUCTION

1. David Van Biema, "The Lost Gospels," *Time*, Dec. 22, 2003, 61.
2. Émile Durkheim, *The Elementary Forms of Religious Life*, trans. Karen E. Fields (New York: Free Press, 1995), 208, 211.
3. David Hawkins, *Power vs. Force: The Hidden Determinants of Human Behavior* (Sedona, Ariz.: Veritas, 1995), 272. I explore the controversies at the Council of Nicaea in chapter 2.
4. Biblical quotations are taken from the Authorized King James Version.
5. Elaine Pagels, *The Gnostic Gospels* (New York: Vintage, 1989 [1979]), 150.

CHAPTER 1. WHO WERE THE GNOSTICS?

1. See *The Nag Hammadi Library in English*, ed. James M. Robinson (San Francisco: Harper & Row, 1977), 117–31. There are other works attributed to Thomas, but for the sake of simplicity, when I speak of *Thomas*, I will be referring to this Gospel.
2. For one example of this argument, see Philip Jenkins, *Hidden Gospels: How the Search for Jesus Lost Its Way* (Oxford: Oxford University Press, 2001), 70.
3. *The Protevangelion of James*. See *New Testament Apocrypha*, ed. Wilhelm Schneemelcher, trans. R. McLachlan Wilson (Edinburgh: T & T Clark, 1991), 1:285–99.
4. *Gospel of Thomas*, saying 14, in *The Nag Hammadi Library in English*, 119. Hereafter references to the *Gospel of Thomas* will be to this edition and will use its verse enumeration.
5. Edward Gibbon, *The History of the Decline and Fall of the Roman Empire* (New York: Harper & Bros., n.d.), chapter 1, 1:214.
6. Plato, *Republic* 476c–d.
7. Plato, *Timaeus* 29e–30a; my translation.
8. Plato, *Timaeus* 41c; my translation.
9. See Plotinus, *Enneads* 2.9.
10. On Simon and his teaching, see Hans Jonas, *The Gnostic Religion*, 2d ed. (Boston: Beacon, 1963), 103–11.
11. This is taken from the *Recognitions* (2.37.6), a work attributed, probably falsely, to Clement of Rome. Quoted in Kurt Rudolph, *Gnosis: The Nature and History of Gnosticism*, trans. R. McLachlan Wilson (San Francisco: HarperSanFrancisco, 1987), 297.
12. See Jonas, *The Gnostic Religion*, 130–46; Rudolph, *Gnosis*, 313–16.

13. On this issue, see *The Anchor Bible: Galatians*, ed. and trans. J. Louis Martin (New York: Doubleday, 1997), 365.

14. See Jonas, *The Gnostic Religion*, 174–205; Rudolph, *Gnosis*, 317–23.

15. Bentley Layton, *The Gnostic Scriptures* (New York: Doubleday, 1987), 248.

16. *The Nag Hammadi Library in English;* Rudolph, *Gnosis*, 91–92.

17. This is mentioned in Marcellus of Ancryra, *On the Holy Church*, 9; in Layton, *The Gnostic Scriptures*, 232–33.

18. See *The Nag Hammadi Library in English*, 309–13.

19. Irenaeus, *Against the Heresies*, 1.24.5, quoted in Layton, *The Gnostic Scriptures*, 424.

20. *The Dialogue of the Savior* III, 138, in *The Nag Hammadi Library*, 235.

21. *Pistis Sophia* 1.17, in Violet MacDermot, *The Fall of Sophia: A Gnostic Text on the Redemption of Universal Consciousness* (Great Barrington, Mass.: Lindisfarne, 2001), 114.

22. *Gospel of Philip* 59, 64, in *The Nag Hammadi Library in English*, 136, 138. Bracketed words have been added by the translator.

23. Pagels, *The Gnostic Gospels*, 76–82.

CHAPTER 2. THE HEIRS OF EGYPT

1. Wayne R. Shumaker, *The Occult Sciences in the Renaissance; A Study in Intellectual Patterns* (Berkeley: University of California Press, 1972), 201.

2. Shumaker, *The Occult Sciences*, 207.

3. Brian P. Copenhaver, ed. and trans., *Hermetica: The Greek Corpus Hermeticum and the Latin Asclepius in a New English Translation with Notes and an Introduction* (Cambridge: Cambridge University Press, 1992), 95.

4. *Asclepius* 24, in Copenhaver, *Hermetica*, 81.

5. *Poimandres* 12, in Copenhaver, *Hermetica*, 3.

6. *Poimandres* 15, in Copenhaver, *Hermetica*, 3.

7. *Poimandres* 9–15, in Copenhaver, *Hermetica*, 2–3.

8. *Poimandres* 15, in Copenhaver, *Hermetica*, 3.

9. *Poimandres* 25–26, in Copenhaver, *Hermetica*, 25–26.

10. *Asclepius* 12, in Copenhaver, *Hermetica*, 74; *Corpus Hermeticum* II, 17, in Copenhaver, *Hermetica*, 12.

11. Herodotus II.123, in *Herodotus*, trans. A. D. Godley (London: Heinemann [Loeb Classical Library], 1931), 1:425.

12. Herodotus II.37, in *Herodotus*, 1:321.

13. Origen, *On First Principles*, trans. G. W. Butterworth, reprint (New York: Harper & Row, 1966), 1.8.3, p. 73.

14. See Wouter J. Hanegraaff, *New Age Religion and Western Culture* (Albany: State University of New York Press, 1998), 321–22.

15. [Valentin Tomberg], *Meditations on the Tarot: A Journey into Christian Hermeticism*, trans. Robert A. Powell (Warwick, N.Y.: Amity House, 1985), 361.

16. For biographical details, see *Clement of Alexandria*, G. W. Butterworth, ed.

and trans. (Cambridge, Mass: Harvard University Press [Loeb Classical Library], 1919), xi–xii.

17. Quoted in Morton Smith, *The Secret Gospel* (New York: Harper & Row, 1973), 15, 17.

18. Clement of Alexandria, *Stromateis* 2.4, 2.11, in *The Ante-Nicene Fathers*, ed. Alexander Roberts and James Donaldson (reprint, Grand Rapids, Mich.: Eerdmans, 1994), 2:354, 358–59.

19. For Clement's views on the Gnostic teachings on sexuality, see *Stromateis*, book 3; on their repudiation of Timothy, see *Stromateis* 2.11.

20. On the watering-down of Origen's texts by his Latin translator, Rufinus, see Butterworth's introduction to Origen, *On First Principles*, xxxv–xxxvi.

21. For my biographical account, I am indebted to Joseph W. Trigg, *Origen* (London: Routledge, 1998), chapters 1–4.

22. This discussion appears in Origen, *Contra Celsum* 5.28–31. The version I am using appears on www.newadvent.org/fathers/04165.htm.

23. Ibid., 5.28.

24. Ibid., 5.30.

25. Joseph Gikatilla, *Gates of Light: Sha'arei Orah*, trans. Avi Weinstein (San Francisco: HarperSanFrancisco, 1994), 174–75.

26. Giovanni Pico della Mirandola, *900 conclusions philosophiques, cabalistiques, théologiques*, ed. Bertrand Schefer. (Paris: Éditions Allia, 1999), 104 (conclusion 402). This edition reproduces Pico's original Latin along with a French translation. My quotations from this work are my own translations from the Latin.

27. *Catholic Encyclopedia*, s.v. "Origen and Origenism," www.newadvent.org.

28. Origen, *On First Principles,* 4.4.1, quoted in Trigg, *Origen*, 24.

29. Origen, *On First Principles*, 3.5.7, Butterworth edition, 243.

30. Origen, *On First Principles*, 1.6.3, Butterworth edition, 57.

31. Origen, *On First Principles*, 3.1.1, Butterworth edition, 288.

32. Gibbon, chapter 21, 2:553. Ibid., chapter 20, 2:457.

33. René Guénon, "*Christianisme et initiation*," in *Aperçus sur l'ésotérisme chrétien* (Paris: Éditions Traditionelles, n.d.), 27; my translation.

34. Richard Smoley, "Heroic Virtue: The *Gnosis* Interview with Brother David Steindl-Rast," *Gnosis* 24 (Summer 1992), 38.

CHAPTER 3.   THE LOST RELIGION OF LIGHT

1. Rudolph, *The Nag Hammadi Library in English,* 326–27.

2. For the following account of his life, I am indebted to Hans-Joachim Klimkeit, *Gnosis on the Silk Road: Gnostic Parables, Hymns, and Prayers from Central Asia* (San Francisco: HarperSanFranciso, 1993), 1–4; and Yuri Stoyanov, *The Other God: Dualist Religions from Antiquity to the Cathar Heresy* (New Haven, Conn.: Yale University Press, 2000), 102–6.

3. *Kephalaia* 14.29ff, in Klimkeit, *Gnosis on the Silk Road*, 2–3. Bracketed insertions are Klimkeit's.

4. *The Gospel of Sri Ramakrishna*, trans. Swami Nikhilananda (New York: Ramakrishna-Vivekananda Center, 1942), 170.

5. Plato, *Cratylus* 400c; cf. *Gorgias* 493a.

6. Plato, *Phaedo* 118a.

7. Mani, as quoted by the *Fihrist* of An-Nadim; in Jason David BeDuhn, *The Manichaean Body in Discipline and Ritual* (Baltimore, Md.: Johns Hopkins University Press, 2000), 76.

8. Quoted in BeDuhn, *The Manichaean Body*, 131.

9. BeDuhn, *The Manichaean Body*, 147; cf. Augustine, *Contra Fortunatum*, 3.

10. Augustine, *Contra Faustum* 5.10; in BeDuhn, *The Manichaean Body*, 103.

11. Swami Vivekananda, *Jnana Yoga* (New York: Ramakrishna-Vivekananda Center, 1955), 15, 86.

12. Klimkeit, *Gnosis on the Silk Road*, 6.

13. See Stoyanov, *The Other God*, 2.

14. Gerald J. Larson, *Classical Samkhya: An Interpretation of Its History and Meaning*, 2d ed. (Delhi: Motilal Barnarsidass, 1979), 75, 96.

15. *Samkhkyarakarika* 56, in Larson, *Classical Samkhya*, 175.

16. See Stoyanov, *The Other God*, 117–19.

17. Frederic Spiegelberg, *Living Religions of the World* (Englewood Cliffs, N.J.: Prentice-Hall, 1956), 466–67.

18. See Gershom Scholem, *Major Trends in Jewish Mysticism*, 3d ed. (New York: Schocken, 1961), 260.

CHAPTER 4. THE WAR AGAINST THE CATHARS

1. For the following account, I am chiefly indebted to Stoyanov, *The Other God*, chapter 3; see also Paul Tice, "Bogomils: Gnostics of Old Bulgaria," *Gnosis* 31 (Spring 1994), 54–60.

2. See David Lorimer, *Prophet for Our Times: The Life and Teachings of Peter Deunov* (Rockport, Mass.: Element Books, 1996); and Georg Feuerstein, *The Mystery of Light: The Life and Teaching of Omraam Mikhaël Aïvanhov* (Sandy, Utah: Passage Press, 1994).

3. Nita de Pierrefeu, "Montségur et le symbole du Graal," *Cahiers d'études Cathares*, series 2, no. 92 (Winter 1981), 60.

4. Stoyanov, *The Other God*, 184–85.

5. Ibid., 189.

6. Ibid., 201.

7. Euthymius of Peribleptos, quoted in ibid., 170.

8. For the following account, I am relying upon Déodat Roché, *Études manichéennes et cathares* (Arques, France: Éditions des Cahiers d'Étude Cathares, 1952), 15–18. Although the *consolamentum* was given to both men and women, for brevity's sake I am characterizing the candidate using the masculine gender.

9. Ibid., 19; English translations of this and other passages from Roché are my own.

10. Quoted in ibid., 19.

11. Ibid., 17.

12. J. Guiraud, quoted in ibid., 19.

13. For further discussion of this topic, see my *Inner Christianity: A Guide to the Esoteric Tradition* (Boston: Shambhala, 2002), chapter 4.

14. Denis de Rougemont, *Love in the Western World*, trans. Montgomery Belgion, rev. ed. (Princeton, N.J.: Princeton University Press, 1983), 83.

15. Quoted in ibid., 34.

16. Quoted in Jean Markale, *Courtly Love: The Path of Sexual Initiation*, trans. Jon Graham (Rochester, Vt.: Inner Traditions, 2000), 86. The bracketed addition is Markale's.

17. Ibid., 209.

18. In ibid., 38.

19. Spiegelberg, *Living Religions of the World*, 466.

20. In de Rougemont, *Love in the Western World*, 88.

21. Dante, *La Vita Nuova*, trans. Barbara Reynolds (Harmondsworth: Penguin, 1969), II:29–30.

22. Dante, *La Vita Nuova*, XI: 41.

23. De Rougemont, *Love in the Western World*, 243.

24. Lynda Harris, *The Secret Heresy of Hieronymus Bosch* (Edinburgh: Floris, 1995).

25. Paul Johnson, *A History of Christianity* (New York: Atheneum, 1987), 191–92.

CHAPTER 5. GNOSIS IN THE MEDIEVAL CHURCH

1. See *Enoch* 6–8; in R.H. Charles, *The Apocrpha and Pseudepigrapha of the Old Testament*, vol. 2 (Oxford: Oxford at the Clarendon Press, 1913), 191–92. According to Charles, different parts of the text of *Enoch* date to different eras. This section is no later than the early second century B.C.

2. Dionysius the Areopagite, *The Celestial Hierarchy*, chs. 8, 9; on www.esoteric.msu.edu/VolumeII/CelestialHierarchy.html.

3. Dante, *Paradiso*, XXVIII: 127–29. My translation.

4. John Carey, "Looking for Celtic Christianity," *Gnosis* 45 (Fall 1997), 44.

5. John Carey, "The Sun's Night Journey: A Pharaonic Image in Medieval Ireland," *Journal of the Warburg and Courtauld Institutes* 57 (1994), 14–34; and personal correspondence.

6. Ian Bradley, *Celtic Christianity: Making Myths and Chasing Dreams* (New York: St. Martin's Press, 1999), 25.

7. Carey, "Looking for Celtic Christianity," 43.

8. Athanasius, *Life of Antony*, §5–9; in Athanasius, *Select Works and Letters*, *Nicene and Post-Nicene Fathers*, vol. 4, series 2, ed. Philip Schaff and Henry Wace, available at www.fordham.edu/halsall/basis/vita-antony.html.

9. *The Philokalia: The Complete Text Compiled by St. Nikodimos of the Holy Mountain and St. Makarios of Corinth*, trans. G. E. H. Palmer, Philip Sherrard, and Kallistos Ware (London: Faber & Faber, 1979–), 1:362.

10. Ibid.

11. Ibid., 1:62.

12. Ibid., 1:271.

13. Ibid., 1:75.

14. For recent views on this subject, see Thomas Lewis et al., *A General Theory of Love* (New York: Vintage, 2001); and Helen Fisher, *Why We Love* (New York: Henry Holt, 2004).

15. *Philokalia*, 4: 418–25.

16. For this account I am indebted to David Vermette's introduction to Gregory Palamas, *The Triads: Book One*, trans. Robin Amis (South Brent, Devon, UK: Praxis, 2002), 19–23. See also Vladimir Lossky, *The Mystical Theology of the Eastern Church* (Crestwood, N.Y.: St. Vladimir's Seminary Press, 1976), 76–77.

17. See *Unseen Warfare, Being the Spiritual Combat and Path to Paradise of Lorenzo Scupoli, as Edited by Nicodemus of the Holy Mountain and Revised by Theophan the Recluse*, trans. E. Kadloubovsky and G. E. H. Palmer (London: Faber & Faber, 1952), introduction, 22.

18. Palamas, *The Triads*, 70.

19. Ibid., 69.

20. Ibid., 71. Italics are the translator's. This three-part characterization of the human structure can be traced back to Plato, who sets it out in the *Republic*.

21. For the following biographical sketch, I am relying upon the introduction to Raymond B. Blakney, *Meister Eckhart* (New York: Harper & Row, 1941), xvi–xxiv. Prof. John Connolly of Smith College has made a number of helpful corrections and additions.

22. Quoted in ibid., xviii.

23. Meister Eckhart, *The Defense*, §39, in ibid., 297.

24. Meister Eckhart, "Justice Is Even," in ibid., 181.

CHAPTER 6. THE SAGES OF THE RENAISSANCE

1. A recent English edition is *Sepher Rezial Hamelech: The Book of the Angel Rezial*, ed. Steve Savedow (York Beach, Maine: Weiser, 2000).

2. See Z'ev ben Shimon Halevi, *The Way of Kabbalah* (London: Rider, 1976), 16–17.

3. Gershom Scholem, *Major Trends in Jewish Mysticism*, 3d ed. (New York: Schocken, 1961), 35.

4. Gershom Scholem, *Kabbalah* (New York: Dorset, 1987 [1974]), 45.

5. Ibid., 50.

6. This account relies upon Chaim Wirszubski, *Pico della Mirandola's Encounter with Jewish Mysticism* (Cambridge, Mass.: Harvard University Press, 1989),

7. Pico della Mirandola, *900 conclusions*.

8. Ibid., 195.

9. Quoted in Wirszubski, *Pico della Mirandola's Encounter with Jewish Mysticism*, 126.

10. Pico della Mirandola, *Heptaplus, or Discourse on the Seven Days of Creation*, trans. Jessie Brewer McGraw (New York: Philosophical Library, 1977), 17.

11. Ibid., 18; cf. Dionysius, *Celestial Hierarchy*, §2.

12. Pico della Mirandola, *Heptaplus*, 16.

13. For a fuller discussion of Kabbalistic doctrine, see Richard Smoley and Jay Kinney, *Hidden Wisdom: A Guide to the Western Inner Traditions* (New York: Penguin Arkana, 1999), chapter 4.

14. Pico della Mirandola, *Heptaplus*, 22.

15. Pico differs from most Kabbalists in seeing the fourth world not as the divine realm, but in terms of man as a microcosm; cf. *Heptaplus*, 25, 26.

16. Quoted in Gershom Scholem, "The Beginnings of the Christian Kabbalah," in Joseph Dan, ed., *The Christian Kabbalah: Jewish Mystical Books and Their Christian Interpreters* (Cambridge, Mass.: Harvard College Library, 1997), 19.

17. See Smoley and Kinney, *Hidden Wisdom*, 196–98.

18. Scholem, *Kabbalah*, 198.

19. Moshe Idel, introduction to Johann Reuchlin, *On the Art of the Kabbalah (De arte cabalistica)*, trans. Martin and Sarah Goodman (Lincoln: University of Nebraska Press, 1993), xix. Both "W" and "V" are used to transliterate the Hebrew letter *waw,* or *vav.*

20. Ira Robinson, *Moses Cordovero's Introduction to Kabbalah: An Annotated Translation of His Or Ne'erav* (New York: Yeshiva University Press, 1994), 113. Bracketed words are Robinson's.

21. Aryeh Kaplan, *Meditation and Kabbalah* (York Beach, Maine: Samuel Weiser, 1982), 185.

22. Joseph Dan, "The Kabbalah of Johannes Reuchlin and Its Historical Significance," in *The Christian Kabbalah*, 56.

23. *The Key of Solomon the King (Clavicula Salomonis)*, ed. and trans. S. L. MacGregor Mathers (York Beach, Maine: Samuel Weiser, 2000 [1888]), 71.

24. For the following account, I am chiefly indebted to Donald Tyson's "Life of Agrippa," in Henry Cornelius Agrippa, *Three Books of Occult Philosophy*, trans. James Freake, ed. Donald Tyson (St. Paul, Minn.: Llewellyn, 1993), xv–xxxvii.

25. There is a so-called fourth book to this work, which consists of several treatises on magic written by Agrippa and others. See Stephen Skinner, ed., *The Fourth Book of Occult Philosophy* (Boston: Weiser, 2005).

26. For my account of Dee I am relying chiefly on Frances A. Yates, *The Occult Philosophy in Elizabethan England* (London: Routledge & Kegan Paul, 1979), 79–94; and Cherry Gilchrist, "Dr. Dee and the Spirits," *Gnosis* 36 (Summer 1995), 32–39.

27. Quoted in Yates, *Occult Philosophy*, 87.

28. For my treatment of this fascinating but ambiguous character, see my book *The Essential Nostradamus* (New York: Tarcher/Penguin, 2006).

29. For my account of Bruno, I am chiefly relying on Frances A. Yates, *Giordano Bruno and the Hermetic Tradition* (Chicago: University of Chicago Press, 1964).

CHAPTER 7. ROSICRUCIANISM AND THE GREAT LODGES

1. *Fama Fraternitatis*, trans. Thomas Vaughan; in Frances A. Yates, *The Rosicrucian Enlightenment* (London: Ark, 1987), 240.
2. *Fama Fraternitatis*, quoted in Yates, *Rosicrucian Enlightenment*, 243. For further discussion of these principles, see my *Inner Christianity*, 233–35.
3. *Confessio* in Yates, *Rosicrucian Enlightenment*, 251–52.
4. *Fama*; in Yates, *Rosicrucian Enlightenment*, 249.
5. For the following account I am chiefly indebted to Yates, *Rosicrucian Enlightenment*, chapter 2.
6. Frederick V to the Duc de Bouillon, quoted in Yates, *Rosicrucian Enlightenment*, 19.
7. *Confessio*, in Yates, *Rosicrucian Enlightenment*, 257.
8. Yates, *Rosicrucian Enlightenment*, 103.
9. *Fama*, in Yates, *Rosicrucian Enlightenment*, 238. The original seventeenth-century English translation has "Porphyry" for "Popery," but this is a mistake: the German original reads "the pope."
10. *Encyclopedia of Philosophy*, s.v. "Bacon, Francis."
11. Yates, *Rosicrucian Enlightenment*, 119. For her views, Yates cites Paolo Rossi, *Francis Bacon: From Magic to Science,* London, 1968.
12. René Descartes, *Discourse on Method*, chapter 1, in *Discourses on Method and the Meditations*, trans. E. F. Sutcliffe (Harmondsworth: Penguin, 1968), 33.
13. Ibid., 33.
14. Ibid., 35.
15. Quoted in Yates, *Rosicrucian Enlightenment*, 116.
16. Quoted in Yates, *Rosicrucian Enlightenment*, 115.
17. Paul Foster Case, *The True and Invisible Rosicrucian Order* (York Beach, Maine: Samuel Weiser, 1985), 5.
18. Tobias Churton, *The Golden Builders: Alchemists, Rosicrucians, and the First Freemasons* (Boston: Weiser, 2005), 133.
19. For the following account, I am chiefly relying on Pierre Deghaye, "Jacob Boehme and His Followers," in Antoine Faivre and Jacob Needleman, eds., *Modern Esoteric Spirituality* (New York: Crossroad, 1995); Cynthia Bourgeault, "Boehme for Beginners," *Gnosis* 45 (fall 1997), 28–35; and Arthur Versluis, *Wisdom's Children: A Christian Esoteric Tradition* (Albany: SUNY Press, 1999), chapter 1.
20. Jacob Boehme, *The Three Principles of the Divine Essence*, preface, quoted in Versluis, *Wisdom's Children*, 11.
21. Ibid., 6.
22. In this sense, *theosophy* as a common noun differs from *Theosophy* as for-

mulated by H. P. Blavatsky in the nineteenth century, which I discuss in chapter 8. To prevent confusion, in this book I capitalize references to the latter.

23. Deghaye, "Jacob Boehme and His Followers," 212.

24. Jacob Boehme, *Clavis*, trans. John Sparrow (reprint, Kila, Mont.: Kessinger, n.d.), 46.

25. Deghaye, "Jacob Boehme and His Followers," 230; Versluis, *Wisdom's Children*, 220–21.

26. Churton, *The Golden Builders*, 122.

27. Versluis, *Wisdom's Children*, 220.

28. Samuel Butler, *Hudibras*, Butler's note to part 1, canto 1, 527–44.

29. Case, *The True and Invisible Rosicrucian Order*, 152.

30. Douglas Knoop et al., eds., *The Two Earliest Masonic Mss.* (Manchester, U.K.: Manchester University Press, 1938).

31. Ibid., 162, 168–70.

32. For further discussion of the symbolism of the Master Mason ritual, see Smoley and Kinney, *Hidden Wisdom*, 261–62; see also my "Masonic Civilization," *Gnosis* 44 (Summer 1997), 12–16, reprinted in Jay Kinney, ed., *The Inner West: An Introduction to the Hidden Wisdom of the West* (New York: Tarcher/Penguin, 2004), 206–18.

33. In my own previous treatments, I gave this theory more credence than I probably should have. Smoley and Kinney, *Hidden Wisdom*, 261–62; see also my "Masonic Civilization."

34. David Stevenson, *The Origins of Freemasonry: Scotland's Century, 1590–1710* (Cambridge: Cambridge University Press, 1988), 49.

35. Quoted in Stevenson, *Origins of Freemasonry*, 126.

36. For a detailed comparison of Freemasonry and Kabbalah, see W. Kirk MacNulty, *Freemasonry: A Journey through Ritual and Symbol* (London: Thames & Hudson, 1991).

37. In Stevenson, *Origins of Freemasonry*, 139.

38. Ibid., 163.

39. For this account, I am relying on Christopher McIntosh, "The Rosicrucian Legacy," in Ralph White, ed., *The Rosicrucian Enlightenment Revisited* (Hudson, N.Y.: Lindisfarne, 1999).

40. For this account of the Illuminati, I am relying on J. M. Roberts, *The Mythology of Secret Societies* (London: Secker & Warburg, 1972), 118–30.

41. Stefan Lovgren, "National Treasure: Freemasons, Fact, and Fiction," *National Geographic News*, Nov. 19, 2004; http://news.nationalgeographic.com.

42. Roberts, *Mythology of Secret Societies*, 154.

43. Ibid., 68–70.

44. Quoted in Yates, *Rosicrucian Enlightenment*, 238.

45. See Robin Waterfield, *Hidden Depths: The Story of Hypnosis* (New York: Brunner-Routledge, 2003), chapters 3–4.

46. Gary Lachman, *A Dark Muse: A History of the Occult* (New York: Thunder's Mouth Press, 2003), 28–29.

47. For a short account of his life and work, see Timothy O'Neill, "Cagliostro: The Grand Copt," *Gnosis* 24 (Summer 1992), 23–29.

48. See my article "The Inner Journey of Emanuel Swedenborg," in Jonathan Rose, ed., *Emanuel Swedenborg: Essays on His Life and Impact* (West Chester, Pa.: Swedenborg Foundation, 2005).

49. Quoted in Kathleen Raine, *Blake and Tradition* (Princeton, N.J.: Princeton University Press, 1968), 1:3.

50. Quoted on the *Antiques Digest* Web site, http://www.oldandsold.com /articles22/honore-de-balzac-8.shtml.

CHAPTER 8. THE GNOSTIC REVIVAL

1. MacDermot, *The Fall of Sophia*, introduction, 22–23. MacDermot's book contains an abridged translation of the *Pistis Sophia* from the original Coptic along with an extensive commentary. Mead's version (a secondhand translation from the Latin) has been reprinted often since it first appeared: one recent edition, a photocopy of the original edition, has been published by Kessinger Publishing Company, Kila, Montana.

2. On this point see Hanegraaff, *New Age Religion and Western Culture*, 382.

3. Rudolph, *Gnosis*, 52.

4. Hanegraaff, *New Age Religion and Western Culture*, 382.

5. Christopher Bamford, introduction to C. G. Harrison, *The Transcendental Universe: Six Lectures on Occult Science, Theosophy, and the Catholic Faith* (Hudson, N.Y.: Lindisfarne, 1993), 8.

6. Countess Constance Wachtmeister et al., *Reminiscences of H. P. Blavatsky and the Secret Doctrine* (Wheaton, Ill.: Quest, 1976), 44.

7. H. P. Blavatsky, *Isis Unveiled: Secrets of the Ancient Wisdom Tradition*, abridged edition, ed. Michael Gomes (Wheaton, Ill.: Quest, 1997), 136.

8. Blavatsky, *Isis Unveiled*, 140.

9. H. P. Blavatsky, *The Secret Doctrine*, 3d Point Loma ed. (Point Loma, Calif.: Aryan Theosophical Press, 1926), 2:389.

10. Blavatsky, *Secret Doctrine*, 2:96. Emphasis here and below Blavatsky's.

11. Blavatsky, *Secret Doctrine*, 2:389.

12. For a succinct treatment of this theory, see Edward Abdill, *The Secret Gateway: Modern Theosophy and the Ancient Wisdom Tradition* (Wheaton, Ill.: Quest, 2005), chapters 4–5.

13. For this quotation and Blavatsky's specific correlation of the two systems, see *The Secret Doctrine*, 2:604–5.

14. Harrison, *The Transcendental Universe*, 89.

15. Hanegraaff, *New Age Religion and Western Culture*, 454–55.

16. Richard Noll, *The Jung Cult: Origins of a Charismatic Movement* (Princeton, N.J.: Princeton University Press, 1994), 69. The reference to "a stepping-

stone to higher things" is taken from Mead's own description of the Echoes of the Gnosis series. See Noll, *The Jung Cult*, 327.

17. C. G. Jung, *Memories, Dreams, Reflections,* trans. Richard and Clara Winston (New York: Vintage, 1989), 190–91.

18. Noll, *The Jung Cult*, 242–43; C. G. Jung, 1917 letter to Alphonse Maeder, quoted in Jung, *Memories, Dreams, Reflections*.

19. Jung, *Memories, Dreams, Reflections*, 192.

20. C. G. Jung, *Collected Works,* vol. 5: *Symbols of Transformation,* 2d ed., trans. R. F. C. Hull (Princeton, N.J.: Princeton University Press, 1967), 100–101, 157–58. Noll, *The Jung Cult*, 180–86, takes issue with many details in Jung's story (which changed in key details over the years as Jung retold it). Despite these discrepancies, the weight of plausibility still lies on Jung's side: it is comparatively unlikely that a schizophrenic patient with only a basic education would have been familiar with an obscure Mithraic text.

21. Jung, *Memories, Dreams, Reflections,* 200–201.

22. C. G. Jung, *Psychology and Religion, Collected Works,* vol. 11, 2d ed., trans. R. F. C. Hull (Princeton, N.J.: Princeton University Press, 1969), 74.

23. Jung, *Psychology and Religion*, 313.

24. Quoted in Robert A. Segal, ed., *The Gnostic Jung* (Princeton, N.J.: Princeton University Press, 1992), 113.

25. C. G. Jung, foreword to Gilles Quispel, *Tragic Christianity*, quoted in Segal, *The Gnostic Jung*, 105.

26. Quoted in Segal, *The Gnostic Jung*, 43.

27. Quoted in Segal, *The Gnostic Jung*, 52.

28. See *The Encyclopedia of Philosophy*, s.v., "Essence and Existence," "Existentialism."

29. Jonas, *The Gnostic Religion*, 327.

30. Jonas, *The Gnostic Religion*, 62–64.

31. Quoted in Clement of Alexandria, *Excerpta ex Theodoto*, 78.2; Jonas, *The Gnostic Religion*, 334, 335.

32. Tau Malachi, *The Gnostic Gospel of St. Thomas: Meditations on the Mystical Teachings* (St. Paul, Minn.: Llewellyn, 2004), xii.

33. Malachi, *The Gnostic Gospel of St. Thomas*, xi–xv.

34. Pagels, *The Gnostic Gospels*, 6.

35. See Smoley and Kinney, *Hidden Wisdom*, chapter 12.

36. David Van Biema et al., "The Lost Gospels," *Time*, Dec. 22, 2003, 56–61.

37. *La Asociación Gnóstica* Web site, http://gnosis.webcindario.com/aboutsamael .htm; http://www.gnosis.org.br/_sawpage/palestra/ingles/imov_gno.htm.

38. Stephan A. Hoeller, "Wandering Bishops: Not All Roads Lead to Rome," *Gnosis* 12 (Summer 1989), 20–25. See also Hoeller's *Gnosticism: New Light on the Ancient Tradition of Inner Knowing* (Wheaton, Ill.: Quest, 2002), 176–78.

39. See *Dictionary of Gnosis and Western Esotericism*, ed. Wouter J. Hanegraaff et al. (Leiden: Brill, 2005), s.v. "Gnostic Church."

40. For a summary of Hoeller's views, see his *Gnosticism*.

CHAPTER 9. GNOSIS AND MODERNITY

1. Segal, *The Gnostic Jung*, 4–7.

2. Charles Baudelaire, *Les fleurs du mal*, no. 119. My translation.

3. On the relation between Blake's political and metaphysical themes, see Robert Rix, "William Blake and the Radical Swedenborgians," www.esoteric.msu.edu.

4. Quoted in Raine, *Blake and Tradition*, 2:13.

5. William Blake, "The Tyger," in *The Complete Poetry and Prose of William Blake*, ed. David V. Erdman, rev. ed. (Berkeley: University of California Press, 1982), 24–25.

6. Raine, *Blake and Tradition*, 2:30.

7. Blake, *The Book of Urizen*, 1.1, in *Complete Poetry and Prose*, 70.

8. See William Blake, *The Book of Urizen*, ed. Kay Parkhurst Easson and Roger R. Easson (Boulder, Colo.: Shambhala/Random House, 1978), commentary, 71–72.

9. Quoted in Raine, *Blake and Tradition*, 1:364.

10. Blake, *Marriage of Heaven and Hell*, in *Complete Poetry and Prose*, 34–35.

11. Blake, *The Marriage of Heaven and Hell*, in *Complete Poetry and Prose*, 43.

12. *Dictionary of Gnosis and Western Esotericism*, s.v. "Carpocratians."

13. Blake, *The Marriage of Heaven and Hell*, in *Complete Poetry and Prose*, 43.

14. William Blake, *America: A Prophecy*, 16.7, in *Complete Poetry and Prose*, 57.

15. Eric Voegelin, *The New Science of Politics* (Chicago: University of Chicago Press, 1952), 164.

16. Voegelin, *New Science of Politics*, 112.

17. Voegelin, *New Science of Politics*, 132.

18. James Joyce, *Ulysses* (New York: Random House, 1961) 34.

19. Voegelin, *New Science of Politics*, 144.

20. Harold Bloom, *Omens of Millennium* (New York: Riverhead, 1996), 23.

21. Harold Bloom, *The American Religion* (New York: Simon & Schuster, 1992), 22.

22. Bloom, *The American Religion*, 32.

23. Herman Melville, *Moby Dick*, chapter 36.

24. Bloom, *The American Religion*, 67.

25. Quoted in Jay Kinney, "The Mysterious Revelations of Philip K. Dick," *Gnosis* 1 (Fall/Winter 1985), 7.

26. "Cosmogony and Cosmology," in *The Shifting Realities of Philip K. Dick: Selected Literary and Philosophical Writings*, ed. Lawrence Sutin (New York: Pantheon, 1995), 281–313.

27. *The Shifting Realities of Philip K. Dick*, 308.

28. *The Shifting Realities of Philip K. Dick*, 288.

29. *The Shifting Realities of Philip K. Dick*, 330. Bracketed material has been inserted by the editor of the volume.

30. Quoted in Kinney, "The Mysterious Revelations of Philip K. Dick," 7.

31. Ibid.

32. Timothy Leary, Ralph Metzner, and Richard Alpert, *The Psychedelic Experience* (reprint, New York: Citadel Underground, 1995), 61.

33. See William Irwin, ed., *The Matrix and Philosophy* (Chicago: Open Court, 2002).

34. See Frances Flannery Dailey and Rachel Wagner, "Wake Up! Gnosticism and Buddhism in *The Matrix*," *Journal of Religion and Film* 5, no. 2 (Oct. 2001). See also Matrix Virtual Theatre, Wachowski Brothers Transcript, Nov. 6, 1999; www.warnervideo.com/matrixevents/wachowski.html.

35. Anonymous, "*The Matrix* and Gnosticism: Is *The Matrix* a Gnostic Film?" www.atheism.about.com/library/FAQs/religion/blrel_matrix_gnos.htm.

36. Quoted in Martin Danahay and David Rieder, "The Matrix, Marx, and the Coppertop's Life," in Irwin, *The Matrix and Philosophy*, 217. Emphasis added.

37. Epiphanius, *Against the Heresies*, 40.2, quoted in Jonas, *The Gnostic Religion*, 169.

38. See his *Way of the Shaman* (New York: Bantam, 1982), 5–9.

39. For Gurdjieff's views on the moon, see P. D. Ouspensky, *In Search of the Miraculous: Fragments of a Forgotten Teaching* (New York, Harcourt, Brace, 1949), 25, 85.

40. Descartes, *First Meditation*, in *Discourses on Method and the Meditations*, 100.

41. *A Course in Miracles* (Tiburon, Calif.: Foundation for Inner Peace, 1975), Workbook, 237.

42. *A Course in Miracles*, Text, 544.

43. *A Course in Miracles*, Text, 364–65.

44. *Apocryphon of John*, 11, in *The Nag Hammadi Library*, 105.

45. Michelle Cracken, "Dan Brown: The Novel that Ate the World," *Time*; quoted in www.danbrown.com/media/morenews/time041505.htm.

46. See the Opus Dei Web site, www.opusdei.org.

47. Dan Brown, *The Da Vinci Code* (New York: Doubleday, 2003), 231.

48. Brown, *The Da Vinci Code*, 248–49.

49. Robert Richardson, "The Priory of Sion Hoax," *Gnosis* 51 (Spring 1999), 49–55. See also Massimo Introvigne, "Beyond *The Da Vinci Code*: What Is the Priory of Sion?" available at www.cesnur.org/2004/mi_davinci_en.htm.

50. Richardson, "The Priory of Sion Hoax," 54.

51. "A Mary for All," *Economist*, Dec. 20, 2003, 25.

52. For further discussion of this issue, see my *Inner Christianity*, 149–51.

53. Brown, *The Da Vinci Code*, 309–10.

54. Jerome, *Contra Jovin*, 1; available at www.newadvent.org/summa/315408.htm. Jerome is quoting a philosopher named Sixtus the Pythagorean.

55. Brown, *The Da Vinci Code*, 444. Ellipsis is in the original.

56. Brown, *The Da Vinci Code,* 454. Ellipses are in the original.

CHAPTER 10. THE FUTURE OF GNOSIS

1. The best recent study of this group is Edmondo Lupieri, *The Mandaeans: The Last Gnostics,* trans. Charles Hindley (Grand Rapids, Mich.: Eerdmans, 2002).

2. On the draining of the southern Mesopotamian marshes, see Christopher Reed, "Paradise Lost," *Harvard Magazine,* Jan.–Feb. 2005, 30–37.

3. See Lupieri, *The Mandaeans,* 38–52.

4. Michael Allen Williams, *Rethinking "Gnosticism": An Argument for Rethinking a Dubious Category* (Princeton, N.J.: Princeton University Press, 1996), 264–65.

5. Karen L. King, *What Is Gnosticism?* (Cambridge, Mass.: Harvard University Press, 2003), 226. Emphasis King's.

6. Pontifical Council for Interreligious Dialogue, *Jesus Christ, the Bearer of the Water of Life: A Christian Reflection on the "New Age,"* available at www.vatican.va/roman_curia/pontifical_councils/interelg/documents/rc_pc_interelg_doc_20030203_new-age_en.html. The passages I have quoted are in §1.4.

7. For descriptions of this system, see Helen Palmer, *The Enneagram* (San Francisco: Harper & Row, 1988); Sandra Maitri, *The Spiritual Dimension of the Enneagam* (New York: Tarcher/Putnam, 2000); Smoley and Kinney, *Hidden Wisdom,* 226–33.

8. King, *What Is Gnosticism?* 227.

9. Marvin Meyer, *The Gnostic Gospels of Jesus* (San Francisco: HarperSanFrancisco, 2005), xii.

10. Werner Heisenberg, *The Physicist's Conception of Nature,* trans. A. Pomerans (New York: Harcourt, Brace, 1958), 28–29.

11. For Eckhart's views, see his essay "On Disinterest," in Blakney, *Meister Eckhart,* 82ff. Blakney translates the German *Abgescheidenheit* as "disinterest," although he concedes that "detachment" is the better term (see ibid., 315). In quotations here I have changed "disinterest" and "disinterested" to "detachment" and "detached."

12. Hanegraaff, *New Age Religion and Western Culture,* 519–20. Hanegraaff is quoting an earlier article of his entitled "A Dynamic Typological Approach to the Problem of 'Post-Gnostic' Gnosticism."

Index